Praise for **SO MUCH TO BE ANGRY**

"*So Much to Be Angry About* is an example of the best impulses of people's history, careful and caring in its attention to people and places, disposing of nothing, casting a loving and critical eye and turning over stones, not just of movement history and its ideas, but also of the labor of the craftspeople, artists, and makers whose work spurs us on but sometimes goes without examination. I love how this book traces generational knowledge, complete with lessons, pitfalls, dynamism, and complication for those of us currently making and joining community, art, and resistance in Appalachia."

—Madeline ffitch, author of *Stay and Fight*

"The Appalachian Movement Press has been an inspiration for almost everything we do. An activist press focused on labor and art, *and* it was based in West Virginia? That's something we all need to hear about! Especially anyone unpacking the region's deep history of exploitation."

—Dwight and Liz Pavlovic, founders, Crash Symbols

"This is a history of Appalachian Movement Press and also a fascinating look into Appalachian history, regional radical politics, and print history. The fire of creation can be passed down through books like *So Much to Be Angry About*, and maybe this retelling of AMP's story could spark something else like it down the line."

—Lucas Church, University of North Carolina Press

"Back before activists used viral memes to reach the masses, the rebels at Appalachian Movement Press used any means necessary to keep their presses running and get information into the hands of all people. I was captivated by the untold story of these scrappy Appalachians who were determined to spread regional pride and history, and who were also completely uninterested in money or fame. Even if they weren't concerned with their names being known, their vision of educating Appalachians on our roots and claiming our identity on our own terms continues today. Ultimately this book is about Appalachia's ability to take what is at hand and use it to support and light a fire under our community."

—Betsy Sokolosky, owner, Base Camp Printing Co.

d before your
ce in single co
mailing cost.
tainee
APPALACHIA
MOVEMENT
PRESS
The Comeback of Midw
tainee
APPALACHIA

so much to be ANGRY about

Appalachian Movement Press and Radical DIY Publishing, 1969–1979

Shaun Slifer

WEST VIRGINIA UNIVERSITY PRESS • MORGANTOWN

First edition published 2021 by West Virginia University Press
Printed in the United States of America

ISBN 978-1-949199-93-2 (cloth) / ISBN 978-1-949199-94-9 (paperback) /
ISBN 978-1-949199-95-6 (ebook)

Library of Congress Control Number: 2020045759

Book and cover design by Than Saffel / WVU Press
Cover image: Appalachian Movement Press logo, early 1970s.

Contents

APPALACHIAN
MOVEMENT
PRESS
LABOR DONATED

Prologue
Digging for Appalachian Movement Press

In the summer of 2016, my partner Becca and I traveled down to the Appalachian South Folklife Center in Pipestem, rural southern West Virginia, for what I later learned from a neighbor became "the rock 'n' roll wedding." Stephanie Tyree and Sam Petsonk, two friends whose social and professional networks, combined with their families, can draw a real crowd, were getting married.

Although by that time I'd been traveling in and out of southern West Virginia for a few years, I'd never been to Pipestem, and the view east off the edge of the hillside was incredible. If you live in an American city, you do well to breathe deep when you get out of one. Familiar with rural camps, communes, rural activist convergences, and various flavors of "folk schools," I still couldn't get a read on my current setting. It felt like a place where kids would come from the city to ride horses, but the field was open with no horses or tack anywhere, no fencing even. I know "folklife centers" mainly as places that people with some money to spend go to take workshops on now-quaint handicrafts, but this place was sparse in that department too—no blacksmithing anvils, no looms. I didn't yet know anything about the history of this place, or the people who founded it.

You probably shouldn't go to a wedding and expect to spend time with the folks getting married, but these two were doing their damndest to make the rounds to every guest anyway. Sam eventually found me standing in the sun and pulled me into the cafeteria building, the largest structure on the ASFC grounds.

"Man you've gotta read up on this place, this guy who founded it, Don West. You'd love this guy!" He pressed a "zine" into my hand, we hugged and chatted for that mere earnest moment you might hope to get from a friend in the midst of a day like that, and then he moved on for more formalities and endless smiling.

A Time for Anger. Don West. Those were the only words on the cover of the thin publication I was left holding. The text was stark, strong. I couldn't ignore the words. White paper, eight and a half by eleven inches folded in half, stapled twice on the fold. Austere, with a look of having been printed and bound in untold multiples.

This zine that I was now holding had been sitting out on a table like someone had just set it down yesterday after their lunch, and yet it felt like it was from another era. On the back cover, there was a logo, just a tiny little icon of a miner's pick. Appalachian Movement Press—Labor Donated.

I took a couple pictures of this logo and the front cover with my phone, and I texted them to two friends who I thought would be intrigued, and who know very little about Appalachia. I knew what a movement press was, but I'd never heard of one in West Virginia. A couple of years later, on a sweltering June afternoon, I would find piles of publications with this logo on them moldering in a basement at this very same folklife center. But evening was coming along, and I returned to the wedding party. The band wasn't holding back anything.

—

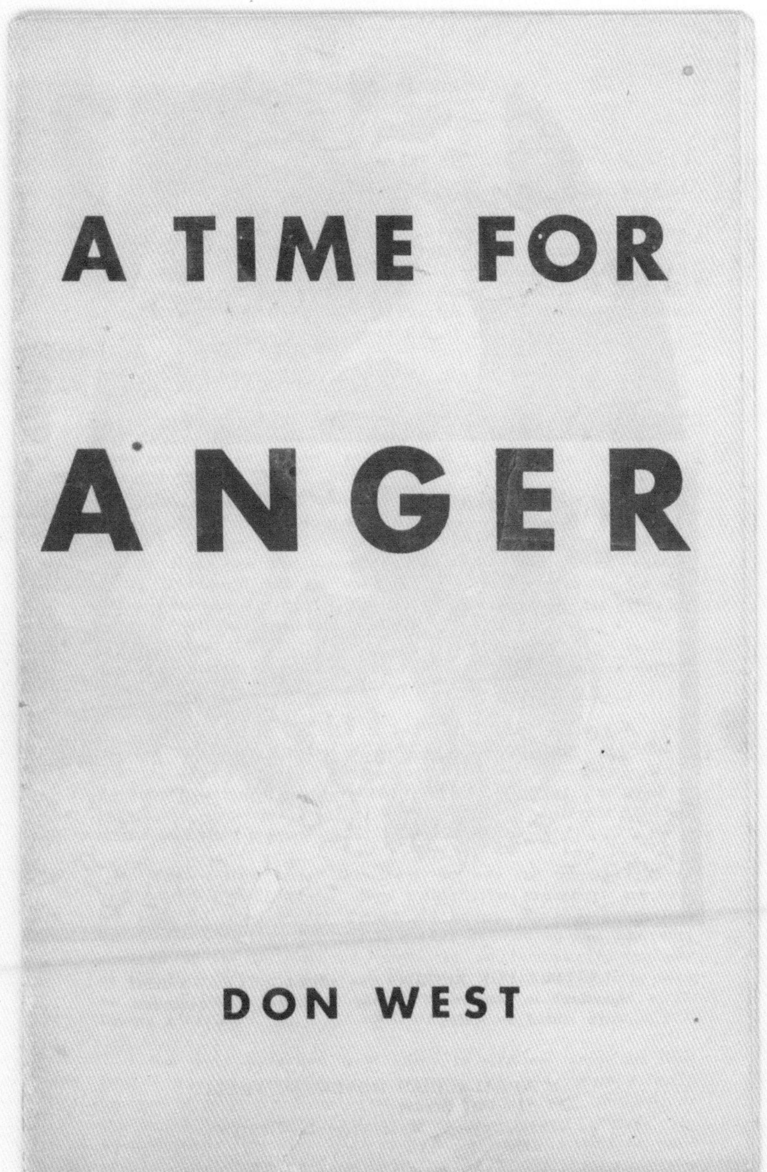

Cover of undated edition of Don West's *A Time for Anger* poetry chapbook as found at the Appalachian South Folklife Center, Pipestem, WV, 2016.

Those two friends that I first sent the logo to were Josh MacPhee and Alec "Icky" Dunn, fellow member/owners in the Justseeds Artists Cooperative and creators/editors/designers of the nearly annual publication *Signal: A Journal of Political Graphics and Culture* on PM Press. I hadn't been back home long before they asked me to find out what Appalachian Movement Press had been and then to write about what I found for *Signal*. I didn't exactly jump at the idea at first because I thought I had no idea where to start looking.

I live and work in Pittsburgh, a city set inside the flexible cultural boundaries of both Appalachia (a name we call The Land and People) and the Rust Belt (a name we call What We've Done to The Land and People). So much of my current historical focus has fallen inside the borders of West Virginia. It's not where I'm from, but if you think a lot more about time, ecology, and human culture than you do about boundaries drawn by colonialism and the nation-state, then your sense of regionality can expand. Although I came to Pittsburgh by way of Nebraska and then western and middle Tennessee, my home for the last sixteen years has been Rust Belt/Appalachia. It's where I have rooted.

My work as the creative director with the West Virginia Mine Wars Museum has steeped me in the Appalachian history of the early 1900s and the deep memories and stories that flow in a place that was riven with guerilla warfare only a century ago. As our museum grew to be an acclaimed destination for school tours and visitors from around the country, this project also helped crystalize a lot of threads for me: about the persistent power of negative regional stereotypes, about stories that are buried by the power of corporations in collusion with state government, about Appalachia as "the region apart." History is not always buried just because we don't write books about ourselves. Sometimes it's buried intentionally.

Where many of the more well-documented "movement" presses in the US during the 1970s operated in cities, Appalachian Movement Press (AMP) was specific to its mostly rural, regional context. I didn't know it at the time, but I'd been handed a piece of a history that had gone almost entirely undocumented, even though the press was right in the middle of some of the most dedicated and successful Left activism the region has seen since.

When I learned that Don and Connie West founded the Appalachian South Folklife Center, where I'd first been handed *A Time for Anger*, I thought that the press had been the Wests' self-publishing house. I spent quite a bit of time looking at Don West's life in particular, especially poring over the declassified online FBI files that had been kept on him and his wife from 1941 through 1984.

But when I started reading Jeff Biggers and George Brosi's anthology of West's work, *No Lonesome Road*, I found the names Danie Stewart and Tom Woodruff, young student activists at Marshall University. They founded Appalachian Movement Press, the book said. Now I had a live thread to follow. I had to find these guys.

Eventually I'd end up back at the Appalachian South Folklife Center, in the basement of the chapel pulling moldering copies of neglected AMP publications out of milk crates next to piles of also-moldering pulp paperbacks that nobody wanted and nobody would throw away. Activists don't always archive themselves, I was learning.

So much of my creative practice is about memory, particularly historical memory, and how this is created both collectively and personally. Pulling together the story of Appalachian Movement Press wasn't easy, not least because no one person that I found and interviewed held a golden key to unlocking the entire story. Rather, my work became the piecing together of a patchwork of clear memories and hazy recollections, conflated stories meshed with the dusty archival record. All of this was made possible by a dozen wonderful people who graciously allowed me to call them up and listen to what they'd been up to well over forty years ago. You'll hear from them all in this book, as this work was only possible from the weaving of all of their recollections.

We've already been shown that history can be taken from us and buried if we don't keep the stories alive. Let me tell you about an activist printshop at the nexus of a remarkable decade of struggle for human and environmental rights in the mountains of Appalachia.

Introduction

A Brief History of the Movement Printshop in the United States

Josh MacPhee

The upsurge in political movements in the 1960s, in the US and around the world, is now a well-worn story. A narrative less told is one focused on the printshops that emerged to produce the leaflets, posters, placards, pamphlets, buttons, and books these movements are best known for. Beginning in the mid-1960s, peaking in the mid-1970s, and petering out in the late 1980s, this country saw the rise of over two hundred printshops dedicated to printing for social movements, from Black liberation to feminism, communism to anarchism, Central American solidarity to Marxist political economy.[1] This shadow industry and national-scale social-organizing phenomenon has largely eluded attention until recently, with the book you're reading being one of less than a half-dozen volumes dedicated to the movement printshop.

Emerging out of the thaw in McCarthyism, small groups of leftist activists began assembling more publicly in the early 1960s. The civil rights movement began to take shape in the South, and in Berkeley, California, the Free Speech Movement put protest back on the geography of the social landscape. The mid-1960s saw the forming of Students for a Democratic Society and the emergence of a New Left, a potent stew of antiauthoritarians, antiwar activists, civil rights organizers, left-leaning liberals, and communists and socialists of dozens of stripes. Many of these quickly learned that while McCarthyism might have been in retreat, racism, misogyny, a prudish conservatism, and anticommunism were alive and well. Many of these new political formations had their posters and publications rejected for printing by traditional printshops and began to take to heart A. J. Liebling's maxim, "Freedom of the press is guaranteed only to those who own one."

By the late 1960s, over one hundred new printshops had popped up, and there likely hadn't been such a fervent resurgence in national print culture since the heady days of the American Revolution. Modern-day Ben Franklins and Thomas Paines churned out thousands of cheap political pamphlets to fan the flames of resistance. Berkeley Free Press, founded formally in 1965 with printing beginning a year earlier, was one of the first, with Glad Day Press in Ithaca, New York, hot on its heels.[2] As the antiwar, student, and civil rights movements evolved and expanded into the feminist, gay rights, Black Power, Chicano, New Communist movements, and more, printshops were founded to meet the needs of these new political formations.

The massive student and antiwar movements of the late sixties and early seventies created more than enough movement print work to go around, and rent and costs were cheap enough that small groups could run presses exclusively focused on agitprop. Members might take turns holding down straight jobs while the rest volunteered their time running the presses. People lived in group houses and apartments or in the shop, sometimes even sleeping above the presses, an arrangement that existed at multiple shops including Appalachian Movement Press and New York City's Come!Unity Press.[3] While a small number of these emerging shops had an organized plan, most evolved out of a need, with one person unearthing an A. B. Dick from a garage somewhere and a group coalescing around it to provide much sought after printing services.

The A. B. Dick Company was one of the major US producers of tabletop and office-scale offset printers in the twentieth century, and as such their machines are often mentioned in the origin stories of movement printshops. When I talk about printshops, I'm talking about people that ran offset presses. The term *offset* comes from the actual printing process, in which the image is photographically burned onto metal plate, the plate is placed on a circular cylinder, and that cylinder is coated with ink. As the cylinder turns, it offsets the image onto another spinning cylinder covered with a rubber blanket, which in turn offsets the image onto paper run underneath the cylinders. This is a relatively complicated process—especially before computers became involved—which entails a significant amount of what is called prepress, including preparing the artwork, shooting a photographic image of it, transferring the image to the metal plate coated with photographic film, and then developing that plate. This would need to be done for each color used in a print job. Many contemporary presses are as long as a warehouse and include the capacity to print six colors in a single pass of the paper. But the smaller, more rudimentary presses most movement shops ran were more likely the size of a large microwave or an industrial refrigerator. The A. B. Dick at Appalachian Movement Press "was kind of this behemoth, you know," Barbara Placier remembered, "clanky and a little temperamental! But Tom [Woodruff] seemed to have the knack for it."[4]

Erica Braun described the founding of Inkworks Press: "Some years ago, probably in the fall of 1973, several of us met to define the basics for a new movement printshop. We'd been presented with an opportunity that may have seemed really appealing only to me: a couple of old offset printing presses, a grand old camera, and a storefront with reasonable rent on Telegraph Avenue in Oakland. While I may have been the only one sure I wanted to do this, there were eight to ten other people sure that they wanted to have such a project succeed."[5]

And that's basically what it took—one or two people with a need and vision and a small community to support making it happen. The extent of the community depended on the press, but Danielle Aubert does a great job of articulating the scale and scope of the one organized around the Detroit Printing Co-op: "Dozens of people poured energy into making the print shop functional. Fredy Perlman would figure out how to operate the Harris press with help from Joel Landy and Carl Smith. . . . A League of Revolutionary Black Workers comrade . . . brought a professional electrician to the Co-op to wire the machines. . . . One friend, Judy Campbell, installed plumbing in the darkroom. Another friend helped them acquire an enormous supply of film, plates and darkroom supplies, purchased for $500 at auction from a bankrupt print shop."[6]

It truly took an extensive network of political projects to raise a printshop.

Different printshops had different focuses. Some, like People's Press in San Francisco or Liberation Support Movement (initially in Richmond, BC, but eventually moving to the California Bay Area), focused on publishing original content, with the group running the presses also taking on writing, editorial, design, and ultimately distribution roles. According to Rick Sterling, "From the beginning [the Liberation Support Movement] ran a printshop. In Richmond there was no movement printshops, so we had to start our own."[7] Other presses, like Red Sun in Boston or Glad Day in Ithaca, printed widely for the movements in their local area, sometimes across wide swathes of struggles and communities. The New England Free Press (Boston), SRAFprint in Mountain View, CA, and the subject of this book—the Appalachian Movement Press—almost exclusively focused on mining the history of political writing and using their presses to reprint easy to distribute and inexpensive versions of existing texts. In a way, they functioned most like the early European printers from the Protestant Reformation, churning out volumes of cheap canonical texts with little concern for copyright. Still others, such as Come!Unity in New York City and the Detroit Printing Co-op, experimented with other models of printing and organizing.

SRAFprint was rooted in an antiauthoritarian commune based in what would become Silicon Valley. SRAF stood for the Social Revolutionary Anarchist Federation, a project developed in the 1970s to give some organizational structure to the anarchist organizations in the US that wanted to think and act more strategically about how anarchist ideas could have a larger impact. Given that SRAF contained groups with extremely varied sets of politics, it not surprisingly had difficulty maintaining itself and eventually split in the early 1980s. While there was no official center for the project, SRAFprint became the informal propaganda wing, almost entirely reprinting a mix of historical anarchist texts and new stand-out anarchist writings from the period. Some of this output was printed offset, and they clearly ran a small press, but other pamphlets appear to be generated on both mimeograph duplicators and eventually even photocopiers.

While some shops coalesced around shared politics or press operators with specific ideologies, others such as New York City's Come!Unity Press functioned with almost no coherent structure at all. Self-described as a queer and anarchist project, Come!Unity came together in the early 1970s with two people—Lin and Debbie—running an A. B. Dick 360 offset press in a small Midtown loft. Both were so profoundly committed to free expression that they allowed anyone to use their press for free as long as (a) they spent the time to learn how to print their materials themselves, and (b) the item printed was either given away for free or sold for a sliding-scale donation. Nothing printed at Come!Unity was supposed to have a fixed price, as evidenced by their equivalent of a union bug that read, "Survival by Sharing/People Before Profit," with a following tagline stating variations on, "This publication is FREE to you if you do not have money—even though contributions ARE NEEDED."[8] One would expect that their stoned, all-night printing free-for-alls might limit those interested in using the press, but instead they have some of the most diverse printing output of all the movement presses. Gay poetry chapbooks, Caribbean Marxist journals, anarcha-feminist pamphlets, Industrial Workers of the World (IWW) flyers, Black nationalist newsletters, alternative education course catalogs, Leo Tolstoy novellas, and Third World lesbian magazines all came rolling off the press for the decade or so that it ran.

A similar cosmopolitanism developed at the Detroit Printing Co-op. The co-op was comprised of an informal collection of publishing projects: the anarchist Fredy Perlman and his Black & Red Press; Bewick/ed, a publishing project of Marty Glaberman, a council communist comrade of C. L. R. James and Grace Lee Boggs; Black Star Press, a publishing wing of the League of Revolutionary Black Workers; in addition to some smaller projects. For a time the co-op printed *Radical America*, a journal of the Students for a Democratic Society; a couple issues of the local literary journal *riverrun*; and a radical paper produced by high school students called *Rebel's Voice*. It was an IWW union shop, and everything it printed featured a union bug that read, in part, "Abolish the State—Abolish Wage Labor."

With a robust armed underground movement in the 1970s (the Weather Underground, the Black Liberation Army, New World Liberation Front, and Symbionese Liberation Army to name just a small number of the dozens of groups committed to armed struggle against the status quo), movement printshops also helped with some of the less-than-legal printing that became necessary—from churning out communiqués taking credit for militant actions to the production of fake identity documents and more. The Weather Underground actually set up their own underground printshop, Red Dragon Press, to print and publish their manifesto *Prairie Fire* and the early issues of their magazine *Osawatomie*. I personally stumbled on evidence of some of these marginal activities when helping to move a printshop in Chicago in the late 1990s. Pushing a piece of machinery away from the wall, we unearthed a long-lost envelope containing dozens of driver's licenses, all featuring the face of the same midthirties Black man but each one from a different state with a different name.

Each of these unique and fascinating ways that shops evolved and organized were also not entirely mutually exclusive. As Shaun has shown with Appalachian Movement Press, not only did AMP produce their own editions of key political texts around labor and social struggle in the region, they also did job work for other political groupings, cultural organizing, and even poetry chapbooks. In another example, by the late 1970s Inkworks had become the go-to printshop for dozens of political organizations across the Bay Area. But this didn't stop the workers from developing their own in-house editorial projects, including the ambitious monthly community calendar broadsheet, produced from 1976 through 1979. On top of all their consistent job work, they collected a robust list of local events, daily historical notes, and unique artwork on a monthly basis. In a mirrored set of actions, People's Press was almost entirely editorially focused, creating unique one-off publications they wrote, edited, laid out, printed, and distributed. But this didn't stop them in the early 1970s from working closely with the Cuban Organization of Solidarity of the Peoples of Africa, Asia, and Latin America (OSPAAAL) to print a North American edition of their influential journal *Tricontinental.*

—

As far as I know, there has been no direct data collection about movement shops across the country. The closest thing to that is Lincoln Cushing's ongoing and informal but quite comprehensive aggregating of information about movement printshops in the California Bay Area. On his website docspopuli.org, Lincoln has organized information on fifty printshops that ran in the Bay Area between 1963 and 2016.[9] Of these shops, twenty-five of them were offset printing, and in terms of internal organization and output, they run the gamut of forms mentioned earlier, from small collective operations that functioned more as publishers than printshops to large shops that ran jobs for thousands of organizations, actions, and campaigns. With seven shops lasting less than five years, and only ten surviving over ten years, the numbers suggest that five years to a decade was about the natural life cycle of a movement shop. While the density of shops in the Bay Area wasn't replicated anywhere else, anecdotal evidence shows roughly the same results. A small number of shops were flexible or lucky enough to survive beyond a decade (a couple are still around), but the majority called it quits within ten years. This is nearly the exact timeline of Appalachian Movement Press, which ran for a decade before the press was handed over to Don West and the Appalachian South Folklife Center.

The 1980s were hard on movement shops. Across the board they had to fight intense pressure from three different fronts. First, social movements in the eighties were shrinking and changing. Second, for relatively small volume printing, the offset press was replaced by the copy machine. Third, operational costs for running a printshop increased exponentially.

1.

The social movements that spawned the shops were in disarray with shrinking memberships. Party-oriented and ideologically focused (whether Maoist, Trotskyist, or dozens of other variations) organization gave way to a new mass politics: the antinuclear movements, more mainstream union drives, solidarity with Central America, and electoral campaigns—including everything from Black mayoral candidates to Jesse Jackson's presidential bids in 1984 and 1988. While these new movement formations still needed printing, much of it needed to be union printed and produced in quantities and scales difficult for the older movement shops to keep up with.

Many shops that couldn't or didn't want to scale up shifted instead to more cultural work, with former activists still involved in the arts, community theater, music scenes, and more. This work kept some shops afloat through the late seventies and eighties, but the culture wars and Ronald Reagan's war on art led to slashes in funding, particularly from the National Endowment of the Arts, which in turn shrunk cultural institutions' budgets across the country and dried up a lot of this work. In addition, the antinuclear, Central American solidarity, and identity-based community movements of the eighties developed their own political culture and were responsible for the creation of a smaller batch of new shops that emerged in the 1980s, including Brushfire Graphics in Boston and La Raza Graphics in San Francisco.

Many activists—especially those that were white and came from affluent backgrounds—turned towards more individuated solutions to social problems: new age gurus, yoga, crystals, Gestalt therapy, and more. This had begun in the seventies but solidified in the eighties with a massive emerging economic infrastructure around self-help and self-improvement. Much of this was profoundly neo-liberal, encouraging individual entrepreneurship. The folks that once printed political posters now needed business cards and flyers with phone number pull tabs. Many political printshops needed to figure out how to survive, so they evolved with their clientele, turning to commercial job work, much of it gleaned from former colleagues who now ran small businesses, restaurants, cultural institutions, and the aforementioned new age industry. But converting to commercial printing was a tricky proposition, and by the eighties many movement shops had already failed to make the shift. Started in 1963, Berkeley Free Press was one of the earliest movement shops, and in 1967 it evolved into Berkeley Graphic Arts in order to capture more nonpolitical jobs. But after hanging on into early 1971 as a commercial printer, "the realities of trying to print competitively with ancient machines and modestly skilled workers caught up with [them]."[10]

The more militant elements of the movements that still existed tended to be seriously underfunded, while movement press operations were getting older, had families, and wanted to make a living wage. Many shops unionized. For some this was an extension of their politics. Erica Braun wrote about Inkworks, "Being in a union was important to us. A couple of early Inkworkers were involved in efforts to organize quick print shops as well as theater workers at a local movie house. Being able to meet the terms of a union contract was part of our notion of viability for our project—besides, we might at any time be out on the streets looking for work."[11] Many of the earlier printshops were all members of the anarchic Industrial Workers of the World I. U. 450, their printing wing. In the 1970s, the IWW even produced a special newsletter with these shops, *The Rebel Printer*. Ross Newport from Santa Cruz's Community Printers said, "When we first got started the AFL-CIO unions didn't want anything to do with worker co-ops so we joined the Wobblies. We kept pushing the conventional unions to accept us, which they eventually did. I wish we maintained our IWW affiliation, but we were looking for recognition of the larger labor movement."[12] This recognition was important because it opened the door to steady, well-paid union printing contracts, which were very important since unions were one of the only elements of the left that still had significant budgets. But this effectively made many of these once do-it-yourself printshops unaffordable to younger activists attempting to continue to do more insurgent work. I remember being extremely frustrated in my late twenties when I approached a printshop that had started out as a movement shop—and still presented as political—about printing some posters about political prisoners and getting a quote back so far out of my price range as to be laughable.

2.

By the early eighties, we saw the triumphant rise of the copy machine. With the turn of the decade, most people had at least some access to office printing technology—either in their workplace or through a family member. Also, copy shops started popping up in the urban landscape, replacing the mom-and-pop offset print infrastructure. An offset press is designed for large volume printing—it takes a lot of labor to set up a job for print and is relatively messy and wasteful of ink and paper, so once you are printing, the economic benefit is in economies of scale. Photocopiers, on the other hand, cost a lot to service but are easy to lease, much more user friendly, and designed to print effectively in smaller volumes. Although the unit cost of a photocopy is ultimately much higher than that of an offset printed page, it is easy to make ten, twenty, or one hundred copies, something completely inefficient and ridiculous to do with a press. This flexibility of micro print runs ended up often better suiting the needs of shrinking movements. The Xerox was the perfect machine for a social context in which movement work was increasingly bifurcated, with massive print jobs by unions, non-profits, and electoral campaigns going to large union printshops and much, much smaller niche activism and its printing needs happening on very local and countercultural levels. The copy machine became the darling of both punk kids and community groups organizing local antidevelopment campaigns, allowing them to print what they needed quickly and exactly when they needed it, with none of the setup that makes offset printing much more time and labor intensive.

3.

The final major change that affected movement shops was a rapid rise of operational costs. I already mentioned the drive to professionalization, so with unionization, families, and a need for stability, the costs of labor often doubled or tripled between the seventies and eighties. Many shops were printing on the same equipment they had been founded with, which ran slower and less efficiently than more modern presses. Because so many movement printers began as activists, not trades or business people, they never created plans for growth, equipment improvement, or lasting for more than what was on the immediate horizon.

With the rise of digital printing, many customers began to desire full-color work, which was difficult to effectively do on old school one- and two-color printing presses. This led to having to charge more, in effect leading all but the most loyal customers to turn towards commercial printshops with much more contemporary equipment, and thus faster turnarounds and higher quality.

As if all this wasn't enough, the shops that did survive the eighties had to face an even bigger challenge in the nineties. Cities saw themselves in the early throes of a new wave of urban development and rapidly moving gentrification. As wealthier people, and commerce, began to return to the urban core, there was a huge spike in rent and cost of living. Light industry such as printing was especially hard hit, as the formerly industrial zones so many shops were tucked into very quickly started the transformation into lofts and eventually condos.

As a case in point, in the late nineties in Chicago, I was part of a small crew of anarchists that started hanging out and being trained to print at C&D Printshop, a small press on Damen Avenue on the Near North Side that had begun as the press of the Sojourner Truth Organization, a seventies communist group. While C&D still did as much movement work as they could, their bread and butter mostly came from printing posters and 7" record covers for the local music scene and a couple large-scale jobs for bookstores and cultural institutions. Five hundred full-color concert posters, which today would be churned out by a digital press within an hour at pennies a piece, back then took days to shoot film for each of the four color separations (all full-color imagery used to be created by mixing four basic ink colors: cyan, magenta, yellow, and black, or CMYK), prep the film in a process called stripping, make aluminum plates for each color, and then print the poster on an old one-color Ryobi press, so that the paper would have to be run through the press four times to assemble the facsimile of full color. The folks that ran the press were getting older and realized that they neither had the capital nor the desire to convert C&D into a modern printshop, so they retired and left the press to our ragtag group. We rechristened the project Bad Dog Press and proceeded to run it into the ground in less than two years. Part of this was the fault of our inexperience and poor business sense, but a large portion of the responsibility also can be placed on external shoulders. The shop was located in a "Business Improvement District," basically a city scheme to boost development, and within months of taking over, we were forced to move locations—which is not cheap when you're talking about equipment with weight measured in tons, not pounds.

In contrast, Inkworks survived into the twenty-first century by quickly adopting digital technologies and transitioning their business into a more environmentally focused model. They were union-organized and worker-run, had local access to one of the larger hubs of social activism and organizing (the San Francisco Bay Area), and had high quality, modern presses. But even this wasn't enough to keep up with rising overhead, leading to the shop closing in 2016.

There are still survival stories. Salsedo Press in Chicago—itself an evolution from an earlier shop called the Print Co-op—was on the brink of folding in the early mid-2000s when they hit an odd stroke of luck. A one-off massive hail storm swept through the Midwest, and Salsedo's skylights were shattered, sending shards of glass into all the presses.[13] They were well insured, and the insurance payout allowed for the purchase of completely new equipment and a newfound ability to meet the needs of a wider customer base with much more competitive pricing. While struggling in some ways, Red Sun Press is still chugging along in Boston, and a handful of other shops with origins in the rise of the movement press are still hanging on. In addition, there has been a recent resurgence in interest in movement and political printing, with small new shops like the worker-owned Radix Media emerging in Brooklyn. Radix runs an offset press but also offers full-service digital printing, oversized banner and sign printing, as well as a complete letterpress shop. It is these new hybrid printshops, merging new and old technologies with social justice orientations, that are the heirs to the movement printshop of the sixties and seventies.

Part I

The Press

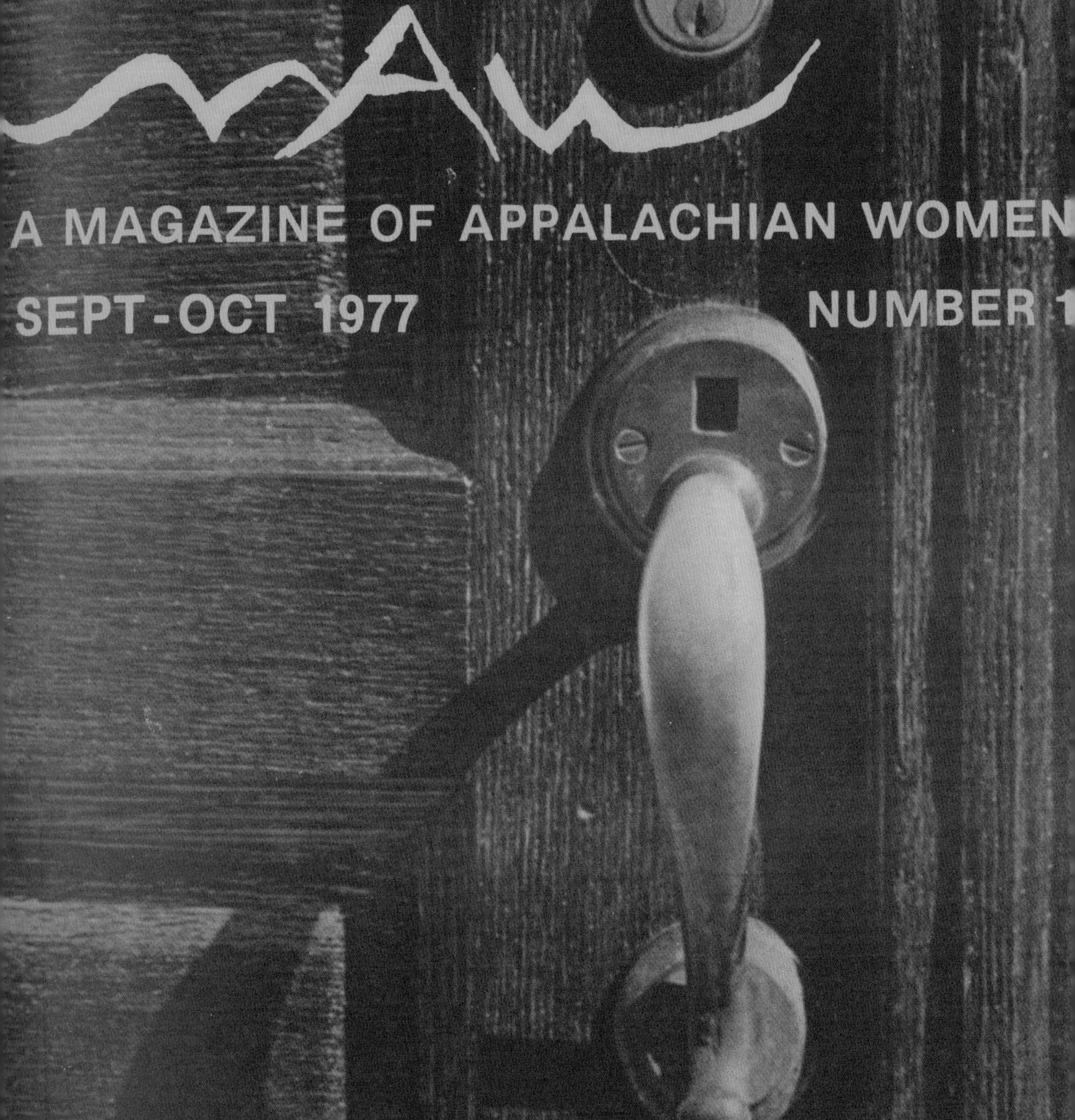

NEW APPALACHIAN WOMEN'S
ORGANIZATION FORMED . . p. 4

To Gain a Greater Degree of Freedom

The Birth of an Activist Printshop in the Mountains

In the fall of 1969, a few of us in Huntington decided we needed a print shop. We decided that this was our only hope in getting correct and full information to all Appalachians. We had been through many years of education in our mountain schools and knew what a complete lack of any information on our culture and history and on our present day political and economic existence there was. We wanted to print pamphlets on famous Appalachians who are ignored in schoolbooks. We wanted to print pamphlets on our Appalachian heritage—on the fight against slavery by mountain people at the time of the Civil War, on the long struggle to gain a greater degree of freedom through organizing unions in the coalfields, and on the general spirit of independence and self-reliance of Appalachians throughout history. We wanted to print pamphlets about how today all our

> wealth is being taken from us—the wealth we produce, with our resources and our labor, that does not benefit us, but is added to the bank accounts of super-rich corporate owners in Philadelphia, New York, and Pittsburgh.
>
> —Tom Woodruff, foreword to *A Time for Anger* by Don West

Early in 1969, after battling years of public resistance and organized conservative red-baiting, a small group of students at Marshall University in the southern West Virginia city of Huntington finally gained official college recognition for their chapter of the national activist network Students for a Democratic Society (SDS). Founded in 1965, the Marshall SDS group's activism sparked a full-blown red scare in Huntington, aggravating rifts that ran along an already existing college/town divide. As opposition to the US war in Vietnam grew nationally and antiwar sentiment came to a Cabell County citizenry that may have seen itself as immune to the New Left, even the suggestion of student organizing at Marshall sparked local fears of violent street protests. The Huntington SDS chapter didn't survive the national dissolution of the SDS as an entity, which occurred soon after Marshall president Roland Nelson granted the group official status. But the local shift in ideas about activism brought on by the relentless battle for recognition from the college and community was profound. The activists were emboldened to develop resources for their movement—and the most crucial of these was a printshop.[1]

By the end of 1969, economics grad student Tom Woodruff and social worker/ex-marine Danie Stewart—both organizers in the resilient Huntington SDS group—began working to put together the equipment to start an activist-run printing press to serve the growing movement that they were working within. Civil rights activist Errol Hess, an electrical engineering and English graduate from Marshall, worked with Woodruff, Stewart, and others for six months to raise the $750 they needed to buy a suite of used but functional equipment. "I shook my head when Tom showed me the press he wanted to buy sitting in the alley behind a printing company. But he got it running," said Hess.[2]

Although Hess remembers that the first thing to roll off the new presses was a pamphlet in support of a Levi's Company strike in North

Carolina, their first long-term objective was to print the regular paper that their SDS chapter had produced since early 1966, *Free Forum*.[3] The young activists had been printing their magazine at the local shop Modern Press, where the owner was sympathetic to both content and cost. Anti-Left pressure on that shop eventually made the relationship untenable, although the owner continued to make printing plates for the paper until Woodruff and the others could get their darkroom up and running.[4]

Published as part literary platform, part political statement, *Free Forum* was actually started by Hess a few years earlier, in 1963, before he handed it off and the SDS activists rebooted it as volume 1, issue 1, in March of 1966. The student editors and writers published under pseudonyms, as they proclaimed that their magazine's policy would be "to create an accessable [*sic*] and anonymous media for the presentation

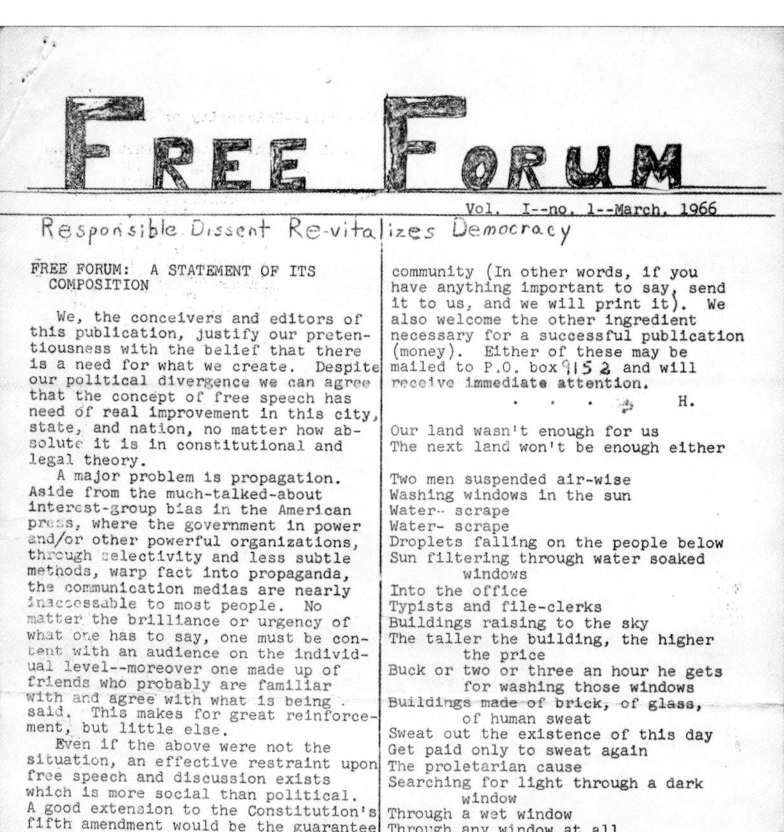

FREE FORUM

Vol. I--no. 1--March, 1966

Responsible Dissent Re-vitalizes Democracy

FREE FORUM: A STATEMENT OF ITS COMPOSITION

We, the conceivers and editors of this publication, justify our pretentiousness with the belief that there is a need for what we create. Despite our political divergence we can agree that the concept of free speech has need of real improvement in this city, state, and nation, no matter how absolute it is in constitutional and legal theory.

A major problem is propagation. Aside from the much-talked-about interest-group bias in the American press, where the government in power and/or other powerful organizations, through selectivity and less subtle methods, warp fact into propaganda, the communication medias are nearly inaccessable to most people. No matter the brilliance or urgency of what one has to say, one must be content with an audience on the individual level--moreover one made up of friends who probably are familiar with and agree with what is being said. This makes for great reinforcement, but little else.

Even if the above were not the situation, an effective restraint upon free speech and discussion exists which is more social than political. A good extension to the Constitution's fifth amendment would be the guarantee

community (In other words, if you have anything important to say, send it to us, and we will print it). We also welcome the other ingredient necessary for a successful publication (money). Either of these may be mailed to P.O. box 9152 and will receive immediate attention.

. . . H.

Our land wasn't enough for us
The next land won't be enough either

Two men suspended air-wise
Washing windows in the sun
Water-- scrape
Water- scrape
Droplets falling on the people below
Sun filtering through water soaked windows
Into the office
Typists and file-clerks
Buildings raising to the sky
The taller the building, the higher the price
Buck or two or three an hour he gets for washing those windows
Buildings made of brick, of glass, of human sweat
Sweat out the existence of this day
Get paid only to sweat again
The proletarian cause
Searching for light through a dark window
Through a wet window
Through any window at all

Masthead of *Free Forum*, March 1966.

of serious thought, whether or not the editors agree with what is said." Readers were encouraged to submit writing, and the editors also welcomed "the other ingredient necessary for a successful publication (money). Either of these may be mailed to P.O. Box 9152 and will receive immediate attention."[5]

Woodruff and the others had their printshop up and running in Huntington by early 1970. Two thirty-year-old A. B. Dick offset

Tom Woodruff, twenty-three years old at the AMP printshop, as photographed for an article in *West Virginia Illustrated*, July–August 1972.

presses, a binding machine, a paper cutter, tools to stock a darkroom, and other related gear eventually formed the basis for a working, if relatively scrappy, printshop.[6] With the no-frills mission of "getting correct and full information to all Appalachians," the young printers named their nascent shop Appalachian Movement Press (AMP), planting a regional flag in the national trend of activist printshops that were run by, and for, the movements in which they were born. As well as filling a pragmatic niche where equipment was needed to realize their own local needs, Woodruff, Stewart, and the others began developing a radical, independent, regional press with the overall mission of uplifting Appalachian people to self-determination.

—

The Appalachian Regional Commission defines the whole of the Appalachian region geographically by drawing clear cartographic lines following the spine of the Appalachian mountain range from southern New York to northern Mississippi. The central Appalachian region, where Appalachian Movement Press was focused, encompasses eastern Tennessee, western North Carolina, eastern Kentucky, parts of western Virginia and eastern Ohio, and the entire state of West Virginia.[7] But

Danie Stewart, yearbook photo from the 1965 edition of Marshall University's *Chief Justice.*

"Appalachia" as a popular concept is maybe better understood as an area of cultural boundaries, and Appalachian Movement Press was born in a context specific to a burgeoning regional identity movement and new theories on the Left about the "colonization" of central Appalachia for resource extraction. The broad cohort that AMP worked within was comprised of organizations that were part of grassroots movements speaking almost exclusively to people living in their home region.

In James Lorence's *A Hard Journey*, activist and librarian Yvonne Farley remembers AMP as part of "an Appalachian intifada": a growing network of leftist activists in central Appalachia in the 1970s who were organizing around (or splintering from) federal War on Poverty initiatives, involved in actions against strip mining, battling corruption in the United Mine Workers of America (UMWA) union, and fighting for recognition and treatment of black lung disease (coal workers' pneumoconiosis) among myriad other struggles.[8] Many of these activists were exploring a newly expressed "Appalachian identity" that resisted mainstream stereotypes of the region as backward and challenged industrial capitalism for its responsibility in creating and maintaining systemic poverty in the region. Counting the victories by the end of the 1970s, George Brosi stressed that "Appalachian activists accomplished more for Appalachian people *on a national scale* in the 1970s than anyone else in any other region," and AMP was critical within these regional struggles.[9]

As well as creating and distributing their own catalog of branded literature as part of the Appalachian Movement Press imprint, AMP served as the regional go-to printshop for many like-minded organizations in the coalfields of Appalachia, and they often charged about half of the market rate. *Mountain Life & Work*, the quarterly magazine of the Council of the Southern Mountains which Woodruff helped to edit, was their first sustaining bread-and-butter printing contract.[10] Variously for the next ten years, AMP workers would continue to print an impressive array of regionally focused publications besides their own, at rates which kept their shop, and these publications, viable on shoestring budgets:

- *MAW: Magazine of Appalachian Women,* the first (and maybe only) feminist magazine of its kind in the region during the 1970s.

- *Mountain Call*, an upstart bimonthly from Mingo County that blended environmentalism and rural lifestyle concerns with working-class, unionist politics.
- *Green Revolution*, the national monthly magazine of the rural cooperative living organization, School of Living.
- *Peoples Appalachia,* the quarterly independent journal of the Peoples Appalachian Research Collective out of Morgantown, WV. "Material may be reprinted for people's struggle purposes."

Unique to the ten years in which AMP operated, the young "New Left" activists who were involved in the printshop notably chose an intergenerational approach to their activism by working with the lifelong "Old Left" activist (and cofounder of the Highlander Folk School) Don West. AMP regularly reprinted West's popular poetry and published the social critiques and historical writings that defined his later work. They were, in practice, West's exclusive sounding board by the 1970s.

"Going through those [AMP] publications and reading them, you would think that the mountains were on the edge of a revolution," writer Jim Branscome told me during a phone interview at the beginning of 2019.[11] But AMP's beginnings were humble, idealistic, and immediate. Without the money to rent an office, and maybe also because the arrangement more intimately positioned their new equipment communally within the daily activities of the SDS-borne activist scene in Huntington, the first Appalachian Movement Press shop was located in a house owned by the father of Dave Workman, one of the original printers.

"I don't think that David ever told his father that [the printshop operating out of his house] was happening," Tom Woodruff told me. "We actually set the darkroom up in the basement—I remember that. And we had the presses in what would have been the dining room and living room. And then there were bedrooms upstairs."[12] Eventually operated aboveboard financially, and organized for tax purposes as a corporation, the printshop's first "stockholders" were Woodruff, Jeanine Stewart (then married to Danie), and Robert Gatewood.[13] "I remember at one time there were four names on the check," Woodruff recalled, including Sherrie Edwards. But, as with many of the people who worked with

AMP or came into contact with their work through the 1970s, many recollections of names, roles, and details have worn down over the years.[14]

When I asked many of the AMP printers what the goal of the printshop had been, the name of revolutionary writer Thomas Paine came up often. Paine might be the first and last famous pamphleteer in the United States—and, typically, it's the big personalities and the events that they inspire that get the focus of the popular history lens.

Cover of *Mountain Life & Work*, March 1971.

Meanwhile, the steadfast resources, like a printshop run by people who weren't concerned to be recognized by name, are easily overlooked. Workhorse activist projects, like a movement press, can often be seen as a means to an end, with their inner workings unimportant to memorialize. Yet in starting and maintaining their own printshop in service to the movements in their time, in the largely rural and working-class central Appalachian context, Appalachian Movement Press became a keystone revolutionary resource on their home turf.

Offset press at the AMP printshop as photographed for an article in *West Virginia Illustrated*, July–August 1972.

Sub includes all pamphlets published over a year (estimated at about 20), plus calendar, plus news and information about mountain people and groups struggling for social change.

Rates: $7.50 for working people
$7.50 for students
$12.50 for professionals
$15.00 for libraries & institutions
$25.00 for wealthy people
(income over $15,000)
$0.00 for unemployed Appalachians

Write to: Appalachian Movement Press
P.O. Box 8074
Huntington
West Virginia 25705
(304) 523-8587

$0.00 for Unemployed Appalachians

Design, Distribution, and People

"They were real troublemakers," John Clark would tell me about the founders of Appalachian Movement Press, "and they had a printing press."[15]

By 1972 the AMP printshop was running "on a full time basis."[16] They had since moved their equipment out of Dave Workman's father's house and were now renting a building at the northeast corner of the intersection of Sixteenth Street and Eighth Avenue. With a couple of boarded-over windows, a cardboard sign in the glass front door, and rent at ninety dollars a month, the new building housed all of their printing equipment and included a "bookstore": several small shelves in the first-floor entryway that specialized in radical literature.[17] "Not that anyone ever came by," remembered Barbara Ervin Placier. "It wasn't exactly the kind of place where you'd get foot traffic coming in to browse."[18] Woodruff, a paid AMP employee on subsistence wages, lived upstairs with the photographer Amos (Bill) Perrine and friends Errol Hess and Bob Placier, who were working as roofers.[19]

Appalachian Movement Press printshop and apartment at northeast corner of Sixteenth Street and Eighth Avenue, Huntington, WV.

"The walls are peeling plaster and the ceiling visibly sags," wrote one mystified reporter for *West Virginia Illustrated* in the summer of 1972.[20] "Probably the fact that [the building] was vacant and cheap was the main motivation" for renting their first office in that particular location, said Hess. "Rent in white Huntington was much higher than rent in Black Huntington."[21] At Appalachian Movement Press, these young white college graduates were now running a leftist printshop situated within the largely African American neighborhood of Huntington, south of the railroad tracks that bisect the city and defined a line of racial and economic segregation. However, with the exception of Hess, who worked as a mechanic at a nearby Volkswagen repair shop, the AMP printers had very little to do with the neighborhood generally.

AMP was a group of young white *men*, to put a finer point on it. Reflecting the entrenched sexism that was only beginning to be significantly challenged within Left movements specifically and American society generally, the Huntington printshop looks to have

Barbara Placier Ervin at the AMP printshop in 1971.

been a less-than-egalitarian organization for most of its ten-year run.[22] Barbara Ervin Placier came to the AMP shop from Ohio University in the summer of 1971 to join her brother and their mutual friends in Huntington. Younger than most of the others at twenty-one, she often helped with childcare for the other printers and lived upstairs at the Sixteenth Street/Eighth Avenue office for several months. During that time, Tom Woodruff taught Placier the darkroom process to make the photographic plates necessary for offset printing. Though she maintains that she respected and admired the men in charge of AMP, Placier felt marginalized: "Even when I started learning in the press, I don't think there was ever an expectation that I would be part of any decision making, or that there was a real future that I would have there. I was window dressing, in many ways."[23] These politics would eventually come to a head at the end of the 1970s, when the AMP printers who

Barbara Placier Ervin and unknown woman (on couch), asleep in the upstairs apartment at the AMP printshop in 1971.

created the first feminist magazine in the region would aggravate these rifts enough to accelerate the final chapter of the printshop.

In these first years, however, what began as an effort to compile the equipment necessary to continue printing *Free Forum* quickly evolved into a fully functioning "movement" printshop within the Appalachian Left. With Woodruff leading the shop, Appalachian Movement Press provided their printing tools and know-how in service to other activists in the region, and AMP became the central job-printing house for organizations like the UMWA reformists Miners for Democracy, the Welfare Rights Organization, the Council of the Southern Mountains, the Black Lung Association, the Workers Alliance for Fair Compensation, and a myriad of other activist groups.[24]

But they hadn't started out with the plan to print their *own* catalog of publications. "To tell you the truth, I don't know exactly where the concept of the Appalachian Movement Press, in terms of publishing our own pamphlets, was born," Tom Woodruff explained. "The original idea was to have a press that would print progressive leaflets and pamphlets and materials for other groups in West Virginia, Kentucky, southern Appalachia."[25] Once they had all of the tools in hand, however, it was only a matter of time before they began cranking out staple-bound pamphlets under the new Appalachian Movement Press imprint. They had started their own publishing house.

Their tone was defiant as the young activists bushwhacked a path for AMP. "We, as Appalachians, are being lied to. Our teachers lie, our school boards lie, our politicians lie, our TV stations lie, books lie, magazines lie—we have heard the same lie so many times that we have come to accept it," Woodruff writes in the 1972 introduction to their *Paint Creek Miner: Famous Labor Songs from Appalachia*. "We, as Appalachians, are seeking out our history, digging through the lies, and coming up with our true heroes, our true heritage, and our true direction for the future."

Now, with their well-worn but functional offset printing equipment, they could easily create and distribute historical writing that they hoped would remedy the lack of education on Appalachian history in their home region and build a fuller picture of the mountains that embraced a more radical past than the broader US culture gave the region credit for. As for documenting the lies happening around them in real time in the 1970s, AMP began republishing anticorruption journalism from other, more widely distributed (and funded) periodicals.

Soon enough, regional bookstores and college libraries were stocking titles from the Appalachian Movement Press imprint, and already by the middle of 1972, AMP publications were being used in classes at Berea College in Kentucky as well as West Virginia University and West Virginia State.[26] The printers booked tables for distributing their pamphlets at music festivals and conferences, and they pushed annual mail-order subscriptions with a tiered pricing structure based on income. Subscribers were promised back orders as well as new materials as soon as the ink dried on them. The back of a 1972 pamphlet advertised an early list of annual subscription rates:

$7.50 for working Appalachians
$5.00 for students
$0.00 for unemployed Appalachians
$25.00 for wealthy Appalachians (income over $15,000)
$15.00 for libraries and institutions

Additional donations towards supplementing free subscriptions for the unemployed were encouraged. In 1972 the Appalachian Movement Press imprint had around three hundred subscribers.[27] As well as receiving new titles as they were produced, readers were also sent some of the other relevant activist job-printing materials coming out of the shop in Huntington. "In this way subscribers are kept abreast of at least a portion of the ongoing community and organizational struggles in the region," says their 1973 catalog.

AMP subscription receipt from 1971, with handwritten note from Jeanine Caywood Stewart to subscriber George Brosi.

APPALACHIAN MOVEMENT PRESS, INC.
P. O. Box 8074
Huntington, West Virginia 25705

Thank you for your subscription to Appalachian Movement Press. It begins on 10/1/71 and expires 10/1/72. The first shipment of our publications should reach you in a few days. There will usually be a mailing every month. Below is a list of publications which were distributed before your subscription came into effect. They may be ordered at the cover price in single copy or bulk (20% discount on 100 or more). Please include 15% to cover mailing cost. Thanks again.

Peoples Cultural Heritage in Appalachia, by Don West	15¢
Thoughts of Mother Jones, edited by Jim Axelrod	10¢
Picking Poverty's Pocket, by Barkan and Lloyd	20¢
Paint Creek Miner, by Charles Patterson	25¢
A Time For Anger, poems by Don West	25¢
West Virginia Wonderland, by William Blizzard	15¢
What's Next?, by Ernest Seeman	75¢
Conspiracy in Coal, by Tom Bethell	20¢
Annhilating the Hillbilly, by Jim Branscome	15¢
Romantic Appalachia, Poverty Pays if You Ain't Poor, by Don West	25¢

By 1974, Woodruff gained over $8,000 in funding through a local Episcopal church, and the shop was able to update and overhaul much of their aging equipment.

George,

This is not a Complete literature list. A new one is being printed and we'll send you some copies of it at the end of the month.

Thanks for your encouragement,

Jeanine S

AMP subscription receipt from 1971, with handwritten note from Jeanine Caywood Stewart to subscriber George Brosi.

A majority of the extant publications on the Appalachian Movement Press imprint are dated from early 1970 through 1974. These are the publications that bear their logo, or printer's colophon, as I'd first encountered it in 2016: a simple drawing of a coal miner's pick, the words "Appalachian Movement Press" striking across the pick handle, with the slogan "Labor Donated" as an inverted arch below, which matches the curve of the pick head above. This logo appears on the front or back cover of nearly every AMP publication, a bold and clear graphic expression of the press's steadfast focus on the history and culture of working Appalachians, which, by and large, had centered on the labor of extracting coal underground for generations.

Although, to say that *all* of the labor that went into AMP's productions was donated wasn't entirely accurate. "People are paid," Woodruff told one journalist in their first few years, "but there are no profits made."[28] In 1972, the AMP logo added the word "Union" before "Labor Donated," reflecting Woodruff's membership in the Workers Education Union Local 189 of the American Federation of Teachers. This subtle change expressed AMP's perennial lack of aesthetic fussiness—the original slogan appears to have just been shifted, by hand, to one side to make room for the additional word. In this way it remained for years, clearly cut and pasted, out of balance, and charmingly uncorrected. Eventually Woodruff would become a member of the Graphic Arts International Union, but because the AMP shop remained too small to take the required number of annual contracts to be a certified union shop, Woodruff fudged a GAIU "bug" that he quietly used on some of their back covers.[29] They still steered their larger commercial inquiries to local union shops. Later members, despite their politics, were not always able (or willing) to afford the GAIU membership dues.[30]

As for their design sense, a few AMP publications reproduced a photo here and there or reprinted classic cartoons from older socialist or communist papers. But the printshop generally never bothered to include many graphics inside or on the covers of their own publications. Until the aesthetics shifted with the influence of new members in the last part of the 1970s, most of their titles had no illustrations at all. Maybe this was part of a desire to keep their pamphlets looking accessible to all and "workmanlike," or maybe the printers just didn't know many artists, even amongst the Marshall University studio art students.

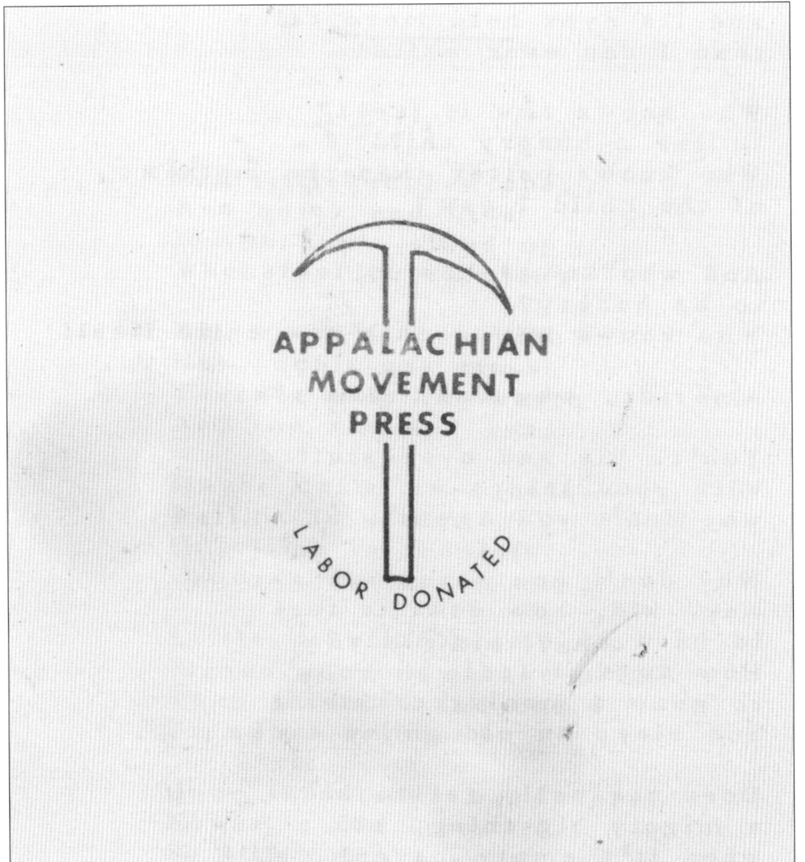

Appalachian Movement Press logo, first version, early 1970s.

Only the art in their 1972 *The Appalachian Struggle: Then & Now* paperclip-bound wall calendar stands wildly apart from the entire AMP catalog, before or since. Detailed illustrations by Malcolm Richards harken to the blatant messaging of the 1930s socialist cartoons that the printshop was clearly fond of and render calendar pages so dense that the whole is nearly unusable as a scheduling tool—even if it *does* make for a nice set of twelve 11" × 17" posters. The captivating effort of *The Appalachian Struggle* to illustrate systematically and literally the concerns of the Appalachian Left at the time presages the large-format allegorical *The True Cost of Coal* poster that the Beehive Design Collective would create in the same region, about many of the exact same social and environmental issues, over three decades later in 2008.

Detail from "The Temple of Conspicuous Consumption," a section of the Beehive Design Collective's "True Cost of Coal" poster (2008), next to Malcolm Richard's "Solidarity Gives Power" (September), from AMP's 1972 *The Appalachian Struggle: Past & Present* calendar.

AMP's follow-up 1973 calendar, however, reins in these aesthetics in the interest of again producing an uncluttered, utilitarian wall calendar, keeping the pages empty enough to function as a tool.

When viewed side by side, the overall look of nearly everything AMP produced begins to suggest an aesthetic of its own. Each title is a declaration. The covers appear to have been printed on whatever color paper stock was available, varying through editions. Pages inside were clear, clean, and uncluttered throughout. It could be that the AMP "look" was largely circumstantial—perhaps they felt that the literature and reporting they published should arrive in packaging that was clear, with the design simple and stark so as not to alienate a wide, working-class readership. It's not uncommon, after all, for graphic arts to be regarded largely, almost exclusively, on utilitarian grounds in leftist circles in the United States.

Detail from "The Dance of Hard Choices," a section of the Beehive Design Collective's "True Cost of Coal" poster (2008), above Malcolm Richard's "Lives Going Up in Smoke" (March), from AMP's 1972 *The Appalachian Struggle: Past & Present* calendar.

In any case, the prevailing aesthetic of the Appalachian Movement Press imprint is decidedly bold and austere, and to my imagination the sensibility feels very immediate, informed by the need to get the publications into readers' hands quickly. This was, after all, revolutionary work in a revolutionary era. There was no time to waste.

Our Wealth Is Daily Stolen from Us

Liberating the Appalachian Colony

The 1973 and 1976 catalogs for Appalachian Movement Press—which appeared on the inside covers of many of their publications and in the folk culture journal *Foxfire* as an advertisement in the resources index for several years—declared AMP politics as such:

> Appalachia is a colony. Our wealth is daily stolen from us. Our natural resources and our labor are exploited by giant corporations whose owners do not live here. Not only do these owners not live here, but they make no contribution to the process of production. Our natural resources rightfully belong to all of us, and it is by our labor alone that they are made useful to us in the form of products. Yet today we receive no value from our resources and a mere pittance for our labor. The greatest share of what is produced from our resources and labor goes into the pockets of these corporate owners who do nothing at all to earn it. They live and have become the richest people in America by

> exploiting us. We at the Appalachian Press [*sic*] are dedicated to putting an end to the exploitation of our land and labor.

An idea had begun taking hold in Appalachia, which was both a response to the endemic poverty in the region and a call to action. What became known as the internal colony theory described the coal-rich central Appalachian areas of eastern Kentucky and most of West Virginia as a resource-extraction colony *inside* the colonial borders of the United States. The mountains of Appalachia, this idea explained, have been taken over by wealthy industrialists from northern urban centers, often in collusion with powerful regional elites, to be exploited as colonies—first for timber, then for coal.[31] The people of the region, who were previously living in a quite different balance with the land, now gain little from this arrangement beyond repression and poverty. They are subjugated to their industrial colonizers, who "prevent autonomous development of the subordinate internal colony."[32]

To many activists and writers on the Left, the internal colony idea helped to explain what they saw as a broad, almost pathological fealty to the coal industry coupled with a pervasive lack of knowledge and pride in the original folkways of Appalachian people carried on from earlier generations. This was Frantz Fanon's psychological analysis of the individual personality of the colonized, applied to home turf. Appalachians were not backward people. They were oppressed colonial subjects, and "the oppressed," as Fanon noted, "will always believe the worst about themselves."

First emerging in the late 1960s, the internal colony idea provided a particularly powerful framework for conceptualizing how it felt to live in the region, codifying and formalizing folk understandings of the historical power of outside industry into a liberation politic that could be easily explained. Activists in Appalachia began to build a movement based on that politic, one that paralleled a broader internationalist, anti-imperialist agenda emerging in the New Left politics of the time.[33]

If West Virginia is a state under colonial rule, then revolutionaries would work towards "the creation of an anti-colonial movement and a radical restructuring of society with a redistribution of resources to the poor and powerless."[34] Appalachian Movement Press thus positioned itself as an anticolonial press, creating both a platform from which

Appalachians could find inexpensive literature to educate themselves and a resource to print the necessary materials for the various movements gaining momentum in the region. Organizations, unions, and communities would become better equipped to act in their collective interest to liberate the region from their colonizers in far-flung and alien urban centers like Philadelphia or New York. If AMP didn't come right out and call their politics "decolonial," they were articulating key elements of the internal colony model from their beginning, and so were many of the authors on their imprint. "We see our region as a colony of a greater nation," says a twenty-three-year-old Tom Woodruff in an interview with *West Virginia Illustrated* in 1972. "Our land and our resources are, for the most part, owned by people who don't live here."[35]

From a contemporary perspective, it's clear that Appalachian Movement Press and many allied thinkers struggled with, or willfully ignored, their modern complicity in the original colonization of the region. If Appalachia was a colony *inside* the colony that is the United States, then one has to ask: Where was the solidarity with the active Indigenous movements of the day? Instead of evidence of reaching out to the national American Indian Movement, or even regional tribes, we're more likely to find writings from white Appalachians of the era comparing their plight to that of the "Indians" who lived on the land before them. These suggested parallels, when they happen, are cringeworthy by today's standards. The cover of 1973's *Fighting for Survival: The Bootleg Coal Industry* features an anonymous quote that screams dissonance from the history of the land itself: "As for the 'stealing' part of it, how did the different companies get their coal lands? In some cases they paid $6 an acre; was that a fair price? In other cases they stole it from the Indians. . . . Well we're the new Indians, taking what coal we can back from the companies." It's a convenient exclusion of the violence of settler colonialism, even if recognizing this doesn't change anything about the reality of the modern lives of Appalachians.

Although you almost wouldn't know it to read most synopses of the history of West Virginia, prior to European settler influx and the federal 1830 Indian Removal Act the mountainous areas of central Appalachia were much more widely populated by a number of Indigenous nations. These were primarily Cherokee and Shawnee people and also included, at different times, Saponi, Lenape, Mingo peoples, and others. But the accepted, generally taught modern history of the state continues to claim that the area that is now West Virginia "was only a 'hunting ground' and that there were no Indigenous Peoples living in the area when the white settlers came."[36] Nobody knows why the place was so empty, the story goes, but in any case the new settlers didn't have to take anything from anyone in order to put down their roots. Displacement was something that settlers *elsewhere* had done.[37]

And so, many pre-coal narratives, like the landscape that serves as the backdrop for AMP's children's story *The Hillbillys*, portray an Idyllic Holler as the beginning of time itself.[38] In this innocent genesis period, white Appalachians are tending to their own quiet lives, and have been for untold generations, before industry shows up to wreck the place. However, as historian Bonnie Brown suggests, even if an area were considered territorial hunting ground before settlers came, this could still mean that Native people were occupying the area for half of any year.[39] Idyllic pre-coal-industry stories provide for a fictional white absolution through the deft erasure of the Indigenous history of the mountains, and from that fallacy one of the foundational building blocks of the mythology of white Appalachian indigeneity has its roots.

At the same time as writers and activists on the Left were building the case for a radical decolonization politic, a distinct Appalachian identity movement was developing, coaxed along within the same theoretical framework as the colonial theory and fueled in part by the various burgeoning Appalachian studies programs developing at regional colleges. As an outgrowth of the internal colony idea, "Appalachian" was conceived as an oppressed minority identity.

As promoted by Appalachian Movement Press in the context of the Left politics of the 1970s, ideas about Appalachian identity drew predominantly from place and identification with the culture of place—namely, the mountains and valleys of the central Appalachian region. But this identity also drew almost exclusively from the Euro-ethnic settler traditions that had generationally assimilated into white culture

Unattributed poster, provided to the author by John Strong Clark and most likely illustrated by him, printed at AMP in 1977–79.

by this time, again to the exclusion of any Indigenous people who either preceded or continue to live in the region. It also tended towards the persistent notion, largely debunked by historians and archeologists, of a commonly held, homogenous regional ethnicity based in Scots-Irish ancestry (a term that is solely an American creation). Notably, since the Appalachian identity movement really grew in popularity in the decade after the outmigration of a significant majority of the African American population to northern industrial centers in the 1950s and '60s, it also doesn't seem to have applied to Black Appalachians in practice. In other words, as Yvonne Farley told me, "Nobody was really calling Black people hillbillies."[40] At the same time, radical writers like Don

West would continue to assert what they believed to be antiracist ideas and to search for abolitionist histories of the region from which to build a historical foundation for this identity—all towards a more just society in Appalachia.

As Elizabeth Catte put it in 2017, "It is important to understand that whatever 'Appalachian' is, it should first be seen as a flexible regional identity that has nothing to do with ethnicity."[41] As the politicized Appalachian identity movement grew in the 1970s, proponents certainly didn't directly claim "Appalachian" as a white identity, but the movement as such was expressing a white identity through the clear absence of a diversity of voices in the majority of the published materials and the language used therein. Many writers often drew parallels to struggles against oppression between Appalachians and, in many cases, African Americans—parallels that define the "Appalachian" of that period as separate from communities of color.[42]

As I'm homing in on the history of Appalachian identity during AMP's time, I want to be clear about something: almost everybody I spoke with when researching this book stressed to me, in different ways, that *their* Appalachia in the 1970s was *not* homogenously white, and that in particular African American (or now, Affrilachian) activists played critical leadership roles in organizing in West Virginia and Eastern Kentucky in that era.[43] Miners for Democracy, as just one example, had many powerful Black leaders, reflecting the history of the United Mine Workers as one of the earliest racially integrated unions.[44] Indeed it is the exclusion of people of color from the larger narrative of Appalachian history that has propped up some of the earliest and most damaging stereotypes that still haunt the region, and the literature about the region, as I write this book in 2020.

What I'm after, specifically, is how Appalachian identity was framed by the people who wrote and published about it and how that effort at solidarity with other identity movements, combined with its utility on home turf, built a definition that looks entirely white by retrospect. We can critique it while looking through a contemporary lens, but we can also, certainly, find much to learn from. This understanding of a regional identity, born from a past identity politic movement but in many ways still with us today, can work unintentionally to hinder a liberatory, antiracist forward movement in the twenty-first century. It can also, most dangerously, be turned against Appalachians with minimal editorial adjustments by white supremacists recruiting, as they so often do, from communities in poverty looking for answers.

The Journal of Appalachian Studies, a locus of academic work in the region, even released a special double-sized issue of their publication dedicated to challenging this issue as recently as 2004. Reflecting on how far this identity had remained unchallenged, at least within the discourse in academic circles during her long career involved in both movements and education, Barbara Ellen Smith called for "a moratorium on glib analogies that compare the rhetorical disparagement of hillbillies to the oppression of people of color."[45] Contemporary cultural organizations like Queer Appalachia have used their popular social media platforms, and their print magazine *Electric Dirt*, to dismantle and complicate these same identities, using a combination of humor, identity reclamation, camp, and current event analysis in a constant attack on the homogenous, heteronormative white Appalachia fallacy.

—

Internal colony theory has fallen out of style, at least in academia, where promoting the idea will, besides raising the incongruencies I've already mentioned, put you just on the wrong side of understanding capitalism. David Walls puts into context that activists like the AMP founders "hit upon the internal colonialism model for reasons that had more to do with the focus of the New Left in the late 1960's—imperialism abroad and oppression of racial minorities at home—than the appropriateness of the model to the Appalachian situation."[46] Walls and others suggest that it is more appropriate to understand the region as part of the typical functioning of any industrialized capitalist state, where peripheral areas are sacrificed to bring resources to core centers—southern West Virginian coalfields, for example, sacrificed to keep the lights on in Philadelphia.

Despite whatever correctives continue to advance within academic journals not widely read by the public, the model still appeals on the ground as an organizing concept even today. It's a useful shorthand, and I was first exposed to the idea of West Virginia as an "internal resource colony" at anti–mountaintop removal info sessions and marches in the mid-2000s. While the colony idea helped crystalize a modern

Barbara Placier Ervin with Tom Woodruff, operating an offset printing press. From a 1975 promotional publication of the Southern Appalachian Circuit of Antioch College in Beckley, WV. Ervin was a student at Antioch, and Woodruff was a consultant for the school at this time.

context for the settings in which I found myself as an activist, I also remember feeling uncomfortable with a kind of cognitive dissonance about white Appalachian indigeneity that I experienced in some casual discussions with other activists during the 2011 March for Blair Mountain. For some, the idea, complete with its baggage, was persistent.

But back in the 1970s, Appalachian Movement Press had several tactics in mind for decolonizing Appalachian people. They would serve as a cut-rate printshop for the radical leftist movements coming alive in the mountains. They would use their offset printing equipment to reprint and distribute original, hard-to-find texts about early twentieth-century Appalachian movements towards workplace determination and unionization. They would republish modern articles on government corruption, coal industry deception, and environmental degradation in violation of any copyrights. And they would continue the publication of Don West's radical, original poetry and nonfiction, securing West's role as an elder intellectual leader of their anticolonial movement.

"Defining Appalachian culture is often a top-down process," writes Catte, "in which individuals with power or capital tell us who or what we are."[47] The birth of the Appalachian identity idea in the 1970s, then, was an attempt at defining Appalachian culture from below. However we might judge these ideas now, the messy formation of an Appalachian identity and the framework of decolonization of the region became a fundamentally useful lens for movement building, for a time. These ideas crystallized a specifically regional movement in a way that might not be as legible outside of the mountains and fueled a literature that may raise some eyebrows decades later. But AMP printed all of their materials as an act of self-determination by Appalachians, for Appalachians. Once liberated, Appalachian people, as a unique cultural identity, would then join the international struggle for justice.

Written in the Midst of Battle

Reprinting People's History

Part of the mission of Appalachian Movement Press was to reprint material "about current and past struggles of workers," according to Tom Woodruff.[48] They republished several writings highlighting key moments in regional labor history, many of which were efforts at cheap reproductions that were easier to get to their readership than the original, often archival or obscure, texts.

From the beginning the AMP printers wanted to propel their largely working-class readership to a collective understanding of their history of workplace struggles for basic rights and unionization. Essential literature about the Harlan Mine War in Kentucky, the West Virginia Mine Wars, and other key events were part of their effort to make this regionally relevant history available to the people whose ancestors had lived it. Their most popularly reproduced edition is a chapbook with a compilation of inspirational quotes from Mary Harris "Mother" Jones, printed in 1971 and again in 1973. "We were trying to keep history alive," said AMP printer John Strong Clark, in an environment where much of Appalachian working-class history was difficult for people outside of an academic context to access.[49]

Many of these pamphlets were printed with the knowledge and consent of allied historians and writers who knew the printers at AMP (or who were at least admired by them) but often *not* with the permission of the original publishers of the articles. For example, two essays detailing the history of the convict lease system and its opposition that led to the Coal Creek War in Anderson County, Tennessee (1891–93) make up the pamphlet *Coal Creek Rebellion: East Tennessee Miners vs. Convict–Labor System*. Philip Foner's essay originally appeared in the second volume of his *History of the Labor Movement in the United States* (1955), and Archie Green's essay originally appeared in his book *Only a Miner* (1972). AMP sold Green's book as well—and at a discount. Ideally the University of Illinois Press wouldn't have known about AMP's anticopyright reprints of Green's other work, but Green himself did threaten to sue when he eventually found out.[50]

In 1971, AMP published *The Socialist and Labor Star, Huntington W. Va. 1912–1915*, the full text of a graduate-school essay by David Alan Corbin, who was, at the time, a student at Marshall University.[51] Corbin is now a well-respected Appalachian historian: as the author of *Life, Work, and Rebellion in the Coal Fields* (1981), a foundational text in West Virginia Mine Wars history, he was one of the first historians responsible for bringing this era of American history back to a public readership after decades of intentional state repression.[52] This essay, as AMP published it, was part of Corbin's earlier research into socialist movement history in West Virginia: the *Labor Star* was a socialist newspaper headquartered right there in Huntington over fifty years before AMP first bought their already-aged A. B. Dick presses.

In 1972, AMP republished significant portions of Tom Tippett's 1931 *When Southern Labor Stirs*, broken up into a series of four pamphlets. The original book is a study of the series of textile workers strikes in 1929 that erupted in the Elizabethton rayon plants in Tennessee; the Loray Mill strike in Gastonia, North Carolina; and the Marion Mills in Marion, North Carolina. It was the Marion strike, where several workers were killed by newly deputized strikebreakers, that AMP luminary Don West claimed as his pivot point into radical politics and organizing. Given West's influential status with the young printers (and the fact that he cited it often in his own writing), it's likely that Tippett's book came particularly recommended by West for distribution. In any case, "it was good history," Woodruff remembered.[53]

AMP would republish the Tippett series again in 1978, with decidedly more lively, illustrative covers. The later crew of AMP printers expressed their hope in aligning with a renewed unrest in the southern textile factories. "The first printing of this pamphlet has been out of print for some time," the inside covers declared. "We are rushing it back into print in hopes it will aid the J.P. Stevens workers in their boycott of the cruel and oppressive J.P. Stevens Company."

Again mining the archives for rare historical reporting that their readers would no doubt find exciting, a trilogy of larger-format booklets were published under the AMP imprint in 1973, each of them a collaged facsimile of articles from *Labor Defender* (published by International Labor Defense) and *Labor Age* (published by the Conference for Progressive Labor Action). These each focused on radical union activities in the Appalachian coalfields in 1931 and 1932. During the era of these original publications, there was considerable critique from the Left of the United Mine Workers (UMWA) union under the leadership of John Lewis, due in part to Lewis's consolidation of power and his active purging of leftist elements from the union. Alternative, Left-led unions were starting to gain considerable rank-and-file popularity across the country (and repression from the UMWA). The AMP pamphlet *The West Virginia Miners Union 1931* details one such effort spearheaded by Frank Keeney. Previously a key militant UMWA organizer during the West Virginia Mine Wars era, Keeney had been central to the militant organizing that culminated in the Battle of Blair Mountain, the largest armed labor confrontation in US history in 1921.

Harlan & Bell Kentucky 1931–32: The National Miner's Union focused on similar activities in eastern Kentucky, which like the textile mill uprisings in North Carolina, Don West had also been involved in. Completing the trilogy, *War in the Coal Fields: The Northern Fields 1931* details a wildcat strike that occurred in the bituminous coalfields of northern West Virginia, eastern Ohio, and western Pennsylvania. Of this trilogy of historical reprints, AMP's 1977 catalog claims, "Seven out of the fifteen journalists in this series are women. What labor paper can make that boast today?" Ironically, however, Appalachian

Movement Press operated as an almost entirely male-run printshop, and their own imprint offered a catalog of all-male writers, with the sole exception of the Mother Jones chapbook.

In 1932 the General Defense Committee of the Industrial Workers of the World (IWW) published *The Shame That Is Kentucky's! The Harlan Mine War* by Edward J. Costello, one-time founder and managing editor of the leftist news service Federated Press. The pamphlet begins by detailing many individual indignities and murders suffered by union organizers in the eastern Kentucky coalfields at the hands of law men and hired security "gun thugs." Costello goes on to describe the precarious legal battle that ensued after the Battle of Evarts, an early skirmish in what became the Harlan Mine War. The IWW's General Defense Committee would have distributed the original of this booklet nationally—not only to stir indignation against the coal operators of eastern Kentucky but to make a direct plea for readers to send aid during the miners' legal battle. AMP republished this pamphlet in its entirety in 1972.

The operators of the AMP printshop seem to have had an entirely utilitarian approach to the design of their publications. But if graphics and photography weren't important to the communication of their ideals, they certainly demonstrated an understanding of the role of creative acts of poetry and song as culturally critical to social struggle, movement building, and the formation of cultural identity. Besides 1973's reprint of Don West's *Songs for Southern Workers: 1937 Songbook of the Kentucky Workers Alliance*, included in this book, they produced two full-sized editions of music books of popular workers' rights tunes that had particular Appalachian significance. Right out of the gate in the first year of AMP's operation came the first slim volume, 1970's *Paint Creek Miner: Famous Labor Songs from Appalachia.* In the introduction, Tom Woodruff writes that "the poetry and songs written in the midst of battle here have been and still are revered by all workers. Appalachians weren't sitting in the back row during this struggle, they were driving the bus."

Written by Charles Patterson, a history major at Marshall University with roots in West Virginia, *Paint Creek Miner* centers on the lyrical work of Ralph Chaplin and his friendship with fellow organizer Elmer "Rummy" Rumbaugh. Chaplin would later become a well-known writer and artist with the Industrial Workers of the World (IWW), and much of his earlier work during his time in West Virginia during the Paint Creek and Cabin Creek strikes (1911–13) is signed only as "A Paint Creek Miner." Chaplin, who was an organizer but not actually a miner, met the writer/photographer Rumbaugh while the two were in Huntington working on the *Socialist and Labor Star* newspaper, where they were employed as field reporters. Later, after leaving West Virginia for his home city of Chicago, Chaplin finished his most famous work, the song "Solidarity Forever," about his time in the Appalachian coalfields. Patterson credits Rumbaugh as coauthor of the tune.

Songs of Freedom: Famous Labor Songs from Appalachia Part II followed after *Paint Creek Miner*, and the descriptions of the included music were taken entirely (and admittedly) from *Songs of Work and Freedom*, edited by Edith Fowke and Joe Glazer and originally published by the Labor Education Division of Roosevelt University, Chicago. Where their first songbook provided only the lyrics and context, *Songs of Freedom* provides the sheet music as well. As was true with so much of what Appalachian Movement Press created, this wasn't only an educational pamphlet. It was meant to be used as a tool.

John Clark, who worked with AMP later in the 1970s, became involved with the printshop partially because of their mission of reproducing these publications from the past. "We just wanted to make sure that the struggle that people went through to get the unions going wasn't lost and obscured, by reprinting the literature. Because once it's gone, if you don't keep one copy and then make copies of *that*, then no one remembers it."[54]

The Rolling Hills . . . Become a Picked Carcass

Anticorruption Journalism and Anticolonial Stories

"We have heard the same lie so many times that we have come to accept it." Tom Woodruff, influenced by the writings of Frantz Fanon, penned these lines in the intro to *Paint Creek Miner*. He was transposing Fanon's ideas on internalized inferiority to what he saw as a "colonized" Appalachian context. In so plainly identifying this psychopathology, he also planted a flag of resistance. Just as they were interested in keeping history alive and distributing it to anyone who would read it, Appalachian Movement Press placed a high value on journalists working to expose industry and government corruption to the public. As they looked back for inspirational stories to tell from earlier generations, they also looked to their current day for those writers who were working tirelessly to keep history from repeating itself. In reprinting this modern journalism, they continued to highlight the disastrous and, as they defined it, colonialist relationship between Appalachian working-class people, the coal industry, and those government officials with whom that industry colluded.

Paul Nyden's reporting is a critical bridge between AMP's historical documentation and the journalism they admired and printed. A career investigative reporter with the *Gulf Times* and later the *Charleston Gazette*, Nyden moved to West Virginia from New York in 1970 following the murder of UMWA reform candidate Jock Yablonski, and he was involved in the Miners for Democracy organization that AMP often ran print jobs for. His 1974 dissertation "Miners for Democracy: Struggle in the Coalfields" serves as a detailed history of the United Mine Workers and the attendant disasters occurring in coal-mining communities of the region, and it's surprising that AMP didn't endeavor to reprint at least excerpts of this work. But earlier, in 1972, they did publish Nyden's article and subsequent dialog with the lawyer and musician Rich Kirby originally from *Mountain Life & Work* magazine as *The Coal Miner's Struggle in Eastern Kentucky*. Giving the 1970s unionizing struggle a grim historical foothold, Nyden calls for tactical changes within Miners for Democracy and a focus on the potential for rank-and-file leadership.

AMP published the journalist Thomas N. Bethell's *Conspiracy in Coal*, which originally appeared in *Washington Monthly*. Based in Washington, DC, Bethell self-published and distributed thirty-one issues of his hard-hitting newsletter *Coal Patrol* from 1970 through 1973 (resurfacing again for a time beginning in 1977). *Coal Patrol* promised "reports and commentary on coal-related developments in labor, industry, and government," and Bethell's one-man operation was known for relentlessly pursuing the news on mine safety breaches and disasters, as well as UMWA corruption before the Miners for Democracy gained in power. Pulled from various writings in *Coal Patrol*, *Conspiracy* documents the lead up to the 1968 Farmington, West Virginia, mine collapse at Consolidation Coal's (now Consol Energy) Mountaineer No. 9 mine, which killed seventy-eight workers.

It was the Farmington disaster that galvanized Davitt McAteer's case study that created the foundation for the Federal Coal Mine Health and Safety Act passed by Congress in 1969, and McAteer and Bethell later collaborated on another piece for *Washington Monthly* in the aftermath of the Buffalo Creek flood disaster, *The Pittston Mentality: Manslaughter on Buffalo Creek*. Published in 1972 and included in this book, *Pittston Mentality* reveals the terrifying timeline leading up to the collapse of a coal slurry impoundment dam in Logan County, West Virginia, on the morning of February 26, 1972. Out of a population of 5,000 people in the area of sixteen coal towns affected by the dam burst, 125 people were killed, 1,121 were injured, and over 4,000 were left homeless. A total of 507 houses, 44 mobile homes, and 30 businesses were destroyed. "We publish it with the permission of Tom Bethell," the inside cover reads, but "it is unauthorized by the magazine."

—

"The only hang-up with automation is that it put tens of thousands of miners out of work," declares the spiky *Picking Poverty's Pocket*, an essay by Barry Barkan and R. Baldwin Lloyd from *Article One: A Magazine for the New Virginia*. The authors rail against the history of absentee land ownership by coal companies and the effects of new mechanized strip-mining practices on union miners, especially taking to task the Pittston Coal Company and the Penn-Central Railroad. As with other AMP publications, the idea of central Appalachia as a resource-extraction colony is a through line, although Barkan and Lloyd cop a more pessimistic stance than typical for AMP publications. After quoting one miner listing the bones he has broken over the years he spent in the mines, the passive tone of which apparently betrays a "kind of acceptance of one's fate [which] weighs heavily on the Appalachian people," the authors conclude that the growing "legacy of this passive way of life makes for good colonial subjects." Or perhaps their challenge was meant to level a question to readers: How much longer will people in the region accept their supposed destiny?

Dark humor is peppered throughout the sardonically titled *Look Out—There's a Profit in Your Appendix!* Originally published in the *Mountain Messenger* and made available on the AMP imprint in 1974, *Look Out* is an anonymous and brief treatise against hospital profiteering in West Virginia. The author(s) show that for-profit hospitals are most concentrated in the southern coalfields, drawing comparisons about absentee ownership in precisely the same areas where outside forces are playing fast and loose with the environment, and thus public health, through strip mining for coal: "These hospitals should be taken

Unattributed poster, provided to the author by John Strong Clark and most likely illustrated by him, printed at AMP in 1977–79.

over and run for the need of the people, not for the greed of absentee owners and home-bred big businessmen who prey off sick and dying people."

The West Virginia Establishment, printed in 1971 and written by Rod Harless, is a deeply researched critique of power players in both Kanawha and Raleigh Counties in West Virginia. At least half of the pages are composed of data tables breaking down a who's who of "The Establishment": regional companies and their top officials and personnel. It's not the most invigorating read if you aren't keyed in to the history of hyper-regional politics, but for context, Harless had recently returned to his home state of West Virginia after working for the US Navy as a budget analyst at the Pentagon in the 1960s. The thick, impressive one-hundred-page booklet's naming of names shows AMP's commitment to exposing corruption on their home soil. Harless would go on to teach at the Southern Appalachian Circuit of Antioch College in Beckley, WV, and to work as the executive director of the Dunbar Housing Authority.[55]

Sometime in the early 1970s, Harless also wrote the standout historical fiction story *The Hillbillys: A Book for Children*, which was lettered and illustrated by Dan Cutler. *The Hillbillys* takes a stark view of prior generations' inability to counter the corporate takeover of the region's mineral resources. Thirty-eight illustrated pages tell a story of "an ancient mountain kingdom called Hillbilly Land." Hailing from the faraway lands of New Rock and Penn Delphia, a ruling-class "order of men called Royal Profiteers," who have an insatiable appetite for eating thin green chips called "Profits," learn from their "Ex-Zecke-Tivs" that Hillbilly Land sits on an underground trove of Profits. Since Profits are mined underground and must undergo complicated processing before being eaten, it's going to be a hard sell convincing the Hillbillies to destroy their homeplace (another version of the Idyllic Holler typical of an internal-colony story) in pursuit of this addictive resource. But the Royal Profiteers send their most resourceful Ex-Zecke-Tiv to do business on their behalf, and pretty soon the Hillbillies are operating scoops and draglines and arguing amongst themselves, wrecking the land while Profits are shipped right out of the mountains daily.

After the land, air, and water are thoroughly destroyed from this mining, the Hillbillies start to organize, and they angrily march to Capital City to speak with the Head Hillbilly (notably *not* a Royal Profiteer, rather a wealthy regional elite). He greets them warmly and talks to them for a full day but secretly casts a "Magic Word Spell" upon all of them. Thus the Hillbillies leave in a daze and later find that if they ever again become angry and turn back around to march on the capital, this spell will take effect when they come within one hundred paces of Hillbilly Mansion.

"After several floundering trips in and out of the powerful force field created by the Magic Word Spell, the Hillbillies journeyed home in dismay and sank into dull despair," the story concludes. "But after awhile, the Hillbillies decided that, after all, every kingdom and all people have their problems, and so they just ordered 1,500,000 gas masks and sets of goggles and left it to the next generation to try to solve the problems of Hillbilly Land."

Not likely to have ever been read aloud during story time in regional day-care centers, *The Hillbillys* still sets up a rather neat theoretical package to explain the mission behind Appalachian Movement Press: the need to create an anticolonial movement concerned with the emancipation of a people led astray by the brutality and false promises of outside industries. But as entertainment, it goes without saying that the book is particularly bleak: in its surrendering finale, the story could even be seen to illustrate the foundational elements of despair that play a part in opioid and alcohol addiction.

The Hillbillys expresses the danger of "shifting baseline syndrome" as well, an ecological concept describing the process by which the events that were previously traumatic to an ecosystem or people become normalized and rationalized by exposure through generations: the new normal. Thus Harless and Cutler painfully illustrate how despair can take hold. The work of changing entrenched power structures begins to seem impossible, and maybe without precedent, if life has always been this way. Written during a remarkable decade of struggle for human and environmental rights in central Appalachia, *The Hillbillys* doesn't offer a happy ending. They left that up to the next generation.

I Think Poverty Won That War on Poverty

Don West as Guiding Light

"Don West gave us the spirit and moral support needed to start and to continue our efforts despite the mass of non-support and criticism all around us," Tom Woodruff wrote, in his characteristically firm tone, in the introduction to Appalachian Movement Press's first edition of West's poetry chapbook *A Time for Anger* in 1970. But when I asked Woodruff about how West had felt about their idea to start a printshop in Huntington when he had first approached the older, seasoned activist, he laughed and tried to paraphrase West: "Well if you're really serious here's some money. But my guess is y'all aren't, and it's just gonna do more harm than good!"[56]

Besides their regionality, one particular detail that set Appalachian Movement Press apart from other movement presses nationally was their mutualistic relationship as a New Left printshop with Don West, an Old Left activist. The younger activists running the AMP shop weren't about to ignore the wisdom of the elder generations, especially not a larger-than-life character like Don West. It can feel reductive to summarize West's life in the struggle for human rights and the decades of work he had already done before Woodruff and others in AMP met him: born in north Georgia, West was a civil rights activist, an ordained Congregationalist minister, a militant labor organizer with the Communist Party, an educator who was, by 1970, the forgotten cofounder of the Highlander Folk School, and an accomplished and published poet. As West himself tells it, he was radicalized in his youth when he witnessed firsthand the lethal violence used against striking textile workers in Marion, North Carolina, in 1929. Here he was exposed to militant union organizing, the violent backlash *against* this organizing from management and the law, and many of the political ideologies that would provide the fundament for his life's work.[57]

West was sixty-three when the young founders of AMP approached him with their plans for a regional movement press. While he may have had some initial misgivings about the "hippie printers" in Huntington, West paid attention to what they were doing and came to believe in the overall value of their mission.[58] In particular, West became a close friend and mentor to Woodruff.[59] Tom Woodruff wrote when AMP began,

> We were broke, so we looked around for people with money who would help us out. We contacted a lot of rich people who gave us no money. We contacted a lot of people with no money, but they gave us no support. We went to see Don West—he had no money, but he gave us what he had. He gave us something much more—he gave us his spirit. . . . A spirit of self-reliance and independence, a spirit of freedom and democracy which enables us to work through any hardships and struggle to reach our goals. Don West is the epitome of that spirit. . . . He is an angry Appalachian, but there is so much to be angry about.[60]

West also saw in AMP an opportunity to publish his own work free from editorial oversight and distribute it directly to Appalachian people. Meanwhile, he had been at the helm or involved with many magazines already. And by this time in his writing career, West had lost most of his earlier tenuous patience for the conventional arena of poetry review and critique in which his creative work had generally been lauded. His poetry style flew in the face of many accepted conventions of literary writing, but AMP provided a direct line to the people he most wished to write for. The young printers in Huntington offered Don West a chance to produce creative work again, unfettered.

Appalachian Movement Press republished West's previous poems and many new ones as well. Their imprint expanded West's printed repertoire to include many of his yet-unpublished research writings on the abolitionist movement in Appalachia during the Civil War, his thoughts on traditional mountain music and customs, and his latest project: increasingly hardline essays addressing the need to motivate Appalachians to practice self-determination and eliminate outside influences and aid. AMP printed more pages of Don West's work than any other single author, and in fact his writing made up the majority of the original material that they published on their imprint. As most of the editors and organizers of the press weren't themselves concerned with being recognized as individuals, West, already a revered character, was often seen as the central figure guiding the Huntington printshop, so much so that some joked that AMP should have instead been called the "Don West Press."[61]

Decades earlier, Don West was a student in the Vanderbilt University Divinity School in Nashville, and he had already been publishing his poetry in several literary journals as well as leftist political papers. Deeply inspired by a trip to Denmark to visit the folk schools there before he graduated, he returned to the US with dreams of creating a folk school in his mountainous home region that would be for working-class Appalachian people, by working-class Appalachian people. He was introduced to Myles Horton because both men had been independently searching for land on which to build similarly minded ventures, and together the two cofounded the Highlander Folk School in Grundy County, Tennessee, in 1932. It was Connie West, the painter and teacher married to Don since 1928, who first suggested Highlander as the name.[62]

Highlander eventually became a critical center of civil rights training and an early model of the center that Don and Connie West would later start in southern West Virginia. But West and Horton had an early and contentious falling out. In part this stemmed from their differing roles—Horton as fundraiser, interfacing with largely middle- and upper-class patrons, and West as shoe-leather recruiter traveling to find prospective students amongst the impoverished working class. The tension was fueled by a growing ideological rift between Horton's relatively reserved socialism and West's increasing faith in communism and growing frustration with the pace of social change in the United States.[63] Perhaps too, as George Brosi pondered, the split was the result of an increasingly unbridgeable personality schism, "the contrast between Myles as a listener and Don as a talker."[64] In any case, West bitterly left Highlander by the summer of 1933, and as biographer James Lorence explains, Horton was the one "privileged by history to tell the story of Highlander's origins," although the two would remain in tenuous but relatively friendly correspondence through their lives.[65]

West's early work as an organizer for the Communist Party in Georgia and Kentucky continually pushed him underground for periods of time, living and publishing under many aliases but rarely slowing down. Don and Connie's lives were threatened several times during his stint as a field organizer in eastern Kentucky mining communities in the 1930s, and in 1948 the Ku Klux Klan burned the couple's home and barn to the ground. His continued connections with the Communist Party, often sub rosa, would haunt both him and Connie for most of their lives—the FBI would deem them interesting enough to track the details of their lives and movements for over thirty years.[66]

In 1965 the Wests bought six hundred acres in Summers County, West Virginia, where they founded the Appalachian South Folklife Center, near the town of Pipestem. Getting the community in rural Summers County to come around to Don and Connie's vision for the ASFC took time, and FBI files from early in its formation focus divisively on community concerns about itinerant "hippies" congregating on the center's acreage, especially during their frequent folk music festivals.[67]

But the Wests, especially Don, forged ahead—this was the folk school that he had wanted to build for over thirty years since before working with Horton in Tennessee. The mission of the ASFC would focus on "the restoration of self-respect and human dignity lost as a consequence of the region's colonial relationship with industrial America," a political outline of the same mission, more or less, that

Appalachian Movement Press founded itself on: decolonization of central Appalachia and decolonization of the minds of Appalachians. Never one to cop an academic dialect, West put it much more candidly in the pages of *Mountain Call*, discussing the cultural focus of the ASFC: "Let me say that a people's understanding of its history is the way that their self-image is created. Your understanding of your origins makes your self-image and your self-image determines what you try to do."[68]

At his core, Don West was driven by a Christian spirituality that developed throughout his life to merge with his internationalist Left politics. West was exposed to the ideas of the Social Gospel by activist faculty at the Vanderbilt Divinity School, where he was a student during the beginnings of the Great Depression. Social gospel offered a kind of "applied Christianity," which appealed to West's growing activism.[69] As James J. Lorence has interpreted, West's philosophy blended "the economic and social determinism of Marx with a uniquely personal interpretation of revolutionary Christianity focused on the comrade Jesus as the prophetic son of man."[70] In his "Jesus the Quiet Revolutionary," an essay based on one of his sermons which he first published in *Orion* magazine in 1967, West outlines much of this ideological and spiritual integration. His focus on "the son of man" minimized the deifying focus on "the son of God" found in so much of the organized Christianity that West despised. Instead, his politics and class consciousness focused on the human personage of Jesus Christ, "the plain Jesus, the carpenter-working-man Jesus, [who was] concerned for and close to the poor and common people." This Jesus, for West, exemplified "the revolutionary quality of love in action," and West had no patience for "pompous efforts to fasten him up in the stained glass windows of costly cathedrals."[71] This Jesus also provided the template by which Don West modeled his *own* life, down to his commitment to wearing plain work clothing daily.

West had become something of a guiding light for many activists in the region, especially those involved with Appalachian Movement Press. Tom Woodruff and the others at Appalachian Movement Press offered this man who had become an elder leader in their movement a powerful

Don West as photographed for the Mountaineer of the Month column in the *Mountain Call*, June 1974 (issue no. 7).

platform from which to preach—although preaching by this time rarely meant the pulpit for West. For his part, West saw an incredible opportunity to collect and republish much of his scattered poetry and articles, pieces of his historical writings, and his own cultural critiques.

Although by the time he met and befriended Woodruff, Don West wasn't concerned to move in the same literary circles he used to, AMP helped him keep his poetry alive and available. Throughout much of his life, West's poetry had regularly appeared in communist, socialist, and religious publications, as well as in regional movement magazines like *Mountain Life & Work* (which AMP printed for a time). He had published several chapbooks and built something of a literary career concurrent with his activism, with the motivations behind both coming from the same wellspring. But by this time, West hadn't focused on creative writing in years. AMP produced *A Time for Anger*, the first pamphlet of theirs I ever encountered, right out of the gate in 1970. The short chapbook pulled poems from West's two most popular books, *Clods of Southern Earth* (1946) and *The Road Is Rocky* (1951). With a blurb often emphasizing that *Clods* had sold more copies in the US than Walt Whitman's *Leaves of Grass*, *Anger* saw perhaps as many as four more reprintings through the mid-1970s while Woodruff was at the helm in Huntington. Meanwhile, through his involvement in the Antioch Appalachia College in Beckley, West Virginia, West renewed his charismatic public performances, especially working with the younger regional writers in the Soupbean Poets Collective.[72]

West's poetry was focused on Appalachia in style, subject, and vernacular, a literature which spoke to his own homegrown audience before (and perhaps excluding) anyone else. Of his uncompromising writing style, Jeff Biggers notes that West would never "elevate his folk traditions to a 'higher art.' . . . Such a rendering would have transmuted the essence of 'folk' culture or 'living word' and denied its inherent value and contributions: *choosing a 'high' form would have been an implicit designation of 'low' to his own vernacular.* West believed that poetry in the language of 'his people' was not only an expression of his own culture, but an act of resistance in turn."[73]

In 1974, Appalachian Movement Press published the bound volume *O Mountaineers!* Both a collection of West's new work and a "greatest hits" of his previously published poems, the book was available in both hardback and paperback. The cover displays several monochrome reproductions of Connie West's paintings, with an introduction (penned much earlier, in 1964) by West's friend and executive director of the New Deal's National Youth Administration, Aubrey Willis Williams. Given that the AMP shop operated on a slim budget and lacked the means to bind larger books, *O Mountaineers!* was one of their most ambitious projects and was outsourced to another printshop, which was never credited. The back cover of this book, West's first in twenty-three years, summarizes much of the sentiment about his work, exclaiming that "the hearts and the guts of people jump out at you from these poems. Read them. They're about real people. About real conditions. And they speak so clearly of the injustice in America yesterday and today."

Consistent with his anticapitalist sensibilities, West's anticopyright ethos was probably a big influence on the printers at Appalachian Movement Press. He rejected copyright to his own work because, as he saw it, to do so would restrict the free movement of art generally. "Poetry and other creative efforts should be levers, weapons to be used in the people's struggle for understanding, human rights, and decency," he wrote late in his life, in 1982. In other words, "Just ignore copyright," Yvonne Farley summarized, "it's a capitalist thing."[74]

Having taught history in many capacities throughout his life, West worked on his own original research into Appalachian history and focused in particular on the early abolitionist movement in the region and the widespread Southern resistance to the Confederacy leading up to and during the American Civil War. West hoped, through this work, to paint a different story of the Southeast to Appalachians and to the rest of the country, a story defining attempts at Southern secession as a battle waged by wealthy elites whose interests (and beliefs) actually ran counter to the majority of the Southern population, particularly those in the isolated mountains of Appalachia. West worked on a book on this history throughout his life, "a long tale still greatly in need of the telling," but he never finished it. He did, however, publish one of the finished chapters and an assortment of excerpts as two pamphlets on the AMP imprint.

One of these, *Freedom on the Mountains* (1973), is full of vignettes claiming the Appalachian region, rather than New England, is the true "Birthplace of Modern Abolitionism."[75] *Robert Tharin: Biography of a Mountain Abolitionist*, which AMP published in 1971, is West's only completed and published section of the book. Twenty-four pages rich with detailed research, the booklet provides a background on West's version of the Appalachian abolitionist movement, including vignettes about individual leaders and an overall analysis of how the "Slavocracy" sought to maintain its power. West uses the story of little-known Alabama lawyer Robert Tharin, who was focused on educating poor white people, to highlight his central thesis: the southeastern region, he believed, should be defined by the class distinctions between the minority slaveholding "Tidewater" aristocracy and the majority poor white population of the South coupled with the population of slaves held in bondage. West argues that there was never a unified South under the Confederacy but rather a violently stratified class system that pitted poor white people against poor Black people and obscured what he believed was their mutual, common interests in liberation. Tharin's work educating and advocating for poor white Southerners to understand these conditions brought violent persecution to him and his family, making him a martyr to Don West.

—

Don West also wrote a number of lively cultural critiques, strong missives against the continued exploitation of the mountains and the people who he saw as the culprits. In his most explicitly anticapitalist pamphlet, *Romantic Appalachia, or, Poverty Pays If You Ain't Poor*, he describes his frustration at the history of perennial outside "discoveries" of Appalachian people and their culture by northern elites and missionaries and, in later years, by federally funded VISTA volunteers and other "poverty warriors." West maintains that the attraction is a romanticization of Appalachia brought on by faulty media stereotypes and that these waves of visitors will never fundamentally alter the poverty they find in the region if they don't challenge capitalism itself. This tract forms the ideological basis for most everything West taught from the mid-1960s, when the Appalachian South Folklife Center was founded, through the 1980s.

Southern Mountain Folk Tradition and the Folksong "Stars" Syndrome was an early 1970s reprint of two essays that first appeared in *Appalachian South* magazine, a journal which West founded concurrent with the birth of the ASFC and which ran for some time. In both pieces, he rails against a new, mainstream interest in what he refers to as the "cult" of "singers of folk songs," which he carefully differentiates from traditional "folksingers." While the latter (like Don and Connie's daughter, the musician Hedy West) were honoring Appalachian traditions, the former were exporting traditional music, perverting it, and cashing in on cultural appropriation. Exasperated by this "extremely vulgar trend," West lets loose his disgust for a music industry he considered to be full of competition and vanity. Most offensively to West, he saw this trend as centered in a New York–based elitist, materialistic society, which he believed ran counter to the original traditions of the folk song custom. "The affluent 'folksinger' is an anachronism."

It can be difficult not to read these later critical works of West's as isolationist, his approach terminally parochial. He trained his focused ire on anyone he saw as perverting or stealing Appalachian culture for personal profit. This could easily include folk musicians who ran afoul of his taste or the itinerant volunteers (mostly white men) from northern states who came to the mountains only concerned with "sowing their radical oats" before returning home and furthering their careers with the cultural cachet of having worked in Appalachia.[76] Even some of his poetry and writing about "the revolutionary Jesus" took asides to deride the fashion and hair styles of the young urban attendees who traveled to attend the folk music festivals that the Wests hosted to help fund the ASFC. The writing is cranky as hell, but perhaps at that point in Don West's life, there was just so much to be cranky about.

While it is true that Don West would always nurse "a lifetime grudge against outsiders," beneath the unrelenting grit that is his most critical prose is a genuine belief in the power of education to motivate mountaineers to self-empowerment and self-determination.[77] West, an internationalist in politics and spirituality, had his eyes on the horizon, where he saw Appalachians joining the transnational class struggle for a better world. The region's history, he firmly believed, proved that this was imminently possible. But he didn't see this deep social change ever happening if Appalachians continued to rely only on outside influence and promises. Appalachian determination had to be homegrown, and his impatient and sometimes sarcastic rhetoric belies a frustrated love weathered by decades of activism, writing, and living a life with Connie that was, in his words, "very close to the raw edge."[78]

It Helped Pay the Bills

The Activist Job Shop in the Hills

"The movement needs printshops," George Brosi stressed to me when we first spoke about Appalachian Movement Press.[79] Late in the digital age, it can be difficult to imagine that in the days before the photocopier became ubiquitous, the offset printshop was the only method that most people had for reproducing anything in multiples, let alone in thousands. If freedom of the press was guaranteed to those that owned one, then owning one was critical to activists globally as well as in central Appalachia.

Huntington and the surrounding region held a loose and dedicated network of activist groups in the 1970s, and in order to function as these organizations invested in changing the region, they needed to be able to print materials. A movement press is meant to be a printshop *for the movement*, and although most of Appalachian Movement Press's historical footprint can be found in the publications they released on their imprint, they consistently printed uncredited job work at cut-rate pricing for allies and associated organizations.

"We did a hell of a lot of printing for Arnold Miller's campaign," remembered Tom Woodruff.[80] All of this work was in the service of the United Mine Workers reformist organization Miners for Democracy, at least until Miller was elected union president in 1972 and the contracts with the small activist printshop quickly dried up.[81] Just a few years later, AMP printer Paul Salstrom remembered printing thousands of leaflets in support of roving picket actions for another UMWA dissident group, the Right to Strike Committee, during one overnight printing session in 1975 and following that job with another for thousands more very soon after.[82]

For some time in the early 1970s, AMP printed the regular paper *Peoples Appalachia* for the Peoples Appalachian Research Collective (PARC) in Morgantown in northern West Virginia. Styled as a quasi-academic journal and, as such, different in approach than anything else AMP printed, *Peoples Appalachia* was produced by a group of activists operating within, and in orbit around, West Virginia University. Much of the spirit of PARC's journal straddled radical academic concerns and frontline activism. They also mirrored AMP's anticopyright stance on their publications: "Materials may be reprinted for peoples' struggle purposes," read boxed text in the first pages of each issue. At one point in the late 1970s, AMP printers were actually in conversation with PARC members about the possibility of transferring ownership of the printing presses and other equipment from Huntington to Morgantown, but the arrangement never crystalized.[83]

But sustaining a shop that serviced the movement required money, and often that could be found, not so much by doing work for allies and cohorts, but by doing jobs for local businesses or anyone else that needed something printed—what AMP printer John Clark called "jackleg jobs."[84] Contracting the printing of menus, symphony programs, leaflets for local churches, and the like, AMP operators needed to keep the bills paid, buy ink and paper, and occasionally pay staff, although it's not clear whether the original corporate model under which Woodruff, the Stewarts, and others founded the shop was maintained throughout the 1970s.[85] Marshall students who wanted to be involved with AMP sometimes came by the shop to lend help with the work, largely by stapling and collating publications after they rolled off the presses. Much, but not all, of the work done with AMP was still essentially "labor donated," as their logo stated, although the logo itself never appeared on any nonimprint job materials.

Meanwhile in the offset printing field, newly invented Japanese plate-making equipment saw the rise of jiffy-print franchise shops across the United States. Locally AMP, with their darkroom and aging equipment, was losing regular business to them.[86] The Huntington shop's equipment was, however, still ideal for printing and binding illustrated magazines. Working with like minds to print their periodicals helped create a larger historical footprint of the activism in the region, much of which survives, albeit dispersed, through various magazines.

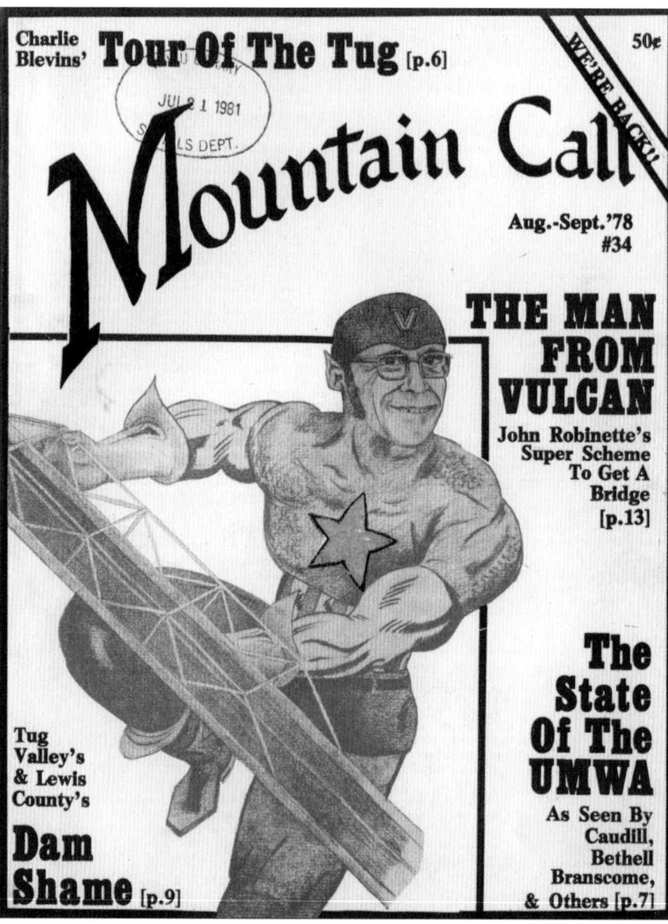

Cover of *Mountain Call* #34, August–September 1978.

For the Mountains, the People, the Culture

The *Mountain Call*, 1973–1978

The *Mountain Call*, a bimonthly magazine out of Mingo County, West Virginia, was one of the longest-running publications that AMP printed for another group, from 1974 through 1975 and again from 1978 through their last issue. "*The Call*" was playful, scrappy, humorous, optimistic, and at times confrontational. Part drop-out yet pro-union, the creators mixed a young, rural, back-to-the-land lifestyle aesthetic with a working-class ethos and respect for the local community in a rare and powerful blend. The *Mountain Call* was a magazine befitting, but also challenging to, the modern culture of the southern West Virginia mountains: "Montani Semper Literati," they insisted.[87]

The early-twenty-something men producing *Mountain Call* lived in "a rambling stone-and-wood house" in an area they affectionately called "the Knob," part of an isolated rural community on Marrowbone Ridge, which was home to Edwina Shepard Pepper.[88] The Knob sits around eight miles east of Kermit, WV, and around thirteen miles north of Williamson, WV, as the crow flies—Marrowbone Ridge is the ridge separating the watershed of Marrowbone Creek from the watershed of Spruce Creek. Pepper had first arrived on this ridgetop in the late 1950s to piece together and eventually settle on land that her father, a local Williamson industry lawyer, had acquired piecemeal throughout his career. A native West Virginian from Huntington who had lived all over the country, Pepper worked hard in the decade leading up to her permanent move onto the land on Marrowbone to integrate herself, as best as possible, into the existing community there. With an eye towards building a mutual aid network of schools, craft centers, and the like, and a savvy ability to find and direct financial resources, she eventually brought electricity and telephone lines to the community along the mountain ridge. In 1962 the land became home to her twin grandnephews, Michael and John Fanning, when Pepper brought them both to live there at nine years old. Both Fannings later attended Marshall University in Huntington, where they befriended Greg Carannante, a "refugee from suburbia" and 1971 journalism graduate of the college.[89]

It was Pepper who conceived of the magazine, and she was "the heart and mind and motivation."[90] The Fanning brothers agreed to help create it. Carannante moved back to West Virginia from a job in New Jersey at Pepper's invitation and became the graphic designer, handling all of the layout and paste-up necessary to get *The Call* to print. Early issues round out the group with artist David Pierce and local resident "friend/philosopher" Herbert Hannah as the creative team behind the *Mountain Call*. With Edwina Pepper, whom they called simply "Ed," guiding their mission in the background, this intergenerational group of friends and family aspired "to create on and about our ridgetop home a subsistent mountain community for free spirits and mountain lovers, consisting of a mountain school, wood and weaving workshops, bee-keeping, and perhaps a natural amphitheater for mountain music and drama, and on and on." As the trumpet from the center of their activities, the *Mountain Call* was their first fully realized endeavor, a magazine which created the public narrative for their grand project in living and serving the community in which they lived. "For The Mountains, The People, The Culture," reads the subtitle on the cover of a 1976 issue.

"We literally began it without a cent," Carannante told me. "None of us had any idea how to run a business. It was all just by the seat of

The *Mountain Call* creators Greg Carannante, John Fanning, and Michael Fanning as photographed in the pages of their magazine in 1975.

our pants: going around, trying to sell ads, and, you know, basically just making it from scratch."[91] The first issue of the *Mountain Call* was printed pro bono in October 1973 at The Bartlett Press in Williamson. The printshop, run by friends Jim Bartlett, Jim Webb, and Don Faries, printed the upstart magazine for its whole first year. But when Bartlett Press closed in 1974, the Fannings and Carannante found Appalachian Movement Press, and Carannante would drive the print-ready magazine up to Huntington every other month. They would later pick up the printed pages and set up shop in the student center at Marshall to collate, staple, and fold many of the issues.[92] From 1975 to 1977, they moved print production closer to Marrowbone by using Logan News Printers in West Logan, WV, before moving back to AMP for their final issues in 1978.

The *Mountain Call* was fully illustrated throughout. Harkening to a West Coast psychedelic style while remaining distinctly homegrown Appalachian, the design was "a reflection of the people who were doing it."[93] Michael Fanning's photography appeared in every issue. Regular features included Rufus Reed's "Ma Natur" column of environmental writing, free/barter columns for local craftspeople, and a longform interview feature called Mountaineer of the Month, which highlighted people the editors looked up to (like Don West and Nimrod Workman) or at least thought would cause an intellectual row amongst their readership (like Harry Caudill). Many issues featured The Wheel of the *Mountain Call*, which determined some of the focus of the issues' articles: topics included Roads, Clean Air, Chemicals, and Forests, among others. Edwina Pepper occasionally contributed her own anonymous writing to the magazine, sometimes under the sly heading "EDitorial." Much of the overall content blends their reverence for the existing culture of the mountains with new ideas on alternative energy and modern attempts at sustainable living—a balance that continues to be delicate for activists today. "These issues of the mountain culture, and preserving the mountains, were very serious to us," said Carannante. "But we came at it from a . . . I don't know if you'd call it a hippie mentality, but we were all longhairs."[94]

If *Mountain Call* was an upstart magazine, then one can understand something about the local support that they had through the breadth of local and regional businesses that supported them by advertising in their pages, some of them consistently for many years. Furniture stores, pizza restaurants, sporting supply shops, office supply stores, and other markets in nearby Kermit, Williamson, Madison, Lenore, and elsewhere placed quarter-sheet ads that sit next to ads for national alternative lifestyle publications and publishers. The owner of Huntington's Pilgrim Glass Company showed consistent support by paying for full back-cover advertisements on every issue from September 1974 through the magazine's end. Although they pounded the pavement to get community-level financial support, the crew at the Knob also received some help from Edwina Pepper's two sons, and at one point in 1976, the Fannings and Carannante each received fellowships from the Robert F. Kennedy Foundation, which also gave them a new Toyota Land Cruiser to share. "That could have just as easily been a helicopter to us," said Carannante. "Compared to what we were doing, literally pushing Volkswagen Bugs up through the snow and the mud every winter. We were that ramshackle of an enterprise."[95]

Although they lived in a rural community on a ridgetop, the younger members of the group at the Knob were also part of a countercultural scene, which held the Lock, Stock, and Barrel restaurant in nearby Williamson, WV, as its nexus. Open twenty-four hours a day and including a menu both eclectic and homey, the restaurant began with an Office of Economic Opportunity grant to train unemployed Appalachians for the food service industry.[96] "The Barrel" advertised (and editorialized) in every issue of the *Mountain Call* and provided a central social hub for a new regional counterculture and multigenerational locals alike. With community help, the restaurant was rebuilt after the 1977 flood that hit Williamson, during which time many local activists founded the community action "muckraking paper" the *Sandy New Era* and "incendiary literary journals" *Stokes* and *Mucked* with Jim Webb and Jim Bartlett from Bartlett Press.[97] Unfortunately the Barrel did not survive the 1984 flood, which hit many of the communities along the Tug River too hard to fully recover.

For her part, Edwina Pepper appears to have occupied something of a parallel role as the inspiring elder guiding light to the Fannings and Carannante that Don West occupied for Woodruff and the founders of AMP. Although, Pepper's politics landed nowhere near the hardline liberation politic that West spent a lifetime fighting for: her community on Big Laurel may have been mutualistic and alternative to the mainstream, but it was "not to be confused with communism in any way, shape, or form."[98]

Mountain Call managed to continue publication until late 1978, when Greg Carannante, newly married and with a newborn baby, left rural West Virginia for Florida and the other members of the group lost steam for continuing publishing. The land trust on Marrowbone Ridge had meanwhile become home to the Big Laurel School of Learning in 1977, founded by Edwina Pepper along with Sisters Kathy O'Hagan and Gretchen Shaffer, now known as Big Laurel Learning Center. The land housing the school is now organized as the John A. Sheppard Memorial Ecological Reservation (JASMER), a 456-acre ecological preserve that Pepper organized and founded in 1976 as a conservation land trust to protect area homes and families from pressure to sell their properties to strip-mining operations.

The Appalachian Movement Press printshop was housed in this building for the second half of the 1970s.

Lifestyle Stuff

Some Changing of the Guard

Most of the original people working in the shop had moved on after the first few years of heavy and consistent activity at Appalachian Movement Press. Tom Woodruff, now working full time as a union organizer, was still willing to teach new printers how to use the A. B. Dick presses to continue AMP's work and learn the printing trade in the process. The AMP imprint as a methodology for educating Appalachians was functionally on hiatus while Woodruff continued building on his career as a full-time union organizer with 1199 National Health Care Workers Union, but all of the printing equipment was available if someone was willing to use it. At some point between 1974 and 1975, the shop itself was moved to its last and longest location at 745 Seventh Street: a red brick building set off of Eighth Avenue with "a nice front office with a large workspace in back" on a street that ends at the railroad tracks, which bisect Huntington from east to west, parallel to the Ohio River.[99] The building was owned by Nelson Nidiffer, owner and operator of the Printer's Product printshop and supply store in Huntington, who was friendly and supportive to the AMP printers.

Paul Salstrom described the interior layout of this building from memory:

> People entered the press into a front office about fifteen feet long and twenty feet wide. Along the left-hand side of the office ran a counter with room behind it to do paperwork. At the back of that

> left side of the office was a small composition room holding the Compugraphic Jr. typesetter—an early-style computer typesetter through which photographic film had to be fed. To the right of that cubicle sat a large light table on which to do layout. Along the right-hand side of the office was a sofa, and there were lots of shelves along that wall. This whole office room was enclosed with wood rafters and boards over its top—but otherwise the rest of the shop was two-stories high.
>
> The door from that office into the larger shop was to the right of the light table. Directly behind the office was a work area where collating and stapling were the main activities. The rest of the shop, the right-hand side of the overall building, contained the offset press and the paper cutter, plus a long mechanical collator—and behind those sat the plate burning set-up and behind *that* was the darkroom, which was sizable but not as big as the front office. In the front wall of the darkroom was a large vertical camera, in front of which layouts would be mounted in order to be photographed, and the resultant negatives were developed there inside the darkroom in trays of developer and fixative. The next step was just outside the darkroom, at the vertical plate-burning set-up, which featured two large old arc lamps that shot off sparks while they were burning the plates. Those plates would then be strapped on the offset press to do the print run. Behind the back wall of the office was a large rack with our supply of our own publications and also the books we didn't publish but distributed—like Mother Jones' autobiography, and *Labor's Untold Story* published by the Electrical Workers Union. The third floor may have held an apartment, but I just don't remember.[100]

Meanwhile, the tone of much of the work coming from Appalachian Movement Press changed somewhat from the original, founding voices. "It morphed from being a left-wing thing to being more of a hippie thing," Yvonne Farley told me about this shift in AMP's output in the mid-1970s. She elaborated that the focus of their publications had moved, perhaps with the absence of Woodruff as a driving force, "from unionizing, hardline stuff to more lifestyle stuff."[101] Perhaps illustrative of this shift, by this era AMP dropped the word *Movement* from their name in some cases and was known only as Appalachian Press. As Salstrom put it, "The word *Movement* wasn't very engaging (in my opinion then) by the mid-1970s."[102]

Miriam Ralston and her husband Paul Salstrom came to the AMP shop from Iowa in 1975, both part of a back-to-the-land rural homesteading movement, which in West Virginia had a locus in Lincoln County, south of Huntington's Cabell County. The couple came to AMP with a contract to print *Green Revolution*—"A Voice for Decentralism" and the monthly periodical from the School of Living, a "cooperative living" organization based in Maryland. Salstrom was also managing editor of the magazine, which differed from most of AMP's jobs in its distinctly nonregional focus. Salstrom described the range of his work for the magazine: "Into the *Green Revolution* I put a lot of how-to-do-it articles, a lot of we-*are*-doing-it articles, a monthly feature on alternative economics by Bob Swann, a monthly piece on alternative energy or technology, and an annotated monthly update on 'rural apprenticeships' available throughout the United States."[103] The checks from printing *Green Revolution* became the primary, most consistent source of income for the shop, and in a short time Salstrom became the de facto manager of Appalachian Movement Press.

Salstrom, already in his thirties and older than most of the AMP printers, mostly worked in the front office, "typing the copy on [their] Compugraphic Junior and doing the lay-out on the big light table in the front office." Miriam, who was in her mid-twenties and had taken "a crash course in printing" at local Huntington East High School, ran the photography and darkroom production, as well as the offset presses.[104] Thomas Gibbs, who had helped peripherally with (and contributed poetry to) *Free Forum* in the 1960s, returned to Huntington in 1977 and worked in the shop with Salstrom and Ralston. His poetry book *No Willows for the Zen Cowboy* would be the only publication to roll out of Salstrom's brief Appalachian Writer's Project, which had been "a scheme to teach writers how to be printers."[105] Charlie Berry and Barbara Frazier were also printers at AMP when Ralston and Salstrom first arrived, as were a couple of other printers whose names I could not recover through my interviews and research.[106]

Eventually, according to Ralston, the shop staff whittled down to just her and Paul. With the couple running operations and Woodruff,

Paul Salstrom, early 1970s.

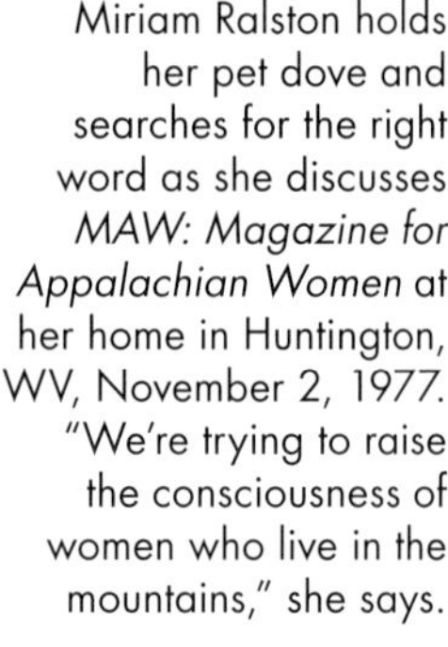

Miriam Ralston holds her pet dove and searches for the right word as she discusses *MAW: Magazine for Appalachian Women* at her home in Huntington, WV, November 2, 1977. "We're trying to raise the consciousness of women who live in the mountains," she says.

as owner, only making an occasional appearance, Appalachian Movement Press as a workplace, while short on printers, "had a balance to it in that era."[107] But from its founding through the mid-1970s, AMP appears to have been a printshop managed almost exclusively by men. "I always felt intimidated when I went over there," Yvonne Farley recalled. "It was a guy place. There were never any women in there, there were never women involved in any decision-making at all."[108] Sherrie Edwards has been claimed as a founding member, but her name doesn't appear often, and her trail was hard to follow up.[109] Although Jeanine Caywood-Stewart—who was married to Danie Stewart when AMP began—is credited as a member of the shop and as a shareholder in AMP's formative years, Farley and others couldn't recall her involvement. Farley in particular disputes that Caywood-Stewart would have been an equal business partner: "Women weren't really considered politically intelligent. We were the worker bees, collating pamphlets."[110]

The environment was one of male dominance, with few women present or ever in positions of leadership, at least in its first few years. According to Farley, "it was very much reflective of the time," and AMP would unfortunately revert to this dynamic before shuttering completely in 1979.[111] But before that could happen, and in one brief but whirlwind year, Huntington became home to the very first feminist magazine in the region, *MAW: Magazine of Appalachian Women*, spearheaded by AMP printer Miriam Ralston.

To Share and Express Themselves

MAW: Magazine of Appalachian Women, 1977–1978

If many in the Appalachian Left in the 1970s argued for the importance of Appalachians creating and maintaining their own culture without the influence of outsiders, *MAW: Magazine of Appalachian Women* complicated that politic. Founded by the tenacity and generosity of a committed midwestern transplant, *MAW* quickly caught welcome fire with the first issue, operating as an open forum "of" women in the region.

Miriam Ralston and Paul Salstrom had taken a break from their work in Huntington, living for three months in rural Minnesota and working on the alternative magazine *North Country Anvil*. "It just popped in my head, basically, I want to start a women's magazine," remembered Ralston, whose mind had been focused on what she could do for Appalachia while she was up north. "There was not anything that I knew of that was a women's feminist journal in Appalachia. I had the access to the press, and Paul was right behind me like 'Go girl!' I printed up a sheet advertising the magazine and went to the women's conference in Huntington that spring and got immense interest in it."[112] Within what is now referred to as the second wave of feminism in the United States, *MAW* could easily be the first, and only, feminist magazine to be published in the central Appalachian region, for an Appalachian audience.

"When *MAW* began, I did not have in mind another *Ms.*, or another *Country Women*," Ralston writes in the introduction to the first issue. The title of the magazine itself was an immediate point of consternation, the colloquial term "Maw," for some, "calls up the sun-bonneted, bare-footed, deprived older woman of the soil-poor, coal-rich hills."[113] In short order, Ralston took flak from those who felt the title of her otherwise progressive publication harkened to retrograde notions of backwards mountain stereotypes. But she heard from just as many who loved it, and she stood firm against her detractors in the magazine's second issue, writing that the "Maw" she pictured as an old grandmother on a porch was "a force that so much life had passed through . . . not a bad image in my mind but a life-giving one." Did readers want to feed the (relatively essentialist) imagery of feminine strength, wisdom, and life of which *MAW* would quickly become an outlet? Ralston implored creative women to get in touch and contribute to the magazine.

The spirit at play on the pages of *MAW* is invigorating and different from anything else that rolled off the AMP presses in the 1970s—if nothing else because it was conceived of and led by women and was, for all intents, the first magazine of its kind in the region. Ralston described their guiding mission so: "From the very beginning, we've tried to solicit interested, creative women who will share their internal feelings and experiences; we've tried to create something that people will keep, something that will command a faith in the values of the inner life."[114] Each issue was full of poetry and illustrations, and regular space was given to multipage photo portfolios, profiles of artists, and fiction. Although the magazine was primarily a creative outlet, perspectives on current politics were woven throughout: "Womanspeak" was one regular column for reader-contributed editorials responding to the issues of the time. Seventy-year-old Clara Cassidy writes in issue 1 that she will never agree with the magazine's title and speculates that her first contribution will thus be her last, but in fact her perspective remained regular in each subsequent issue. If it wasn't "hardline" leftist material, then what *MAW* was doing takes a wholly different tack with liberation: with the personal understood as political, *MAW* demands the validity of a woman's experience.

Appalachian Movement Press had recently lost the critical *Green Revolution* printing contract at the end of 1976, and *MAW* brought some much-needed overhead funding at exactly the right time. Salstrom continued his work running the presses as *MAW*'s only male employee, and Ralston assembled a group of women not otherwise involved in the AMP shop who could help make the magazine happen: Jean Darcy (associate editor) and Marilyn Putz (fiction editor) were both assistant professors in English at Marshall University. Elizabeth Nordeen, who had no prior experience at magazines or in academia, worked as poetry editor. *MAW* had original artwork throughout, with Yvonne Aslip as regular staff photographer and Vicki Gibbs, who was married at the time to AMP printer Tom Gibbs, serving as art editor and illustrator. Ralston told the *Huntington Advertiser* that the first issue had taken the work of twenty people, "mostly the staff and their children," working for two weeks to print, staple, and fold the first issue of *MAW* for distribution.[115] That cover is dated September/October 1977—it retailed for one dollar.

Soon excited reviews of the magazine and new contributions from Appalachian women were coming in. Strat Douthat's profile of Ralston circulated by the Associated Press "sent it further into space!" according to Ralston.[116] *MAW* was distributed by AMP into many regional stores and was picked up for selected magazine racks by a magazine distribution company out of Charleston, WV, guaranteeing that the AMP shop would be printing large press runs.[117] Valerie Staats (who would go on to found the *MAW*-inspired midwestern feminist publication *Iowa Woman*) and Barbara Young soon joined the expanding *MAW* staff.

Concurrent with the launch of the magazine, Miriam Ralston founded Appalachian Women Incorporated as a body for organizing *MAW* and also to quickly manage all of the adjacent activity she predicted would surround her new endeavor. AWI would hold workshops and organize a Women in Psychotherapy Conference in Huntington in November of 1977. They announced an interest in producing films on social issues concerning the region (" 'child abuse' and 'women in prison' have been suggested as good topics").[118] They would produce a book of photography and advertised that they would consider publishing other manuscripts if the writer could help subsidize the cost until the organization was on firmer financial ground. They printed a 1978 calendar. They dreamed of buying a parcel of land, "for arts and crafts festivals, for retreats, or even for homesteading by women."[119] The women who comprised the AWI and were involved in producing *MAW* dreamed big from the beginning, and the pages of the magazine called out, constantly, for expanding all of their ideas into mutual endeavors by asking for help, more ideas, content contributions, printing, and assembly labor. If Miriam Ralston, with her regular editorial pages and position at AMP, was the managing editor, she pushed constantly to make these projects into collectivist endeavors. "Help us raise and nurture *MAW*," Ralston writes on the first page of the first issue, "so that she can raise and nurture all of us."[120]

Meanwhile, Ralston became pregnant after the second issue—she and Salstrom would soon be raising a baby girl. "I actually remember the smell of ink while my belly was swollen and I was thinking if it would do harm, but at the same time I was thinking the sound of the press and my mental activity would inspire my firstborn Eve!"[121] The tone of each issue of *MAW* roiled forward on the momentum that the first issue generated but also expressed the genuine exhaustion of actually producing the magazine on a shoestring budget.

The magazine was launched in autumn of 1977, and already by the fourth issue in the spring of 1978, Barbara Young mentions trouble, writing cryptically of their desire to move the magazine to a new printshop—or perhaps purchase their own equipment. Young went on to write that, of course, if anyone else was game, they'd certainly love to see someone open a "women's press" in the area. Ralston echoed much of this in her editorial page, attempting strategically to take her own step back in the months before her daughter would be born.

What was happening behind the scenes was an increasingly confrontational atmosphere in the Huntington printshop between the midwestern couple Ralston and Salstrom and Jack Frazier, a new arrival to the Appalachian Movement Press shop who had recently moved back to his native West Virginia from New Orleans. "I totally enjoyed being pregnant and running the press," Ralston reflected. "I thought it was quite symbolic giving birth to a magazine while also giving birth to a child. When Jack came in, it became very heavy."[122] Frazier, originally from Madam's Creek in Summers County, WV, started working for AMP doing mostly collating and stapling. A writer and researcher with a critical focus on environmental destruction in his Appalachian homeland, he was planning to continue his own publishing imprint to be printed on the AMP equipment: Solar Age Press.

What caused the tensions between the printers wasn't recorded directly in the pages of *MAW*, and Ralston, Salstrom, and AMP printer John Strong Clark each remember the next couple of months differently.[123] Clark remembers that, quite plainly, Frazier "hated feminists" and did not want to help print *MAW*. "We worked with her, but Jack hated her," said Clark, who positions himself as a mediating force. "I just said, 'Jack, stay away from her man—we're all working in the same underground nonprofit organization, right?' " Although the pages of *MAW* express a growing momentum behind the magazine, Clark also says that the printshop had taken a risk in funding the printing of the new magazine and claims that *MAW* never did became solvent (which Ralston also confided in private correspondence), thus heightening the tension in the shop.[124]

Salstrom also remembers Frazier's attitude becoming increasingly hostile to the couple, even though he says that he had given Frazier permission to live and sleep in the loft over the printshop office and that, when Frazier's Volkswagen had broken down, they had made room for him to park it inside in the back of the production room. While Clark believes that Frazier was capable of operating the printing presses, Salstrom's memory differs. Salstrom remembers Frazier mainly working on collating and binding the contract jobs AMP took on.[125]

For her part, Ralston recalls this era much more vividly as a time of threats and increasing tension. Everything finally boiled over between Frazier and the couple in the summer of 1978. One morning, she remembers, they arrived at the Appalachian Movement Press shop to find that everything had been sabotaged: "Literally, we came in one day to the press to continue working, and the machines were damaged—all the issues and printing materials were strung all over the floor of the press. It was a complete anarchy. I don't remember the details after that, but it was impossible to work."[126]

Paul Salstrom dashed out a one-color cover for issue 4 using the AMP presses in an effort to get the edition finished, and the couple made preparations to leave the printshop with Miriam eight-months pregnant. As it was arriving in mailboxes and on magazine racks, "friendly but discerning critics told Miriam that *MAW* 4 was the best issue yet for content," according to Salstrom, and despite problems unknown to the broader readership, the consensus was that the magazine kept improving with each new issue.[127] But inside the Huntington printshop, *MAW* was on the rocks, and the people producing it were packing their bags.

In her final editorial in *MAW* 5, Miriam Ralston raged. After calling *MAW* readers to remember the crippling sabotage of the feminist Diana Press in California in the past year, she takes a broad view and speculates on the fear and jealousy at the root of male violence. *MAW* had been attacked: "Her volunteers were physically threatened. Papers were stolen. Equipment was sabotaged. Half-printed sheets were strewn on the floor."[128] Phone calls, messages, and mail were never forwarded. The last issue of *MAW*, its fifth in the summer of 1978, was printed with a $1,000 private loan from a family member at another nearby commercial printshop.[129] This double-sized issue combined materials and reader contributions that were originally meant to have constituted an upcoming, but now uncertain, sixth issue. A photograph by Yvonne Aslip of the chain-link fence surrounding the prison yard at the Federal Prison for Women in Alderson, West Virginia, splashes the front cover of *MAW* 5, the "Women and Violence" issue.

Although she never calls Jack Frazier out by name, Ralston does, in her final editorial page, wish retroactively that the magazine hadn't been dependent on the AMP printshop and thus "vulnerable to the workings of male chauvinism."[130] Meanwhile, as early as January of 1978, Ralston was clearly reading the writing on the wall and had reached out to negotiate the possible sale of the magazine to the relatively new Council on Appalachian Women (CAW), based in western North Carolina.

Hoping to keep *MAW* alive even if she could no longer steer the magazine herself, Ralston's backup plan included selling the naming rights, their subscription list (numbering almost five hundred), and all of their remaining back issues—even encouraging the council to hire Valerie Staats to continue publishing the magazine. Selling *MAW* would also, she hoped, recoup some of the cost of the loan she had received to produce the final issue.[131] As winter thawed into spring, Ralston waffled back and forth on the prospect of handing the magazine over to CAW, unsure of whether she could trust the organization's intentions with a project to which she had become so intimately attached.[132] But the environment at the AMP shop continued to deteriorate, and Ralston eventually conceded to an unrecorded deal with CAW to sell *MAW* and keep some version of the magazine in print. "Even with our future plans and hopes," she wrote to Jeanne Hoffman at CAW in July of 1978, "to continue the magazine from [Huntington] would be a threat to my health." [133]

In a letter sent to all *MAW* subscribers in November 1978, Jane Weeks, then president of CAW, announced their newly renamed magazine *Appalachian Women*, which would begin production soon as a quarterly in the same spirit as *MAW*. However, by the next summer, institutional subscribers were writing in to the council wondering where their first issue was. The whole effort lasted less than a year and produced only two issues, and the Council of Appalachian Women, stretched too thin and beset by leadership turmoil and financial difficulties from the beginning, folded in 1981.[134]

The story of these fundamental conflicts that boiled over inside Appalachian Movement Press parallel the world outside the Huntington activist printshop's walls: a patriarchal social order rooted in male violence had inspired the need for Miriam's vision for a feminist magazine in the first place, one which would unwaveringly declare the validity of women's experience in that world. And then, despite (or because of) the growing support her magazine was receiving, that same force had squashed their voice and evicted their vision. *MAW: Magazine of Appalachian Women* flamed out within its first year, but not because of organizational burnout, or lack of funding, or a deficit of equipment. The magazine folded because of unworkable tension and sexism wrought out in their small, collectivized work space, and Miriam Ralston and Paul Salstrom's ultimate mutual need to find what they felt would be a safer place to raise their child pushed them to move on.

We Printed the Radical Stuff

1978–1979

Appalachian Movement Press came to a close soon after Paul Salstrom and Miriam Ralston left the printshop, although much of what went on between the summer of 1978 and the end of 1979 isn't clear. If Tom Woodruff knew about it, then he, still acting as owner of AMP but rarely involved in the weekly operations, never stepped in to mitigate the conflict between the printshop operators. After turning in their keys, the couple moved to a house in Mason County where Ralston gave birth to their daughter Eve. Salstrom finished a degree at Marshall University, after which the family moved to Boston to continue pursuing academics: Salstrom to Brandeis University, Ralston to Emerson College.

As a native West Virginian with a lifetime in the Appalachian Left, Yvonne Farley, who didn't know the AMP printers in that later era, offers a different take on the fundamental conflict between Frazier and Ralston/Salstrom. Her perspective highlights a perennial tension in the region and a rift that Don West, in particular, was happy to aggravate. Farley points out that Ralston and Salstrom were "outsiders" from the Midwest and that, when they decided that they needed to, they were able to move away from Appalachia to continue their academic pursuits. Many in the region, for various reasons, lacked this flexibility. Farley merges academic mobility with existing tensions between native regional activists and the influx of back-to-the-land homesteaders in that era—many of whom, she claims, did not stay long: "We believed that the movement should consist of lifetime Appalachians. We thought that Appalachian people needed to stand up for themselves without the help of outsiders."[135]

From John Strong Clark's perspective, it wasn't that nuanced. Clark liked Salstrom and Ralston but maintains that Jack Frazier simply despised the idea of working with feminists and was stressed about the time and money that *MAW: Magazine of Appalachian Women* was taking to produce.[136] In any case, Frazier and Clark, both from Summers County, West Virginia, took the wheel and operated Appalachian Movement Press on their own during the printshop's final year.

Clark became involved in AMP in late 1977, after spending a couple of years in art school at Marshall University: "I was a hippie from Summers County, and I went to Marshall to take courses. They said they would teach me how to print at the underground printing shop, Appalachian Movement Press. So I started sleeping on the couch there, and I learned all the darkroom work and how to make plates and print on the A. B. Dick."[137]

John Strong Clark in 2017 at the Hinton Marble Works in Hinton, WV, where he keeps a studio and a garden.

Clark calls Frazier the VP of the printshop and himself "the president, of a sort," perhaps because his know-how with the printing presses exceeded Frazier's. Clark loved the mechanics of running the presses, and he was moved by the original mission of AMP. "My grandfather died of black lung in the Pennsylvania coal mines before the union. I remembered that from when I was five years old. Both of my wife's parents lived in coal camps." At Appalachian Movement Press, Clark told me, "we printed the radical stuff." [138]

Jack Frazier had his own personal focus, his Solar Age Press imprint, on which he launched his first publication, *The Marijuana Farmers: Hemp Cults and Cultures*. Self-published in 1973, during his time in New Orleans, *The Marijuana Farmers* is an early, historically rooted missive against marijuana prohibition and in support of a reinvestment in industrial hemp production in North America. Jack Herer, author of the lauded *The Emperor Wears No Clothes* (1985, Ah Ha Publishing), began his own decade of compiling research for his seminal book the year Frazier's booklet was released in underground circles, and he later cited Frazier's work extensively in *Emperor*. According to Clark, Frazier "was ahead of his time." [139]

Jack Frazier, unattributed photograph from a 1987 article about his reprint of Huey P. Long's "Share Our Wealth" platform, visible on the table.

Frazier's follow-up on Solar Age, *West Virginia Green: Part 1*, rolled off the presses at Appalachian Movement Press in 1976 and was popular regionally within the central Appalachian environmentalist milieu. A review of the sixty-two-page publication in the *Mountain Call* that year calls Frazier a "diehard bohemian and nitpicking researcher" who "lived like a self-made pauper" while researching and writing *Green*. In several issues of *The Call* leading up to the printing of his first book, Frazier placed advertisements attempting to sell off his full collection of over a thousand "rare blues, jazz, gospel and folk" 78 rpm records from over a decade of his own roving collecting. The ad claimed "the money will be used to sustain a destitute writer writing a book on the ecological rape of West Virginia by multinational corporations and to support the Alternative Energy Center."[140]

"Social skills. He didn't have none. But I got along with him because I really appreciated what he was doing," remembered Clark.[141] Clark admired the dedication of his friend and coworker as much as the editors of *The Call* did, while also conceding that Frazier was, at best, difficult to work with. "He was a hell of a researcher. He was a pain in the ass, but he was a hell of a researcher."[142] *West Virginia Green* ended up divided into thirds due to Frazier's lack of funding, and the first edition was the only one to see print. Given his focus on his own research and writing, it's possible that Frazier had involved himself in AMP primarily as a means to produce *Green* and to eventually expand Solar Age Press in Huntington.

The new operators, Clark and Frazier, pursued their environmentally focused politics and experimented with formats beyond staple-bound pamphlets. They produced a calendar, *Stop the Stonewall Jackson Dam: Save Our Heritage*, and distributed it for free. Clark in particular experimented with printing posters and small illustrated cards. Their 1977 catalog offered batches of stickers that were "suitable for placing above faucets and water fountains, particularly in public places." Emblazoned with "CAUTION: POISON," the stickers' fine print reads, "The Environmental Protection Agency has determined that this water contains carbon tetrachloride, chloroform, and other cancer-causing chemicals." This design and the similarly accompanying text have, sadly enough, been appropriately reproduced and reapplied in the modern day natural-gas-drilling regions of New York and Pennsylvania.

In Appalachian Movement Press's final year, Clark and Frazier also changed the printshop's logo: replacing the miner's pick with a strutting black cat. The two friends resumed maintaining the full AMP imprint, available through mail order, which by the late 1970s still offered over forty titles and now included some fresh editions with illustrated covers. They continued printing a small annual catalog, and it was Frazier's idea to mail this catalog out to libraries around the country in an effort to sell more publications to fund the shop. Indeed, by the

CAUTION

DRINK AT YOUR OWN RISK

The Environmental Protection Agency has determined that this water contains carbon tetrachloride, chloroform, and other cancer causing chemicals.

POISON

3x3½-inch stickers suitable for placing above faucets and water fountains, particularly in public places.

1-9 copies .... 10 cents each
10-49 copies .... 6 cents each
50-100 copies .... 5 cents each

Packets of these stickers were available from AMP's 1977 catalog.

end of 1978, once *Green Revolution* and *MAW: Magazine of Appalachian Women* were no longer being produced at AMP, library purchases and small local commercial contracts were one of the only sources of income for the printshop, and Appalachian Movement Press was losing momentum.

Appalachian Movement Press logo in the final year of the printshop.

Young, Wild, Impractical Ideas

Appalachian Movement Press folded up a decade of operations in Huntington in late 1978 or early 1979—exactly when and why has been lost to memory.

Michael Fanning said that the community at the Knob had to stop printing at AMP because the printshop was shuttering at the same time as he was looking to print what became the final issue of *Mountain Call* in autumn of 1978—not long after Miriam Ralston printed the final issue of *MAW* at another nearby commercial printer before she and Paul Salstrom moved on.[143]

Salstrom claims that Jack Frazier, and by extension John Strong Clark, had no idea how to fund the printshop after he and Ralston left.[144]

Clark, who claims that publishing *MAW* had drained the AMP bank account, told me that he also believes that the shop had simply run its due course, with the printers burned out and unwilling to keep the presses going.[145]

Yvonne Farley theorizes that Tom Woodruff, under some collaboration from his friend and mentor Don West, reclaimed the shop from the various "lifestyle" magazines that West would have barely tolerated. Since the printing equipment was transferred to the West's Appalachian South Folklife Center, perhaps West, as AMP's original guiding light, had sought to put the printshop back on a particular political track.[146]

But for his part, cofounder Woodruff can't remember much more than packing up a truck with all of the printshop equipment. Meanwhile, he was proving to be a successful and talented union organizer. Now working full time with 1199, the Health Care Workers Union, Woodruff was elected union president in 1980. According to a modern profile from the Service Employees International Union (SEIU), he "successfully initiated the first major service-sector organizing drive in a region in which hostile laws historically prevented all but workers in the mining industry the freedom to form a union. In addition," the profile goes on, "he focused on helping mostly working-class women in hospitals and nursing homes unite their strength to have a voice in the quality of care, which in turn raised standards for both patients and caregivers in Appalachia."[147] Woodruff went on to climb to the executive ranks of the SEIU, resigning as an officer in 2013 but continuing to work full time as a consultant.

After the printshop in Huntington closed, Clark returned to his hometown of Hinton, West Virginia. There, he and his wife Teri founded and operated the Bluegrass Printing Company, primarily a letterpress printshop. Clark continued his friendship with Jack Frazier, and three more Solar Age Press books were printed at Bluegrass in Hinton. *Auto Fuels of the 1980s*, a seventy-one-page treatise and manual on methanol as a petroleum alternative for vehicles, came first, around 1979. A couple of years later, looking to promote Huey P. Long's 1934 platform on wealth redistribution, "Share Our Wealth," Frazier photocopied an entire edition that he found in a New Orleans Public Library, wrote a biographical introduction about Long, and republished *Share Our Wealth: Every Man a King* in two thirty-two-page editions of 1,500 each. A decade later, in 1991, Frazier's comb-bound 110-page *The Great American Hemp Industry* would round out the Solar Age Press imprint on Bluegrass, pulling together earlier writings from *The Marijuana Farmers* and a collection of research papers on marijuana and hemp. "[Jack] don't get enough credit," Clark reflected. "He was an asshole, but he don't get enough credit for what he did."[148]

All of Appalachian Movement Press's equipment was either given, or sold, to Don and Connie West, and Woodruff himself helped pack and move everything from Huntington down to the Appalachian South Folklife Center (ASFC) in Pipestem. The plan was to set up the print-shop inside a two-story building on the ASFC grounds that already housed a darkroom and several weaving looms. The addition of a full suite of printing equipment was meant to diversify what could be produced at the West's folklife center and to begin a new publishing arm for the work already happening there.

An undated early ASFC newsletter highlights the center's activities and resources—including a library, a summer camp, regular folk festivals, and other burgeoning projects—and describes "a complete offset printing plant [that] publishes pamphlets, booklets and other materials on Appalachian history, heritage and people."[149] For the newly renamed Mountain Freedom Press, the listing of available publications via mail order were clearly the remnants of the AMP imprint catalog as transported from Huntington.

Don West hired an unattributed printer through the Comprehensive Employment and Training Act (CETA) program to run the A. B. Dick offset presses he had inherited.[150] In November of 1979, they finished producing *Gospel Millions*, a sprawling fifty-four-page collection of a

The Mountain Freedom Press logo, from the inside of *Gospel Millions*, 1979.

series of articles, including photos, detailing the inner workings and funding/donation infrastructures of regional evangelical churches and gurus by investigative reporter Jim Haught. These articles were originally published in the *Charleston Gazette* earlier that year, and Haught's work focused on precisely the sort of spiritual corruption that was right in line with the kind of deceptive, exploitative systems of organized religion that West hated most.

Gospel Millions is an exceptional piece of underground bootleg literature, packed so dense with information and images that it likely stressed the shop's long-arm stapler just to bind the pages. With its cut-and-paste facsimile approach to the reproduction of the articles inside, hand-drawn satirical cover, and continuation of an unapologetic anti-copyright ethos, *Gospel Millions* wouldn't look out of place in an early 2000s punk zine collection. But it was the only full-fledged publication to roll out on the Mountain Freedom Press imprint and the last bound booklet produced on the repurposed Appalachian Movement Press equipment.

Pete Laska, of the Soupbean Poets Collective, told Yvonne Farley that the building at the folklife center that housed the printing equipment was, unfortunately, unheated. In those conditions, a winter frost quickly cracked many of the bearings on the A. B. Dick offset presses, effectively destroying them in an environment where funding for repairs on equipment nobody knew how to operate was scarce. Laska had worked and performed with West since they met at Antioch College's Beckley Center, where the Soupbean group formed, and a book of his poetry would have been Mountain Freedom Press's next publication.[151]

—

When I visited ASFC in the summer of 2017 to look for remaining evidence of Appalachian Movement Press, the building that had housed the printshop was no longer standing and only a concrete foundation remained. Then-director Roger May told me that I should have a look in the basement of the chapel, where there was overflow storage from the center's library. There I found the last remnants of Appalachian Movement Press's publishing imprint in the back corner of that humid cinderblock room. Stacks upon stacks of covers, sheets, catalogs, and unfinished reprints of songbooks and essays were piled inside a pair of purple plastic storage bins. Several milk crates were next to these with bound and finished pamphlets bent over on themselves, their binding staples consumed with a rust that stained the folded spine of their covers. A few finished titles were piled on the top ledge of a metal bookshelf, right under the floor joists of the chapel above. It looked like nothing had been touched in almost forty years.

Woodruff had already left behind some of the ideals that seeded Appalachian Movement Press, and when he moved the equipment to Pipestem in 1979, he closed that chapter of his life entirely. "We wanted to start an Appalachian rights movement that didn't quite start," he told me about the original intentions for AMP and the environment that the press was born in. "There was even a theory at one point that we ought to secede from the country, but those are kind of young, wild, impractical ideas. We'd hoped for an Appalachian revolutionary movement, but that didn't happen."[152]

Most, if not all, of the better-documented movement presses in the US during the 1970s operated out of large urban areas, but Appalachian Movement Press was specific to its rural context in central Appalachia. As a publishing imprint, they may not have left their name in the region's history as such, perhaps because the printers and other people involved over the years saw their operation as, simply, a means to an end. But AMP's mission was to put thousands of powerful, independently produced publications directly into people's hands, not to create their own legacy. In that, they succeeded. And as a printing outfit serving the Appalachian Left, they were indispensable in the region during a critical, revolutionary time in the struggle for human rights and environmental justice.

The politics undergirding Appalachian Movement Press were, ultimately, internationalist, but they defined a specific regional and class-conscious audience. During their decade-long run with very little sustaining income, AMP provided a platform that strengthened a burgeoning Appalachian identity, became an outlet for mountaineers to access investigative articles on regional corruption and previously suppressed working-class history, and, perhaps most lastingly, served as the steadfast platform for the later work of Don West.

Their small activist printshop in Huntington, West Virginia, may have never sparked an Appalachian Revolution, but Appalachian Movement Press succeeded in its mission of fostering the resistant culture at the heart of modern Appalachia.

Part II

In Print

Hillbilly Ain't Beautiful

Jim Branscome's *Annihilating the Hillbilly*

A Tuesday night in September in Arlington, Virginia, 1971. Sitting on the floor of a small, barely furnished apartment on Fort Myer Drive, near the US Marine Corps's iconic Iwo Jima War Memorial, Jim Branscome handwrote what would become one of the more widely read salvos of the burgeoning Appalachian identity movement on a yellow legal pad.

At the time, CBS ran a Tuesday evening primetime program that featured a trifecta of popular comedy shows, back to back, which drew most of their premise and humor from ridiculing rural American stereotypes (Appalachian and otherwise): beginning at 7:30, *The Beverly Hillbillies*; next up, *Green Acres* at 8; rounding out the program at 8:30 was the hour-long *Hee Haw*.

Sitting through these shows that evening, Branscome grew more and more incensed: "I just started boiling over! What in the *fuck*—this is part of our oppression! And so I just started writing."[1] Branscome's essay became *Annihilating the Hillbilly: The Appalachians' Struggle with America's Institutions,* an exposition that exploded into the middle of a growing regional movement towards considering Appalachian folk-ways and modern-ways as culturally distinct, valuable, and even worth fighting for: an Appalachian identity movement, defined from the bottom up.

It feels complicated to apply a modern lens to Appalachian identity as it was forming in the 1970s. To start with, it appears to have functioned as a primarily white identity, if nothing else because the authors were mostly white and because many of them, Branscome included, would draw comparisons that paralleled the plight of Appalachians with the plight of African Americans or American Indians. A fumbling gesture at solidarity, the comparison itself *becomes* the definition. As such, "Appalachian" generally meant the white inhabitants of the region during this time, although in *Annihilating* Branscome stands out for at least mentioning Black Appalachians *as* Appalachians.

In building on the idea of a distinct Appalachian identity, white radicals in the region—cognizant of war and genocide around the globe, as well as the brutalities of racism at home—were trying to create a new bedrock of pride in culture and place that would both bulwark against degenerative stereotypes of working-class Appalachians and provide fuel for a progressive political movement on home turf. Though, a contemporary audience will rightfully shudder when Branscome describes CBS's Tuesday primetime line-up as "the most intensive effort ever exerted by a nation to belittle, demean, and otherwise destroy a minority people within its boundaries."

Again, putting this into a frame that feels useful to any modern reader while also pointing to the clear racial components can be tricky. So I'll call in an example from another work by Branscome, who, along with many activists, was working to reimagine how the US education system could work better for otherwise disinvested rural Appalachians. In his oft-circulated essay "The Case for Appalachian Studies" (1974), Branscome argues that the education curriculums that were forced upon children in the region were part of a colonialist program of assimilation and that high drop-out rates "are indications of the failure of

American education to assimilate the mountain individual into mainstream American society." Dropping out of school wasn't a sign of an individual's failure, it was direct resistance to outside oppression.

Branscome homes in on vocabulary and dialect, well understood as cultural indicators of difference and leverage for stereotype from the outside (as with the CBS programming that spurred him to write *Annihilating*). A spoken accent would bring immediate ridicule to Appalachians when they would visit or relocate to a larger urban center for work, Branscome points out. He offers a radical solution that presages the contemporary practice by which speech therapists no longer pathologize dialect: "There must be a curriculum change to meet the needs of the people, not the needs of the national norms. . . . By giving Appalachian students an awareness of the structure and origin of their own particular speech patterns, and at the same time giving them instruction in standard English, which might necessarily be taught much as one would teach a foreign language, they could deal with writings and other communications from outside the region but would not be forced to adopt speech patterns alien to them unless and until they so choose." In this model, the primacy of the regional culture would be celebrated, and students would learn to meet outside cultures on their own terms.

"When I finished it," Branscome told me about *Annihilating*, "I didn't know if I wanted to publish it or not." The young writer was in touch with Jim Holloway, one of the editors of *Katallagete* magazine, a journal of Southern liberal Christian thought and, at times, argument. Holloway was interested to publish his essay in the magazine, and Branscome agreed. "That would just be the end of it," he thought. But in fact he had struck a chord, and requests to reprint the essay would come to him for years. Appalachian Movement Press put *Annihilating* into its rotation of perennially available booklets from the beginning, around 1971. "I never made a nickel from it!" Branscome told me in 2019, as he always granted republication permission for free. Now, sought-after printed versions still surface as collectibles online and in specialty bookshops.

These days, Branscome says, "I look at it and shudder. But then I go back and look at the context. Was I writing something that other people felt? I think the Appalachian identity movement was on a tipping point. Every time I think, 'That was pretty naive, James,' I realize also that there were lots of kids that grabbed on to that and said, 'I understand, this is giving me some insights into who I am.' "[2]

Annihilating the Hillbilly has, as mentioned, been reproduced countless times in various forms. We reproduce it here as a historical document for the first time since the publishing of the important academic survey *Colonialism in Modern America: The Appalachian Case* by Helen Lewis, Linda Johnson, and Don Askins (Boone, NC: Appalachian Consortium Press, 1978).

ANNIHILATING
THE
HILLBILLY:

THE APPALACHIANS'
STRUGGLE WITH
AMERICA'S
INSTITUTIONS

James Branscome

15¢

Annihilating The Hillbilly

Cover

Annihilating The Hillbilly

Inside Front Cover

This article is published with permission of the auth
James Branscome is director of Youth Leadership
Developement of the Appalachian Regional Commissi

1970
Katallagete

Annihilating The Hillbilly

Page 1

In September CBS began its new television season with the theme "Let's All Get Together." If you watch television on Tuesday nights, you know that who got together, back-to-back, were the stars of three of America's most popular TV programs: "The Beverly Hillbillies," "Green Acres," and "Hee-Haw." Each week millions of Americans gather around their sets to watch this combination, which has to be the most intensive effort ever exerted by a nation to belittle, demean, and otherwise destroy a minority people within its boundaries. Within the three shows on one night, hillbillies are shown being conned into buying the White House, coddling a talking pig, and rising from a cornpatch to crack the sickest jokes on TV—all on the same channel, all only a short while after Eric Sevareid has completed his nightly lecture to the American public on decency, integrity, dignity and the other great American virtues to which he and his network supposedly adhere. If similar programs even approaching the maliciousness of these were broadcast today on Blacks, Indians or Chicanos, there would be an immediate public outcry from every liberal organization and politician in the country and a scathing editorial in the *New York Times* about the programs' "lack of taste." The new culture people would organize marches and prime-time boycotts and perhaps, even, throw dog dung at Eva Gabor as she emerged from her studio. They might even go a step further and deal with that hillybilly-maligning patriot, Al Capp. But, with this, as all things Appalachian, *silence*. America is allowed to continue laughing at this minority group because on this, America agrees: hillbilly ain't beautiful.

The treatment given by the media to Appalachia is only one example of the massive failure of America's institutions for over a century to meet the needs of the people of the region. From government at all levels, to churches, private welfare agencies, schools, colleges, labor unions, foundations, newspapers, corporations, *ad infinitum*, the region has received an unequal share of exploitation, neglect, unfulfilled promises and misguided assistance. This is not to deny that America is interested in Appalachia. It has been for some time, in the peculiar American way—in Appalachia's worth to industry, of course; only erratically in the plight of the people. General Howard of the Freedman's Bureau is said to have convinced Lincoln that he ought to try to do something

Annihilating The Hillbilly

Page 2

for the poor mountaineers after the Civil War. The New Deal brought the then rather progressive Tennessee Valley Authority to one part of the region, but TVA's recently developed capacity to burn lower-grade strip-mine coal brought the hellish human and material waste of that process to Central Appalachia.

If the ability of institutions to respond to people's needs is judged on the basis of the federal government's enforcement of the Mine Health and Safety Act of 1969, then the answer to this question is *No!* Loud and Clear. The death of the 78 coal miners in Farmington, West Virgina, in November 1968 led to the passage of that Act which is the strictest mine safety legislation ever to get through Congress and be signed by a President. The public outrage over Farmington gave government one of its few opportunities to wrestle successfully with the powerful American coal-oil conglomerates. But, something did not work: either there is no will, or desire, by the bureaucracies (*the* institutions) of the federal government to go to the mat with the conglomerates. Perhaps their interests are so inseparable that no contest is ever possible. In any case: since the disaster, more than 300 miners have been killed *in the mines* and more than 10,000 have been crippled or injured. There has been no public outcry to avenge the death of these men.

Moreover, the Social Security Administration's own Bureau of Disability Insurance provides some statistics which indicate how the bureaucracy of one fundamental institution—government—deals with one crisis which the 1969 Act sought to meet: compensation for miners disabled by "black lung" contracted after long years and long hours inside the mines. The national average of claims under the black lung provisions of the Act processed by the Bureau of Disability Insurance is 43%. However: only 22% of the claims from eastern Kentucky and 24% of those from West Virginia had been processed by early November 1970. And: 32% of the processed claims of West Virginia miners have been denied; 57% of Kentucky miners have been denied. The figure for claims denied for the rest of the nation is only . . . . 20%!

If one reflects on the fact that in the past seventy years there have been 101,000 mine deaths, a number larger than the total of miners now working in Appalachia and double the number of Vietnam deaths, then the inability of the government to enforce regulations, which are mild by international comparison, strikes one as not speaking well for the capacity of political institutions to use the very arena of action which is theirs, by democracy's mandate, or for the American public's capacity to care for anything more than the dramatic, never the substantial.

And with the death of thirty-eight men in the Finley mines near Hyden, Kentucky last December 30, the nation was once again reminded about the plight of miners in Appalachian coal pits. The President of the United States himself announced that he would have visited the scene of the disaster. . . . if it had not been for "the bad weather." The more important visits, however, those of inspectors from the Bureau of Mines, were not made to the Finley mines on schedule some few days before the disaster in order to check compliance with violations of regulations in the 1969 act cited on earlier visits. It was the same, old refrain: new priority guidelines for violations under the new Act had just come down from Washington to the Bureau's regional office in eastern Kentucky, necessitating a new schedule of visits; the office itself was short-handed because some of the inspectors had taken "Christmas leave"; the mine operators complained that some provisions of the Act were a peril to the safety of miners and mines; that no one, not even the inspectors, understood all of the provisions of the Act. Etc. Etc. In any event, the Finley mines near Hyden, Kentucky, were permitted to operate up to the disaster on December 30. They did so in large part because an inspection required under the 1969 Act was subjected to the administration of a bureaucracy which, perhaps unwittingly but in fact, vetoed the will and intention of the Congress and the President and—if representative government is still taken seriously—the will of the people. Thirty-eight men dead. And the litany of charges: families of the dead miners exploited by funeral operators, insurance claim men and government officials; cover-ups and double-dealings and politics involved in the "hearings" to inquire into the disaster; illegal "primer cord" and "dynamite" had (and had not) been used in the mines; an inspector "who didn't want his name used" said a simultaneous explosion ten times the legal limit was set off when the men were killed. . . .

The complete failure of the American corporate structure to accept even a charitable responsibility for the region that it has raped so successfully is hardly arguable. Since men like General Imboden in the late nineteenth century went before the state legislatures to argue that ". . . within the imperial domain of Virginia, lie, almost unknown to the outside world and not fully appreciated by their owners, vaster fields of coal and iron than in all England, maybe, than all Europe" the American corporate community has wrenched resources estimated at a worth of nearly one trillion dollars from the mountains. While these companies pay some of the highest dividends of any company in the world to their already wealthy shareholders, the *communities* in Appalachia where those resources originated survive on a subsistence economy if "survive" is the proper verb here. Often more than half of the money in circulation comes from state and federal welfare coffers. This fact alone tells us something about the American Way, if not the American Dream. Three months after the June 30, 1970 deadline for reducing the amount of hazardous dust in the mines as required by the 1969 legislation, 2800 of the 3000 underground mine operators had not complied. It is these same companies which have continually opposed severance taxes on coal and medical benefits for the more than 100,000 disabled miners who suffer permanent lung damage from poorly maintained mines. Apparently when these corporate institutions of American free enterprise become incredibly wealthy, they cannot be expected to have conscience even to allow *government* to pay the tab for the damage they have caused. Somewhere that "pursuit of selfish interest accruing benefits to all" went astray in Appalachia.

It has always been asserted with pride that America takes great interest in its children. "Dr. Spock" has been a best-seller for over a decade. But this "child-dominated" society has interest only in certain children. Of the more than 925,000 poor children under six in Appalachia, as estimated by the Office of Economic Opportunity, only about 100,000 receive cash benefits in their home from Aid For Dependent Children or other similar welfare programs. While the national participation rate of children in Head Start programs decreased three percent between 1967 and 1969, the Appalachian participation decreased fifteen percent. The greatest decrease in Appalachia, significantly, was in full-year programs, those regarded as most beneficial to poor children. What other group in the country received the benefits from the cutbacks in Appalachia is unimportant here; that "hillbillies" were not on the priority list is obvious.

In the area of prenatal and infant care, the situation in Appalachia is even more alarming. Examinations of children in several areas of the region have shown that as many as seventy percent have "parasitic infestation" (the euphemism for "worms"), one of the contributing causes to Appalachia's unusually large number of retarded and "slow" children—"worms" abounding in the miserable shacks and grassless yards American free enterprise has put aside for the hillbillies. If the Appalachian infant mortality rate were reduced at the same rate as East Germany's in a five year period as reported by the World Health Organization, then the lives of more than 1,000 children a year could be preserved. In certain areas of the region, as a matter of fact, the situation worsened over a decade. In Lamar County, Alabama, for example, the infant mortality rate rose from 32.5 percent to 40.9 percent in ten years. Hancock County, Tennessee's rate rose from 21.4 percent to 42.2 percent in the same time period. While increased attention to child development at the national and regional level promises to better the situation, for many lives and for many minds the help comes too late. Perhaps if it were possible to estimate the number of mountain children who would be alive and healthy if Appalachia had received and retained a more equitable share of the nation's wealth, certain institutions could be persuaded more easily to invest in saving children. Until the case is made, however, we all labor under the curse of the prophets and the admonitions of the poets (increasingly, it seems, the only sane people), that the final judgment on civilizations and their institutions rests on how well they treat their children, who are—in appeal at least—the "least of these."

The Appalachian child who makes it to school does not find the institution America has charged with equipping youth with basic "survival" skills any better prepared to serve his needs. The inability and unwillingness of local governments to tax the property and extractive resources of large corporations has resulted in an educational system in Appalachia that can only be compared with that in the so-called "underdeveloped" nations. Add to this the fundamental resistance of middle-class teachers to acknowledge the unique cultural heritage of the Appalachian youth, and you have a laboratory for studying one of the classic, historical struggles between a nation intent on erasing a minority from its midst and a people intent on preserving their identity and life style at any cost to themselves. In an Appalachian school, the middle class aspiring, teacher is just as insistent that the student be aggressive, obedient, joyless—in short, everything that his culture tells him he is not—as is the teacher in the Bureau of Indian Affairs school on a reservation. No wonder then that as many as 65 percent of the students drop out of school before graduation—a figure 25 percent higher than the national average.

Responding to the fiscal needs of the Appalachian educational system alone is overwhelmingly beyond the capacity of government agencies as they are presently funded. In 1967, for example, the Office of Education estimated that the construction needs of the 13 Appalachian states represented over 42 percent of the total school construction needs of the entire country. It would require the additional expenditure of $363 million annually just to raise the per pupil expenditures of Appalachian schools to the national average. Title I of the Elementary and Secondary Education Act, designed to increase the amount of funds available for the teaching of disadvantaged students, will spend more money on an equal number of students in the schools of Westchester, New York, where the number of poor students is about three percent of the student body, than it will in a county in Appalachia where more than half of the student body is poor. Talent Search, a special college recruitment and placement program funded by Congress for high-risk students, spends only 3.8 percent of its money in Appalachia, compared to the 10 percent the region deserves. Simply to make the Appalachian educational system equal in educational resources to the nation will require a political miracle at a time when no miracle workers are to be found.

While Appalachia is heavily populated with institutions of higher learning supported by various religious denominations and state governments, the region's students are no better served here than in the secondary institutions. Neither is the region's needs for professional and para-professional manpower. No institution of American society, in fact, is more divorced from Appalachia than the higher educational system which resides within it.

Forced by accrediting agencies, visiting boards, and hundreds of other pressures to maintain a facade of "academic excellence" and "a sound liberal arts education," usually with Christ thrown in somewhere, the church-supported schools spend little time thinking about the community below their own mountainside. Their emphasis on admitting Appalachian students is so small, their tuition so high, and pressure so intense from church supporters outside the region to admit their sons and daughters, that most of these colleges have an inordinately high percentage of students from states like New Jersey. Certainly to these colleges, "Christian" education has nothing to do with serving the victims of Caesar's educational system.

The "open door" policies of state universities are often, in actuality, "revolving doors" for the Appalachian student. Once the student is admitted and the fees collected either from him or the state, the more aggressive and well-trained student from another section of the state or nation, and the freshman composition teacher, can be expected to send the Appalachian student scurrying

Annihilating The Hillbilly

Page 8

home. In January 1968 the National Association of State Universities and Land Grant Colleges summed up the record of their members in the region with: "To maintain quality they raised student charges substantially, turned away qualified students, limited enrollments, and refused urgently needed public services."

The regional universities and colleges place little emphasis on promoting a regional consciousness on the part of their students. In fact, there is not at present a single Appalachian studies program in the region which could begin to rival the offerings in Far Eastern studies or astronomy. One, Eastern Kentucky University in Richmond (which in reality is in "Blue Grass," not "eastern," Kentucky) prides itself on its training and research in law enforcement and police work. All this continues and intensifies a channeling process begun by the elementary teacher to send the Appalachian student —ashamed of his background and ill-equipped to meet the needs of his region—into middle-class society outside the region. The sixteen-year process of credentializing that the student has been subjected to, becomes finally a ticket to the world of Dick and Jane, Support-Your-Local-Police and the affluence of America built at Appalachia's expense. So, a region which needs more than 200,000 college graduates—a minimum of 5,000 physicians, many more thousands of nurses, teachers, businessmen, government leaders, *ad infinitum*—finds no help in another of America's institutions.

The young Appalachian left behind by the higher educational system is destined to be the object of a number of complicated channeling devices. Certainly the male youth, if he can pass the examinations, is eligible for one of the more obvious youth channeling programs in the country, the draft, and, too, the volunteer army. Selective Service does not maintain records on Appalachians as a group, but the number in the service is estimated to be higher than their percentage in the population because the armed forces represent the only opportunity available to many young mountain men to be assimilated into mainline America. For example: recent Department of Defense figures report that West

Virginia led the nation in per capita Vietnam deaths. *Twenty-five* West Virginians per 100,000 population had been killed, compared to *seventeen* per 100,000 nationally. For the youth who seeks opportunity and training in some special opportunity program, such as the Job Corps, the fate may not be a great deal more encouraging. Because of the Job Corps' resistance to establishing a Center especially for Appalachian youth, they are sent to camps both within and outside the region where the population may be largely urban and black. Combine his unfamiliarity with urban life and blacks with his affinity for home and family, and one can easily understand why the Appalachian youth drops out of the program in equal frequency with his Indian counterpart. Even if he lasts the program out, according to Joint Action in Community Service, the agency which contracts with the Job Corps to place and counsel graduates, it is very difficult to find him a job or to locate a person or agency willing to assist him in the mountains.

For the youth who has not dropped out of school by the ninth grade and who has no prospect of attending college, vocational training represents the only channel open to him. Many find it a wicked channel indeed. Three years ago the Education Advisory Committee of the Appalachian Regional Commission reported that 50 percent of all vocational training programs in the region consisted of agriculture and home economics—areas in which there were almost no job openings. Since that report the Commission and the states have required all 235 vocational programs which they have funded to teach job-relevant skills. While only half of the schools are now open and no thorough evaluation has been reported, it is expected that the schools will be significantly better than their predecessors.

As late as 1968, however, the West Virginia Commission on Higher Education reported that only about 18 percent of the students in that state had access to vocational training. Given the fact that post-high school vocational training is still not available to the majority of Appalachian youth, this major channel of supposed opportunity still has a long way to go to overcome the serious handicaps it has represented in the past. And with improvement, vocational education's role may be to channel all the so-called disadvantaged students into neat

Annihilating The Hillbilly

Page 10

slots, thereby diminishing not only the student, but vocational education as well. Additionally, so long as vocational school graduates must leave the mountains to find jobs, the region will remain a loser. It is already estimated that 900,000 high school graduates will have to leave the region to find jobs in the decade of the 70's. They will thus become the people the cities do not want and the people the region cannot afford to lose.

The fact that a mountain youth takes advantage of the opportunity to finish high school and apply to college does not guarantee that the tentacles of the system will let him go. For instance, one of the high-risk students I taught in the Upward Bound program at Berea College applied and was accepted last fall at that college. During the preceding spring he was approached by a recruiter for the FBI who gave him a hard sell on the benefits of working for the Bureau in Washington. He dropped the idea of college and is now a low-paid clerk at FBI headquarters. Since this incident I have checked with school personnel in other areas of the region and found that intensive recruitment of high school graduates in rural areas is now carried out by the FBI and other government agencies who are not finding recruits for their clerk and typist posts in urban high schools. The law, it seems, does have a long arm and no qualms about modern forms of impressment.

Most high school dropouts—except those who marry and somehow find work or welfare payments—and unemployed high school graduates eventually end up being forced to migrate to find work. In West Virginia, for instance, 70 percent of the young people leave before they reach the age of 24. Usually referred to as "migrants" instead of more accurately as economic refugees, these youth join the more than 2,000,000 other mountaineers who have preceded them to northern cities such as Cincinnati, Chicago, Indianapolis and Detroit. If they have a skill and happened to move during a period of relative economic prosperity, or are willing to accept a job run by the stopwatch and a minimum wage employer, as many do, then their chances for survival are good. If, on the other hand, circumstances deem that they have to move in with kin in the "back home" ghetto, then the situation is different.

The unemployed and unassimilated mountain youth finds himself in a bewildering ghetto that defies description, and usually comparison, with the ghetto life of other minorities. He also finds that in the city there is one thing more unacceptable than a black man—a hillbilly, a ridgerunner, a briarhopper. For the first time in its history America has recognized him as a cultural minority. If he ends up in juvenile court for stealing hubcaps, he is offered leniency with his promise to go "back home." Judges make this offer to youth whose families may have been in the city for three generations and can only consider themselves Cincinnatians or Chicagons. If he enters school, studies show that its foreign nature drives him out faster both psychologically and physically than it does his black migrant counterpart. For the mountain youth who is unable or unwilling to assimilate into the life of the city, there is little help from the social service agencies who understand much more about blacks than they do about him. He is thus not only without help, but—perhaps more appallingly—without an advocate in a city that he does not understand and that does not understand him.

One group of Appalachians who are consistently overlooked and underserved by the institutions of the region are the blacks. As a matter of fact, both government and the so-called "private" welfare agencies refuse to acknowledge the existence of blacks in Appalachia. While the percentage of blacks in the region as a whole is low —about eight percent—they comprise the total population in many small, isolated hollows and ghost coal towns abandoned by the corporations and welfare and poverty agencies. Because the backbreaking jobs that brought black imports into the region are gone and because of the discrimination and competition with the majority of poor white people for jobs and welfare funds, their existence is a poor one, indeed. As yet no agency report or journalist has documented the presence and needs of these people, let alone described the culture of a minority group in the midst of another cultural minority.

Annihilating The Hillbilly

Page 12

America's unwillingness to deal with the Appalachian as he asks to be dealt with is probably no more baffling than America's seeming obsession to study and understand his unusual life style and values. Even before the Russell Sage Foundation published John Campbell's *The Southern Highlander and His Homeland* in 1921, writers and sociologists were making forays into the mountains to alternately praise, condemn, and collect the mountain culture. The studies are still being made today in the midst of the technological revolution that is, for all practical purposes, making "Middle Americans" all alike. The conclusions of modern studies do not differ from those made in the last century. The Appalachian is different: he is existence-oriented, independent, has close family ties, is fatalistic, cares for his elderly, *ad nauseum*. If, as Robert Coles and others have written of late, the Appalachian has a life-style, a culture, that America would do well to listen to if not opt for, then why has America failed so miserably at times to meet his needs?

Part of the answer is, obviously, that Appalachia in the main has been a colonial territory for America within her own boundaries. The life style of the region served well the need of the mining and lumbering corporations for a subjugated people willing to be peasants in their own land. Even after the bloody struggles to unionize the mines, the capacity of America's institutions (including its labor unions) to contain the people's struggle remained intact. So what on the surface appears to be quaint people, to be explained away by their isolation and independence may, in fact, be more accurately described as the historical reaction of the people to colonialism.

What on the surface may strike Jack Weller, author of *Yesterday's People* (published jointly by the University of Kentucky and the Council of the Southern Mountains) as ignorance which keeps people from taking polio shots even when they are offered free transportation, may, in fact, be better explained by Frantz Fanon, a physician himself, who argued (in *The Wretched of the Earth*) that the Algerians resisted "modern medical techniques" so long as the French were in control of them, but adopted the new practices immediately when they felt themselves to be in control. I have seen parents who refused to have their children vaccinated at the public health clinic, willingly have them vaccinated when it was "our" medical students who were giving the shots.

One has to understand how the medical profession in Appalachia operates to appreciate fully this phenomenon. He has to sit with a young father in the mountains and hear the story of how his pregnant, now deceased, wife was turned away from the hospital because he did not have the hundred dollars that the doctors demand as a downpayment for those who do not have medical insurance. It is these same compassionate doctors who have, rather than reform their own practices to meet the needs of people, turned the Medicaid program into a thriving business. The potential earning from the health support programs is so great that a recent government report on physician manpower in Appalachia suggested that it was one of the most lucrative enticements to get doctors into the region—another colonial characteristic. A largely overlooked article in the Louisville *Courier Journal* in the Spring of 1970 described how doctors and pharmacists have turned Medicaid recipients in eastern Kentucky into addicts and junkies. It repeated reports from law officers and nurses who had seen "whole families lying around in a stupor" and "glassy-eyed teenagers and small children wobbling or passed out along the roadside" because they took narcotics prescribed by their physicians. One eastern Kentucky pharmacist admitted that 65 percent of his business came from Medicaid dues. "The poor people are substituting pills for faith," he explained. He went on to describe why the abuses are allowed to continue: "It would cost the pharmacist a great deal in time away from work to keep a check on abuses. They are just too busy."

By and large American institutions can be said, then, to have held no respect for the mountaineer other than for his use as an object. Richard Davis notes in his recent *The Man Who Moved a Mountain* (Fortress Press), large metropolitan newspapers used the notorious Allen feud of the second decade of this century in my hometown of Hillsville, Virginia, to interpret the Appalachian to their urban readers. Said one:

Annihilating The Hillbilly

Page 14

> The majority of mountain people are unprincipled ruffians. They make moonshine, 500 horsepower, and swill it down; they carry on generous and gentle feuds in which little children are not spared, and deliberately plan a wholesale assassination, and when captured either assert they shot in self-defense, or with true coward streak deny the crime. There are two remedies only—education or extermination. Mountaineers, like the red Indian, must learn this lesson.

Another editorial in a northern newspaper on the same event went on to conclude:

> The Scotch-Irish mountaineers are more ignorant than vicious, victims of heredity and alcohol, and now that their isolated region has been invaded, must change or perish.

One of the often overlooked aspects of the outsiders' fetish for Appalachia has been the premises which underlie their own prescriptions for the people's future. One finds in Jack Weller's influential writings, for instance, comments such as these:

> There is little in the mountain child's training that would help him develop self-control, discipline, resolution, or steadfastness. Thus the way is prepared for future difficulties in the army or at work.
>
> Since the culture inadequately prepares its members to relate to "outsiders," there is a great need for "bridge" persons, who can help the suspicious and fearful to respond more positively to persons and institutions which will increasingly be of help and resource—doctors, psychiatrists, clinics, hospitals, government in the form of agency officials, policemen, public health nurses, welfare workers, and recreation leaders. The mountaineer's suspicion of these persons limits his use of them to crisis occasions, when, in fact, their purpose is to be of assistance in many ways at other times. He needs help in understanding that government and other institutions cannot be run in person-oriented ways but must be conducted in great measure on an impersonal objective basis. He needs help in seeing that a certain amount of bureaucratic organization is a necessary thing, and that a government does not exist for an individual person's benefit (*Yesterday's People*, pp. 157-158).

Responding to the Appalachian culture, outsiders are sometimes incapable of interpreting the evidence because of their own training in research procedures. One, for example, while, of course, repeatedly enjoining his readers that he is passing no judgment on the culture—describes mountain music and literature as "regressive looking", "nostalgic and melancholy," over all, "repressive." Thomas Merton, on the other hand, after hearing some mountain music for the first time at the Abbey of Gethsemani, gave the correct interpretation and exclaimed, "It's apocolyptic!" Perhaps the only fair hearing the culture of the people of Appalachia will receive is from persons, like mystics and contemplatives, who do not assign ultimate importance to the things that the modern State and today's seminarians have blessed as divine.

The churchmen, educators, welfare agents, independent do-gooders, journalists and novelists, and the institutions which pay their salaries—that is, those who have made an extraordinarily good living trying to "understand" the mountain man—have studied the Appalachian not to learn from him, but rather to "teach" him, to "school" him, to "doctor" and "save" him by making him into what they already are: Middle America, assimilated into the America of the television and Holiday Inn—the America which Tocqueville and Faulkner warned was founded by those who sought not to escape from tyranny, but to establish one, in their own image and likeness.

Only in Appalachia, for example, have the mainline churches come upon a "Christian" religious expression which stands four-square against what they expect religion in America to "do." The rejection of the "Christian century" by Appalachia has baffled and annoyed the mainline churches, their agencies, theologians and sociologists. And because the Church in mainline America is unable to understand the Church in Appalachia, they have so far been unable to assimilate it. They have failed, in other words, to make it over into another of the agencies of social welfare which stands alongside HEW, Social Security, the Council of the Southern Mountains, the Commission on Religion in Appalachia, the Home Mission Board(s), etc. The mainline churches have tried to obliterate the Appalachian churches with demands for expressions which are "progressive," "rational," "contem-

Annihilating The Hillbilly

Page 16

porary" and "relevant". What more haunting, and in many instances disgusting, examples of the philosopher's "ambiguity of reason" or the theologian's "original sin" could be asked for? The liberal churchmen—Catholic and Protestant—insist that the snake-handling of the mountain man must come to an end (as must the "emotionalism" and "irrelevance" of the Black church). And all the while the mainline, liberal Church ignores the more dangerous "snakehandling" which defines their very efforts to "save" "yesterday's people"—a phenomena described precisely in the early years of this journal by the contemplative, the mystic, Thomas Merton, in "Events and Pseudo-Events: Letter to a Southern Churchman" (*Katallagete,* Summer 1966).

The answer to the question of why mountain culture must be destroyed is to be found in the fundamental truth about the technological society: the techniques which undergird all our institutions are assimilating all of us into, as Jacques Ellul puts it, "a society of objects, run by objects." Institutions in the technological society —and this means not only those of the state and its welfare bureaus, but the do-good agencies which include churches, schools and colleges—can respond only by and with the techniques of the impersonalized, bureaucratic means, procedures, formulas. Technique cannot discriminate between right and wrong, justice and injustice. That is why the same technique that gives and takes away the health card from an ailing miner, assimilates the pious mountaineer into the five-point grading system and the Uniform Sunday School Lesson.

The meaning is clear: institutions working in Appalachia today can work for only *one* end: the extinction of the Appalachian people. The extent to which these institutions have so far failed in the venture is the extent to which this people and culture have successfully resisted the formidable pressures of the institutions of contemporary technological society. Why institutions—political and private, church and business, industrial and charitable—have responded and can respond to the Appalachian the way they have tells us something very important about power—and powerlessness—in the technological society.

For those of us who believe that the struggle is for the soul of man in the technological society, the resistance of Appalachian culture against assimilation into middle America demands earnest, indeed prayerful, attention. The struggle of the mountain man against the institutions of the technological society is the struggle to deny their right to define any man by his relationship to Middle America. The struggle—whether one believes that it comes out of resistance informed by left-wing Protestantism or opposition to colonialism and genocide — has implications for all who question not only the possibility, but the quality and character of any resistance to the totalitarianism of the technological society. □

Annihilating The Hillbilly

Back Cover

Other Pamphlets Available From AMP:

Thoughts of Mother Jones, edited by Jim Axelrod
Romantic Appalachia, by Don West
Picking Poverty's Pocket, by Barkan and Lloyd
Poverty and Affluence in Appalachia, by Harry Caudill
Paint Creek Miner, by Charles Patterson
A Time For Anger, poems by Don West
West Virginia Wonderland, by William Blizzard
What's Next?, by Ernest Seeman
People's Cultural Heritage in Appalachia, by Don Wes
Conspiracy in Coal, by Tom Bethel

SUBSCRIBE TO AMP ! ! !

rates: $7.50 for working Appalachians
$5.00 for students
$0.00 for unemployed Appalachians
$25.00 for wealthy Appalachians
(income over $15,000)
$15.00 for libraries and institutions

write to: Appalachian Movement Press
P. O. Box 8074
Huntington, West Virginia 25705
phone (304) 523-8587

In a World of Plenty We're Hungry as Hell!

Songs for Southern Workers: Don West and the Kentucky Workers Alliance

In the second half of the 1930s, Don West worked as a field organizer for the Communist Party of the United States (CPUSA) in the Southeast, first in North Carolina's textile mills and then in Kentucky. A stint working as a coal miner while organizing with the National Miner's Union in Harlan and Bell Counties eventually landed both Don and Connie West in jail in Pineville, Kentucky. Don recounted the couple's arrest:

> One night about dark, six deputies came out. They were hired by the coal operators. I looked up and through the window, there was a man with a six-shooter in his hand. There were six of 'em all around. They said I was under arrest. They came in and got all my books off the shelves and put 'em in the trunk and carted 'em off to Pineville, and took my wife and myself—I asked 'em, what about the baby, they said they didn't give a damn about the baby. But some of the neighbors saw us and came down and took care of her.[3]

West was charged with criminal syndicalism for his organizing efforts, and particular to his Christian preaching of the Social Gospel as part of his organizing work, he was also accused of conspiring to "overthrow the government by use of the churches." After over a month in jail, he was eventually bailed out by local citizens. But the conditions of his bail included that the family must leave the state of Kentucky—and Don was already wanted in Georgia as well. Leaving Pineville, the Wests' car careened off the road dangerously: the lug nuts on all four of their wheels had been surreptitiously loosened in an attempt on their lives. Soon after, Don was captured by "gun thugs" (private coal mine security guards) in Hazard, Kentucky, who beat him severely and left him for dead in the woods.[4]

Undeterred, once he healed, Don moved to Louisville while Connie took their young daughter Ann and began a job as an instructor at the radical cooperative Commonwealth College in Arkansas. It was common over lifetimes together (they were married for over sixty years) that Connie and Don would part ways so that she could earn money to support the family and Don could continue organizing. And as he often did in this era, Don returned to his work under a false name. As "George Brown," he quickly rose within the racially integrated Kentucky Workers Alliance, a regional political pressure group developed as a division of the communist-led Workers Alliance of America. The KWA became a powerful (if relatively short-lived) unemployed workers' organization fueled in large part by the work of West, whose charisma, experience, and southerness made him quite popular. He was so supported in the Louisville community that once, when jailed, West was quickly freed by three hundred of his working-class supporters who convinced the judge and sheriff of their potential to riot on his behalf.[5]

During his time with KWA, West was also actively recruiting for the Abraham Lincoln Brigades, the volunteer US soldiers who joined the International Brigades during the Spanish Civil War and fought alongside Spanish Republican forces against the army of the fascist General Francisco Franco. The CPUSA was actively funding transportation for volunteers to reach Spain and engage with the Republican battalions there, and West was able to recruit over twenty Kentuckians, including Connie's brother Jack Adams, to join the brigades.

When Jack was killed in battle in 1938, it created a rift between Don West and Connie's family that never fully healed, and in later years West sometimes used "Jack Adams" as an alias while continuing his workplace organizing. West's public admission of his associations with the CPUSA, or communists generally, was typically evasive in later years, but "Don was a member of the Communist Party, he never dropped out," Yvonne Farley told me, speculating that biographers have left out this critical detail in an effort at making West "more appealing."[6]

While working with the Kentucky Workers Alliance, Don West created *Songs for Southern Workers* as an imminently accessible tool for working people to carry in hand to picket lines, sit-ins, demonstrations, and marches. Nearly every song within it is set to tunes that workers and their families would already know by heart, making these new often-humorous variants easy to learn and teach. The booklet is a prime example of West's creative skill at merging ground-level organizational work with his natural eloquence for meeting people right where they were at with his poetry and prose.

Songs for Southern Workers was first published by the Kentucky Workers Alliance in 1937 and republished, as you find it here, by Appalachian Movement Press in 1973. This is the first time it has been reproduced since that printing.

This introduction relies heavily on James J. Lorence's thorough biography *A Hard Journey: The Life of Don West* (Urbana: University of Illinois Press, 2007). In particular, Lorence had access to "They Fought Hunger! The Story of the Kentucky Workers Alliance during the 1930s," an unpublished manuscript by KWA state chair Giles Cooper and secretary-treasurer Allen McElfresh.

SONGS for Southern Workers

1937 Songbook of the Kentucky Workers Alliance

Prepared by
DON WEST

$.25

Songs for Southern Workers

Cover

Songs for Southern Workers

Inside Front Cover

The Kentucky Workers Alliance was a strong and militant organization of unemployed and WPA workers during the height of the depression. It was able to mobalize thousands of people to push for fair treatment of WPA workers, and for social legislation such as Social Security and Unemployment Compensation. It helped striking union members, and prepared unemployed workers for union activity when they got jobs again. It kept local, state, and federal relief agencies honest by exposing graft and corruption. And it demanded equal rights for black workers and an end to Jim Crow laws.

In 1937, the Kentucky WA published a songbook prepared by Don West, its state organizer. Using familiar tunes, Don and others substituted words which expressed the thoughts of people towards unionism, bosses, exploitation, etc. At meetings, rallies, and demonstrations these songs were sung to inspire people to continue struggling, to help draw new members to the organization, and to let officials, bosses, and thugs know that people demanded action —and were going to stick together to win their goals.

1st printing, August, 1973

Appalachian Movement Press, Inc.

P.O. BOX 8074 • 1600 8th AVE.

HUNTINGTON, WEST VIRGINIA 25705

PHONE: (304) 523-8587

SONGS

FOR

Southern Workers

Prepared by

DON WEST

STATE ORGANIZER

Kentucky

Workers Alliance

PRICE 10 CENTS

Songs for Southern Workers

Page 1

Songs for Southern Workers

Page 2

UP! UP!

Up, up, you toilers
And hear what I tell.
In a world of plenty
We're hungry as hell!

We dig and we shovel,
We weave and we sweat.
But when comes the harvest
Its little we get!

O this is the story
Of you and the rest--
And if I am lying
My name's not Don West!

DON WEST

Don West was born in the mountain country of the south. He was brought up in poverty. By hard work he managed to get an education. He won a scholarship to travel and study in Europe. His opportunity to "rise" in the world was good. But he realized if he "rose" financially, it would be at the expense of stomping his fellow worker down deeper into poverty. Don could never do that.

He gave up what many would consider an easy life and fine opportunity for "success", and came back to live with his people. "When I rise," he says, "it will be when the great mass of my own common people rise in one big united movement. No honest son of toilers will ever crush his fellows down for greedy financial gains."

Don West is a poet. He has had two books published. Even at this young age he has long been a leader of southern workers. His honest nature has endeared him to thousands over the south. His ability and courage to lead, even in the face of jails and gun thugs, has won him confidence and respect. Don is at present State Organizer for the Kentucky Workers Alliance. We are glad to have him working with us.

—GILES COOPER, President
Kentucky Workers Alliance

Songs for Southern Workers

Page 4

NOT GOING TO WORK AND STARVE NO MORE

WORDS BY DON WEST

(Tune: Study War No More)

Going to build up our union
Many thousand strong!
Many thousand strong!
Many thousand strong!
Going to build up our union
Many thousand strong
To lead us on our way.

CHORUS

We're not going to work and starve no more
Not going to work and starve no more
Not going to work and starve no more
We're not going to work and starve no more
Not going to work and starve no more
Not going to work and starve no more!

SOLIDARITY FOREVER

(Tune John Brown's Body)

When the union's inspiration
Through the workers blood shall run
There can be no power greater
Anywhere beneath the sun,
Yet what force on earth is weaker
Than the feeble strength of one?
But the union makes us strong.

CHORUS

Solidarity forever
Solidarity forever
Solidarity forever
For the union makes us strong.

Giles Cooper, President

Jim Simmons, Louisville

Songs for Southern Workers

Page 6

I LOVE MY UNION

WORDS BY MILDRED AND ETHEL SLONE

(Tune: I Love Little Willie)

I love my union I do-- Ma, Ma,
I love my union I do -- Ha, Ha.
I love my union--and you can tell Pa,
For he will like it you know.

REFRAIN
It fights for me it does Ma Ma,
It fights for me it does Ha Ha.
It fights for me--and you can tell Pa,
For he will like it you know.

I'll ask him to join--I will Ma Ma,
I'll ask him to join--I will Ha Ha.
I'll ask him to join--and you can tell Pa,
For he will like it you know.

He sent for the leaders he has--Ma Ma,
He sent for the leaders he has--Ha Ha.
He sent for the leaders--and you can tell all,
For they will like it you know.

Now we have joined, we have, Ha Ha,
Now we have joined, we have, Ha, Ha.
Now we have joined, and I'm glad I told Pa,
For he sure likes it you know.

MY COUNTRY 'TIS OF THEE

WORDS BY DON WEST

My country 'tis of thee
Land of mass misery,
Of this I sing,
Land where the workers toil
And bosses reap their spoil
Where children starve and freeze
From fall 'til spring.

My native country thee,
Our fathers fought to free
You from a king.
And in their steps we tread,
Fighting for meat and bread,
Workers, lift up your head-
Let freedom ring!

The union now, you see-
Our hope for liberty,
Of it we sing!
Let Southern voices sound
With union all around
The mountain side rebound
With songs we sing!

Songs for Southern Workers

Page 7

Songs for Southern Workers

Page 8

WE ARE BUILDING A STRONG UNION

WORDS BY DON WEST

(Tune: Jacobs Ladder)

We are building a strong union
We are building a strong union
We are building a strong union
Workers of the world!

Every new man makes us stronger
Every new man makes us stronger
Every new man makes us stronger
Workers of the world!

Black and white unite together
Black and white unite together
Black and white unite together
Workers of the south!

Come on brothers, Join up with us
Come on brothers, Join up with us
Come on brothers, Join up with us
Workers of the world!

Come, we'll break our chains of bondage
Come, we'll break our chains of bondage
Come, we'll break our chains of bondage
Workers of the world!

OH, WORKING MEN UNITE

WORDS BY DON WEST

(Tune: Red Wing)

A worker's lot is hard
Without a union card,
Oh that is why our children cry
For food and clothes that we can't buy
A worker's life is tough
Our grub is slim and rough,
And it will be as long as we
Bow to our enemy . . .

CHORUS

Shall we always bow down before the
bosses
Like they were crosses--and take our
losses
This world and its wealth belong to
workers
And not to shirkers who live in ease!

Oh working men unite
Together we shall fight
Like men of old in battle bold
Against the class that hoards the gold.
They rob us of our toil
And live upon the spoil,
But we will fight for truth and right--
The earth belongs to us!

Songs for Southern Workers

Page 10

MY UNION CARD

(Tune: Hand Me Down My Walking Cane.)

Oh, write me out my union card
Oh, write me out my union card
Oh, write me out my union card
Organize, we'll all fight hard--
Time to turn those hungry blues away.

In '17 we went to war
In '17 we went to war
In '17 we went to war
In '36 the cannons roar--
Time to turn those guns the other way.

In bosses war the worker gets
In bosses war the worker gets
In bosses war the worker gets
A belly full of bayonets--
Time to turn those guns the other way.

Allan McElfresh, Secretary

F. C. Sloane
Hueysville Organizer

IN THE UNION'S RANKS

WORDS BY DON WEST

(Tune: Tramp, Tramp, Tramp)

In the union's ranks we stand,
Firm and steady to a man
While the bosses shake and tremble
Full of fear!
For they know when we unite
We can wage a mighty fight,
And the day when they shall cease to
Rule is near!

CHORUS

We are building up our union,
Fellow worker, do your part!
Join together in the fight,
For the jobs which are our right.
It's the only way to break the bosses
heart!
Like a workers' army strong
We shall fight to end the wrong
Of the masses crushed in misery
By the few,
Who have gobbled up the wealth
At the price of workers' health--
We'll replace this world of sorrow
With a new!

Songs for Southern Workers

Page 12

GIVE ME BACK MY JOB AGAIN

BY JIM GARLAND

(Tune: Of Greenback Dollar)

I don't want your millions, mister,
I don't want your diamond ring.
All I want is the right to live mister--
Give me back my job again.

We worked to build this country, mister,
While you enjoyed a life of ease.
You've stolen all that we built mister,
Now our children starve and freeze!

Yes you have a land deed, mister,
The money all is in your name,
But where's the work that you did mister,
I'm demanding back my job again.

Think me dumb if you wish, mister,
You may call me green or blue or red,
There's just one thing that I know, mister,
My hungry babies must be fed.

HOLD THE FORT

We meet today in freedom's cause
And raise our voices high.
We'll join our hands in union strong
To battle or to die . . .

CHORUS

Hold the fort for we are coming,
Union men be strong.
Side by side we battle onward
Victory will come!

Look, my brother, see the union's
Banners waving high.
Reinforcements now are nearing,
Victory is nigh.

Fierce and long the battle rages
But we will not fear.
Help will come whenever needed,
Cheer my brother, cheer!

Songs for Southern Workers

Page 14

RISE UP, YE WORKERS

WORDS BY DON WEST

(Tune: Stand Up for Jesus)

Rise up, rise up, ye workers
Rise from your misery
Shake off the chains that bind you
The union makes you free.
From victory unto victory
The union banner leads
'Til every child that hungers
Shall have the food it needs.

Rise up, rise up, ye workers
Rise up in union strong
Fling to the boss this warning--
Our judgement wont be long.
We'll gird ourselves with power
That many gives to onc.
We've got the world before us
Our job is just begun.

Stand up, stand up, my brothers,
The battle won't be long--
Set all the hills a ringing,
Call up a mighty throng.
Our banner leads to victory
Each man must take his post--
Into the final conflict
Against the robber host!

DOWN TO FRANKFORT TOWN

BY THELMA SLONE and AVENELL SEXTON

(Tune: Derby Town)

When I went to Frankfort Town
Many workers I did pass,
'Twas there I saw the Governor,
And I kicked him on the--Hocus, Pocus,
Sonny Bocus
And you may think I lie
But if you'd been down in Frankfort Town
You'd done the same as I . . .

There's a Billy Goat in Frankfort Town
In the Mansion by the pass
His coat is on his shiny back.
While his pants are on his--Hocus, Pocus,
Sonny Bocus
And you may think I lie
But if you go down to Frankfort Town
You'll see the same as I . . .

The Goat that wears these shinny clothes
Is surely not so rich
The bosses call him loving son
While workers call him son of a--Hocus,
Pocus, Sonny Bocus
And you may think I lie
But if the rich were poor like us
They'd call him same as I . . .

Songs for Southern Workers

Page 16

IT TAKES UNITY

WORDS BY DON WEST

(Tune: Worried Man)

CHORUS

It takes u-ni-ty
To build the union strong
It takes u-ni-ty
To build the union strong--
We're starving now,
But we won't be starving long!

The pot-bellied boss
Thinks he is so strong.
Smokes a big cigar--
Thinks he is so strong.
He's bossing now,
But he won't be bossing long!

CHORUS

Preacher of the rich
He shouts so loud and long
Tries to shield the boss
And tells us we are wrong--
He's preaching now,
But he won't be preaching long!

BUILD THE UNION

WORDS BY DON WEST

(Tune: Battle Hymn of the Republic)

We have toiled in every weather
Labored hard from sun to sun
We have mined and built the railroads
Cleared the fields and wove and spun--
Now we see our children ragged,
Slowly dying one by one
While wealth keeps rolling up.

CHORUS

Brothers, come lets build the union
Brothers, come lets build the union
Brothers, come lets build the union
For it is our only hope!

We have seen our masters gorging
We have seen them wine and dine
While we live on bull dog gravy
And go down into the mine
Where we've clawed into the mountains
For the wealth that makes them fine
And our children starve and freeze.

Songs for Southern Workers

Page 18

THE COMMONWEALTH OF TOIL

BY RALPH CHAPLIN

(Tune: Nellie Grey)

In the gloom of mighty cities
Mid the roar of whirling wheels,
We are toiling on like chattel slaves of old.
And our masters hope to keep us
Ever thus beneath their heels,
And to coin our very life blood into gold.

CHORUS

But we have a glowing dream
Of how fair the world will seem
When each man can live his life secure and free!
When the earth is owned by labor
And there's joy and peace for all
In the Commonwealth of Toil that is to be.

When our cause is all triumphant
And we claim our Mother Earth,
And the nightmare of the present fades away,
We shall live with Love and Laughter,
We, who now are little worth,
And we'll not regret the price we have to pay.

WE SHALL NOT BE MOVED

WORDS BY DON WEST

The union is our leader
We shall not be moved
The union is our leader
We shall not be moved
Just like a tree planted by the water
We shall not be moved.

Black and white together
We shall not be moved
Black and white together
We shall not be moved
Just like a tree planted by the water
We shall not be moved.

We're fighting for our freedom
We shall not be moved
We're fighting for our freedom
We shall not be moved
Just like a tree planted by the water
We shall not be moved.

Songs for Southern Workers

Page 20

POOR MINER'S FAREWELL

BY AUNT MOLLY JACKSON

Poor hard working miners, their troubles
are great
So often while mining they meet their
sad fate--
Killed by some accident, there's no one
can tell
Their mining's all over, poor miners
farewell.

CHORUS

Only a miner, killed under the ground
Only a miner, but one more is gone.
Only a miner, and one more is gone--
Leaving his wife and dear children alone.

They leave their dear wives and little
ones too
To earn them a living as miners all do.
Killed by some accident, there's no one
can tell,
Their mining's all over, poor miners
farewell.

GONE ARE OUR JOBS

WORDS BY DON WEST

(Tune: Old Black Joe)

Gone are the days
When we drew a weekly pay.
Gone are our jobs
From the mines and mills away.
Gone from this land
Where we live in want and dread,
We hear our children's voices calling
"We want bread!"

CHORUS

We're coming, we're coming,
In union proud and strong!
We're fighting for our kids and homes--
We'll end this wrong!

When we were young
Here we labored everyday
Down in the mines
Or the mills for little pay.
When we grow old
There is naught for us to do
We hear the bosses' voices saying
"You are thru!"

Songs for Southern Workers

Page 21

Songs for Southern Workers

Page 22

INTERNATIONAL

Arise ye prisoners of starvation
Arise ye wretched of the earth
For justice thunders condemnation
A better world's in birth.
No more tradition's chains shall bind us.
Arise ye slaves, no more in thrall!
The earth shall rise on new foundations
We have been naught, we shall be all.

CHORUS

'Tis the final conflict
Let each stand in his place
The International Union
Shall be the human race.

(Repeat)

AT DOES THE KENTUCKY WORKERS ALLIANCE WANT?

Our immediate demands are simple and reason-le. We are asking for:

Jobs for every unemployed person in need. This n be done by expanding WPA.

Trade union hourly wage scale on all WPA jobs.

A minimum of at least $40.00 a month for all PA workers.

Adequate relief for the disabled. Adequate pen-ns for the aged.

That monthly wages be paid in full and without d up every month; that Administrative Order . 44 which docks workers for time lost through fault of their own, be wiped off the books.

That WPA workers be given full right to organ- without discrimination and that their represen-ives, as named by the Workers Alliance, be ced on all Labor Policy Boards.

For the appropriation of 5 million dollars by state for direct relief.

A minimum old age pension of $30.00 a month Kentucky.

For no discrimination against Negroes.

Songs for Southern Workers

Page 24

Songs for Southern Workers

Inside Back Cover

Songs for Southern Workers

Back Cover

I Know All the Trout by Their First Names, Every Tree by Its Shape of Leaf

Margaret Gregg and Michael J. Clark's *Lazar & Boone Stop Strip Mining Bully*

Appalachian Movement Press published *Lazar & Boone Stop Strip Mining Bully to Save Apple Valley & Buttermilk Creek* in early 1973. A charming collaboration between the artist Margaret Gregg and *Baltimore Sun* journalist Michael J. Clark, the fully illustrated "story for children & mature adults" stands out especially from the rest of the AMP catalog. Clark told me that he wrote the story very quickly, based on "an intuitive feeling," and his friend Gregg was happy to illustrate it—she still feels that the story "gives parents a way to present something that has political significance, environmental significance, and translate it for children."[7]

In their early thirties, Gregg and Clark were older than many of the other AMP operators in the early 1970s, and neither remembers how they eventually came to publish their collaboration with the Huntington printshop. Gregg had been exposed to AMP in Knoxville, where she was living as a Glenmary Catholic sister working with their Federation of Communities in Service. She had already seen and read several of their pamphlets and encountered the AMP distribution table at music festivals. "Oh, these were the guys that were hardcore radicals, they know what's going on," she said of Tom Woodruff and the others. "They were edgy, interesting people!"[8]

Meanwhile, Michael J. Clark spent one year living in Appalachia, traveling there for a service-focused sabbatical from his career as a journalist in Baltimore. Along with his wife and two of their (eventually three) children, Clark worked with the Brethren Volunteer Service project of the Church of the Brethren's Appalachian Caucus.

Clark and Gregg both work from distinct spiritual backgrounds, which clearly ground them in social justice service work and an ethic of nonviolence. The same spring that *Lazar & Boone* was published in Huntington, Clark traveled to Washington, DC, to testify at a House subcommittee hearing on the moral mandate to abolish strip mining altogether in the region. He spoke as part of a delegation that presented the issue as a spiritual conflict and as a fundamental violence to the land and people that no amount of profit could validate. Explaining church divestment at home and his own travels through Appalachia to bear witness, Clark called strip mining "quack surgery on blue green ridges" and addressed much of the same social and environmental devastation that he and Gregg decry in their children's book. Quoting the words of deep miner John Tiller, academic researcher Timothy Albright, and folk singer John Prine in front of the House subcommittee, Clark flatly concluded in support of the abolition of strip-mining.[9] Industry representative and president James Wilkinson, at the same hearings, balked at talk of abolition and cynically dismissed it as an "extremist solution to what is essentially an esthetic problem."[10]

Lazar & Boone, a children's storybook, presents a moral argument against surface mining for coal. But the story also suggests the incredible lengths that people may go to towards the preservation of their homeplace. As is typical with many pre-coal Appalachian stories, fiction and nonfiction alike, this settler community has been in harmony with the land since time began. Apple Valley is idyllic, to say the least, and the residents' interconnection with the local ecology runs charismatically deep: when running through the forests, the energy of their ecstatic laughter is directly transmuted to the flora, creating the palette of colors that the trees' leaves will eventually turn to each autumn. "They played on the mountain because they loved it."

On the day when strip-mining equipment suddenly arrives to destroy, in pursuit of coal, Apple Valley and everything that Lazar, Boone, and Farmer Caudill know, Lazar first tries diplomacy.[11] When that fails, because Strip Mining Bully turns out to be an inert bulldozer "without the brains necessary to smile and cry," the trio turns to dynamite to save their homeplace.

The practice of strip mining for coal seams had already been increasingly and violently forced into normalization across Appalachia, and it was met with protests both violent and nonviolent. Gregg and Clark based the central action in their book on the very real news accounts of machinery sabotage that had become common in the rural Appalachian region in the past decade.

"It's basically an antigreed story," Clark told me. "We, in our craze for mineral, material wealth, have sometimes forgotten the true beauty and value of the environment that surrounds us." Gregg and Clark hadn't intended for sabotage to be *the focus* of the story, only for it to get readers' attention. "I knew there'd be some heat involved in writing it, because people would be looking at the *destructive* aspect of it and not looking at the *constructive* aspect. Clearly a way of life is being threatened."[12]

In an afterward written by Mike Clark, then executive director of the Highlander Research and Education Center, he maintains that the Apple Valley sabotage, fiction or not, isn't unique. Summoning "General Lazar" for comfort whenever one hears the distant ring of an explosion at night in the mountains, he places Lazar in the folkloric tradition of other mythical quasi-military guerilla leaders like General Ned Ludd and Captain Swing: two characters who each served as the figureheads for communities in 1800s England that, failing in their efforts at redressing their grievances through official means, turned to property destruction as a last resort against oppressive technologies. In order to save their communities and lifeways, their devotees signed declarations in their names and waged guerilla wars against destructive forces that they couldn't otherwise reason with.

"These animals are not only saying that they have a right to exist but that the environment is essential to our well-being, and if we screw that, we're really ultimately screwing ourselves."[13]

Lazar & Boone saw only one print run with Appalachian Movement Press and is seeing its first reproduction since 1973 in the pages of this book.

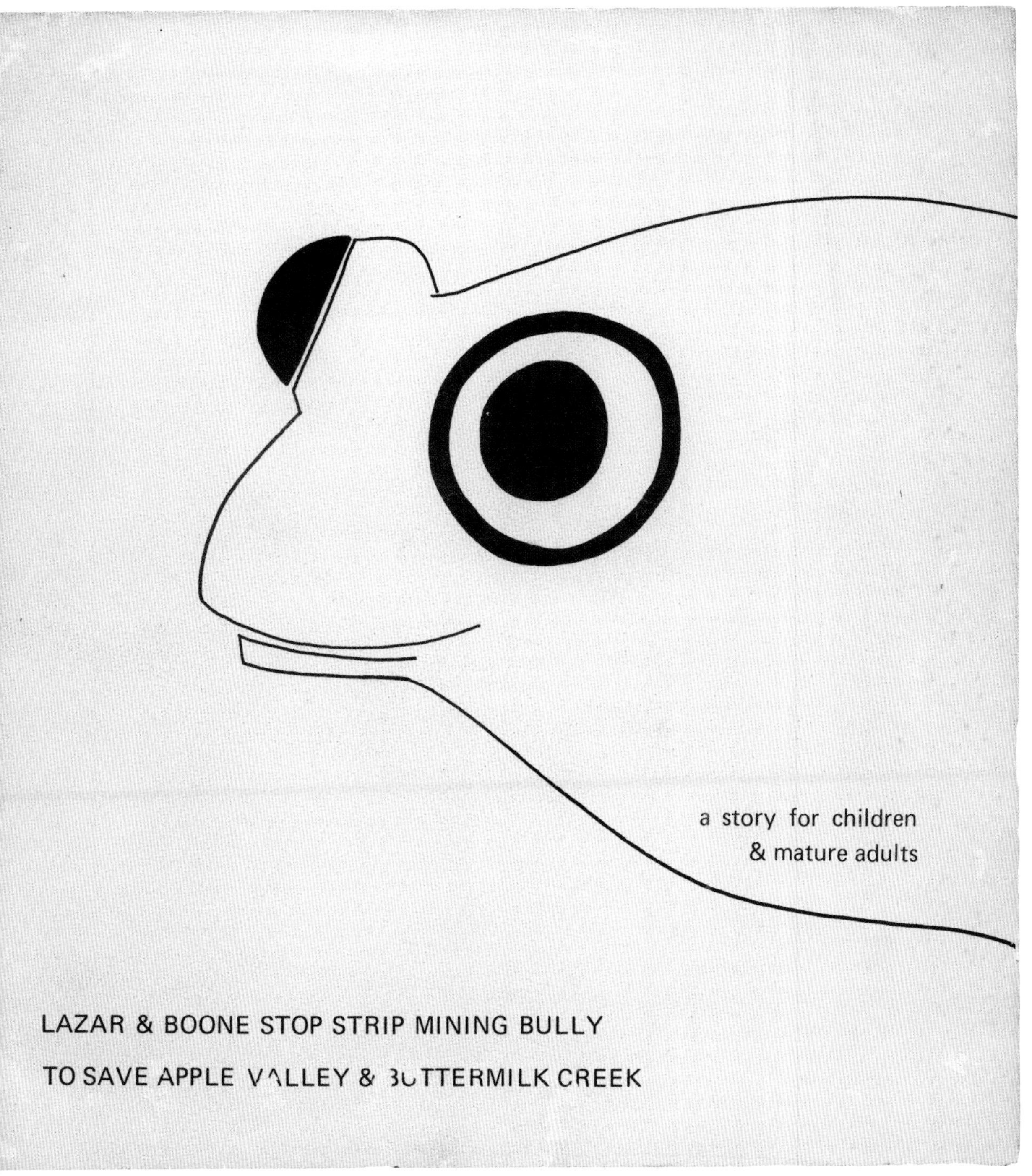

Lazar and Boone Stop Strip Mining Bully Front Cover

Lazar and Boone Stop Strip Mining Bully Inside Front Cover

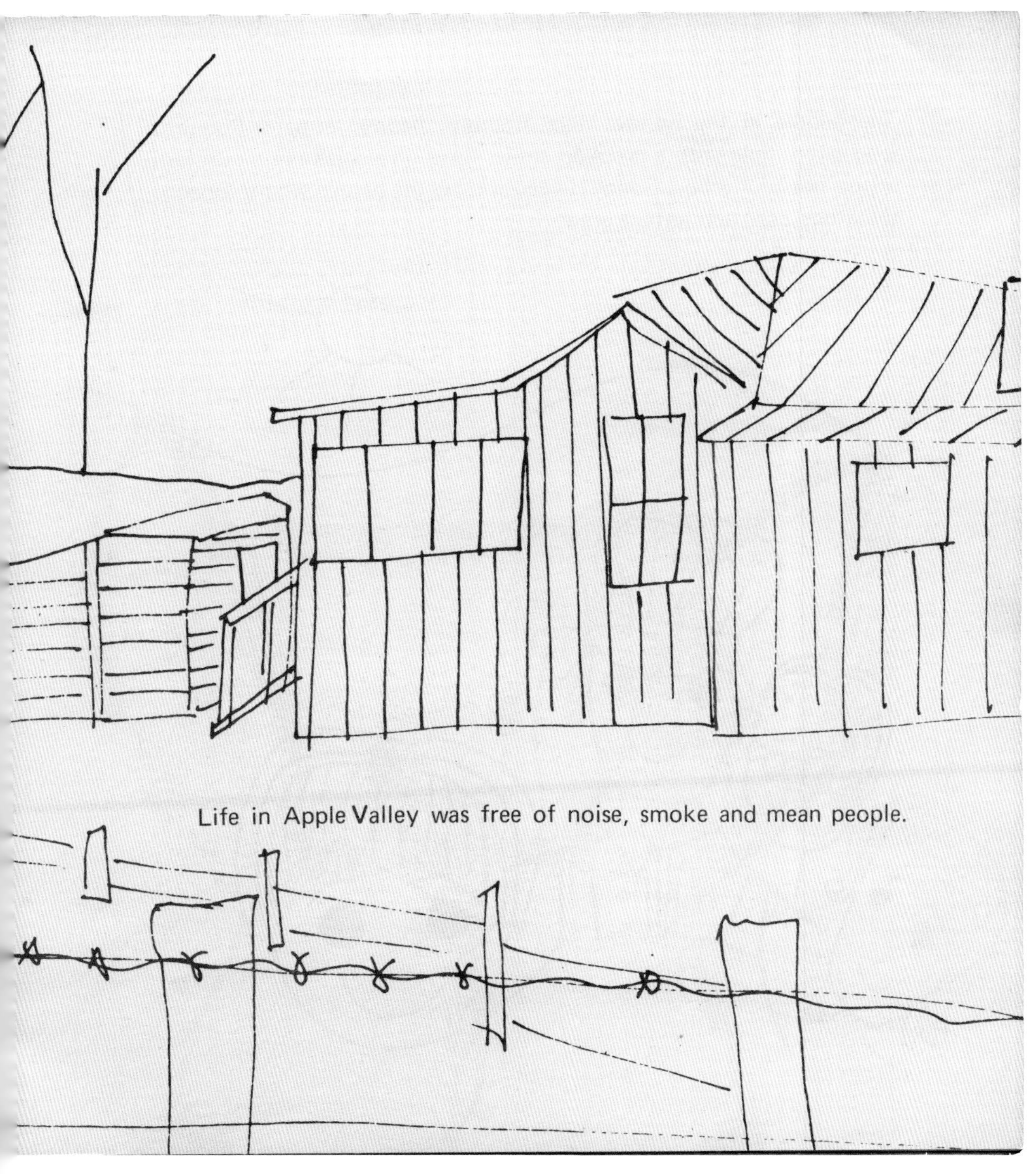
Life in Apple Valley was free of noise, smoke and mean people.

The people in the hollow were friendly, happy farmers. Boone, a long-eared mule with a crooked smile, lived on a small mountain farm in the peaceful valley. Boone helped furrow the garden where tobacco, tomatoes, corn and lettuce grew.

Boone's best friend lived near Buttermilk Creek. That was Lazar, the toad, a little fellow who liked to roll over and let Boone sniff hot air from his nostrils onto his speckled belly. Lazar usually could be found tucked between Boone's long floopy ears. They were close friends. It was not unusual for Lazar to spend weeks at a time on Boone's soft furry head.

Lazar thought a lot. And he read a lot. He had the biggest home library of any toad on Buttermilk Creek. He had one book. It was a dictionary. Lazar knew every word in it.

Boone was not exactly dumb. But after all he was a mule. The humans who kept him had low expectations of Boone. So Boone did not try to think or act smart. Boone was free not to put on airs.

Every living thing was happy in Apple Valley. Even the humans. They had sewing bees, barn raisings and community suppers. Life was dandy.

Lazar and Boone would frolic in the stream that looked like glass and tease the rainbow trout swimming past them. Lazar would jump off Boone's back and ride a trout downstream for minutes. But the trout with their quick fins would throw off their rider and "splash"—Lazar would get dunked. Boone would come along with his head down and Lazar, wet from the cold stream, would scramble aboard.

The two friends would run through the woods, singing their favorite song:

Buttermilk Creek and Apple Valley
Let us be free together, let us
Dance and sing and play and pray.
We will never go away.

Running through the stand of spruce and fir and bunches of bunchberry and bead lily and groves of white pine, yellow birch, sugar maple, oak, beech and tulip trees, they played on the mountain because they loved it. All the trees and plants waited eagerly for Lazar and Boone to come for a visit. The laughter of their animal friends helped the trees turn joyful colors when Fall came to the mountain. Their Autumn reds, yellows and oranges were feelings of joy. Lazar sometimes came to the shadowy forests alone to meditate and roll a new word he just learned over his tongue. After practicing the word, he would return to the grassland meadow of Apple Valley and impress Boone with his discovery of a new word.

"A...XXXX...EEEE," Lazar told Boone. "A...XXXX....EEE?" Boone asked. "It is a sharp implement used for chopping," Lazar answered. "Oh," said Boone. "That's good to know. AA...XXX..EE."

As the two friends were talking, farmer Caudill came by wiping tears from his eyes. Boone never saw his farmer friend cry before. So he wondered what was the matter.

"Boone," Farmer Caudill said, "it is going to be a sad day for Apple Valley. The strippers are coming. They will level our trees, strip away our mountains, ruin our streams and scare us away by setting off dynamite and having rocks and mud slide into our valley."

Farmer Caudill did not know that Lazar, the intelligent toad, was sitting nearby under a floppy ear, hearing all this. Boone never told his human friends about his untamed friend from the creek. They might think him strange.

Farmer Caudill went on to say, "It is all because of the coal in our mountain. Coal means money. Money means power. We are just poor farmers. What can we do?"

Boone knew that if what Farmer Caudill said came to pass then all his friends—the shiny trout, the black bears, the singing trees (when there was a stiff breeze) and even he and his friend Lazar were in trouble.

Of course Lazar knew that, too. He was already thinking beyond that. He was making plans to save Apple Valley from the strip mining bully.

"Don't despair Farmer Caudill," Lazar spoke up in his squeaky voice.

"What?" Farmer Caudill said. "Did you say something Boone? Of course not. Mules don't talk." Boone just smiled knowingly.

Boone trotted off as soon as Farmer Caudill left. He went into the woods just as Lazar had told him. "What are we going to do?" he asked his friend. Tiny Lazar, sticking his head into his friend's ear, told him not to worry.

"I got it all figured out. We will talk with the bully. He won't want to destroy Apple Valley after we tell him how happy we all are," Lazar said. Lazar was by nature an optimist.

So croaking out "Giddyap," Lazar got Boone to move up the mountain where the stripper was said to be.

It took them a long time to move through the forest. It was as if they were cautioned by their plant friends to go slowly. Trees swung their leafy branches into Boone's eyes. The mountain flowers rose up almost a foot, sticking out their blossoms, causing Boone to stumble a lot. They were warning their two friends. "Strippers are not ordinary life forms. Beware. Beware." they seemed to say.

Night had fallen when Boone and Lazar got to the top of the ridge. They all looked all round them, expecting trouble. But all was quiet. The huge platter moon looked down kindly on the two little creatures . . . Little to the big moon so far away yet so close to Apple Valley and Buttermilk Creek.

As Boone clopped along the ridge, Lazar crept down to the posterior position so together they could see fore and aft. Lazar was the one who spotted strip mine bully with its huge blade pressed against the mountain soil. Strip mine bully was a bulldozer. The bully had not the brains necessary to smile and cry.

Lazar and Boone Stop Strip Mining Bully Page 10

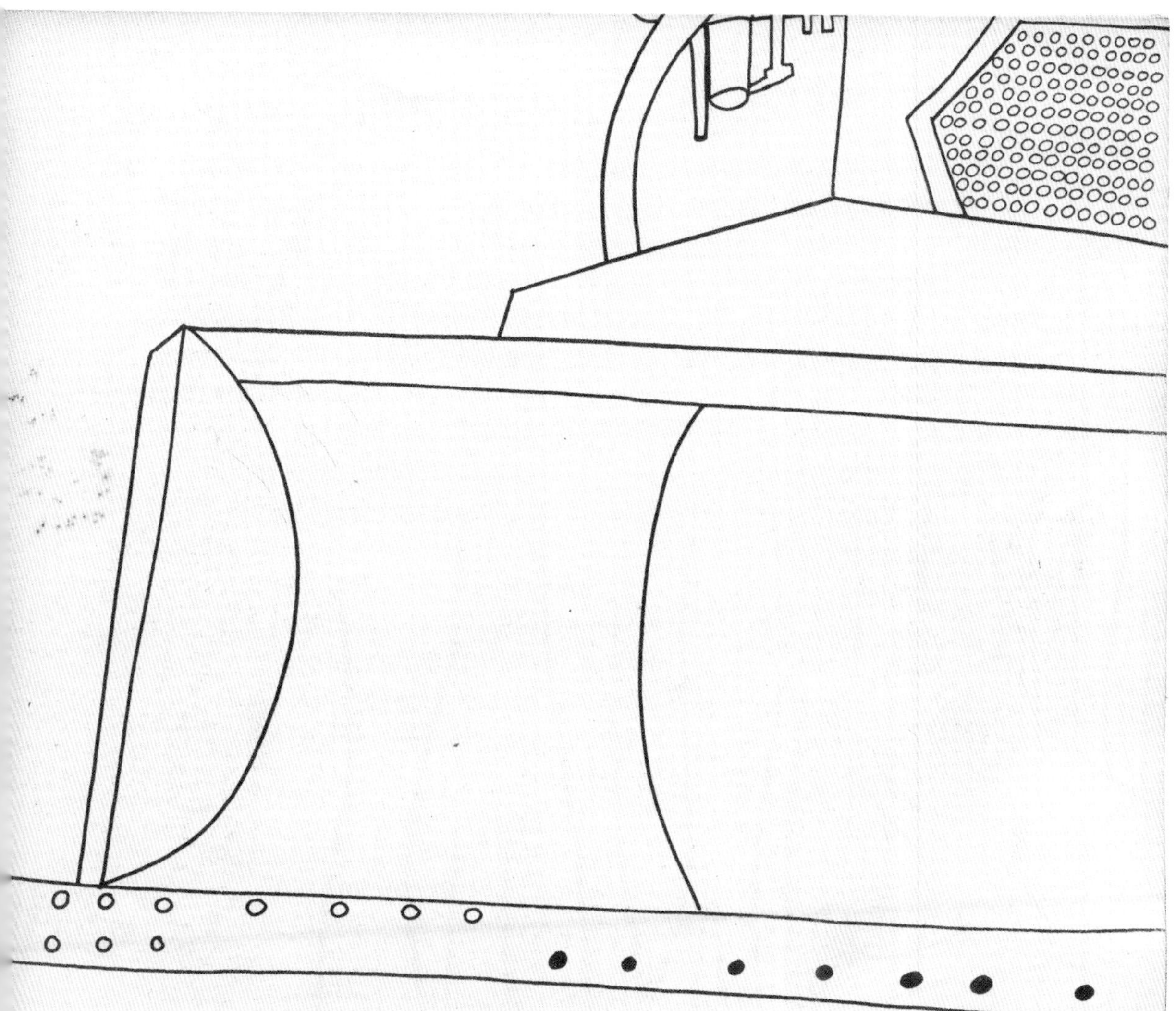

Strip mine bully was the biggest creation—outside of the moon and the blinding sun—that Lazar and Boone had ever seen. And here it was showing no signs of friendliness like the sun and the moon. Strip mine bully just stood on their ridge. Strip mine bully was there to tear down Apple Valley and chase away all the loving plant and animal life.

But Lazar did not think life was that simple. "You can reason with it," he whispered to Boone. "Once it learns that we are happy and it will bring us sadness, it will leave us in peace."

So Lazar told Boone to get up real close to the bulldozer so that he could have a discussion. But Boone balked. "No. No. No." Boone was not going anywhere near that strip mining bully. Lazar, the diplomat, took matters into his own hands. He jumped off his friend, landing harshly on the ground. He rubbed his head and wandered off in a daze to chat with the bulldozer.

That was quite a sight. There was little Lazar perched in front of the big treads of strip mining bully. Skipping over to the dozer's blade, Lazar looked right into the gleaming steel.

Lazar started talking. In fact, Lazar did all the talking. Strip mine bully could not talk and could not hear, it seemed. Boone ran off into the forest. Lazar could see him. Boone had his head poking out of a bush, making sure the dozer did not hurt his only true friend in all the world.

"Look here bully," Lazar said boldly. "We are the friends of all living things here. I know all the trout by their first names and every tree by its shape of leaf. I know the wind and the tunes it hums. I know the water by its ripples and crispness. It is home here for us. Why are you here? Don't you want to be loved and living, too? We could use a dozer here to reflect the sun off your blade so we could send messages to God in heaven. We have always wanted to send God a message of thanks. We are happy and knowing that God should be happy that we are happy, too. Of course, God is always happy. Anyway . . . You know what I mean."

The bulldozer said nothing. Lazar talked all the night and on into morning until the bully's masters came up the ridge to start the bully and attack Apple Valley and Buttermilk Creek. Poor Lazar. He got out of the monster's path just in the nick of time.

His friends the trees were the first to go off the high ridge and down the mountain. Then the earth holding tight to trees was pushed over the side. Coal, dark as night, was dug out. Big trucks drove away filled way over their pans with the black gold. Dynamite going "BOOM!" sent rocks flying high and down into Apple Valley.

Lazar and Boone Stop Strip Mining Bully Page 14

Lazar and Boone and Farmer Caudill were together in the hollow watching silently.

"Words won't work. Words won't work," little Lazar said.

"What's that?" Farmer Caudill asked.

Boone confessed. It was Lazar, his little friend, who was talking. Boone nudged his shoulder, pointing behind his sagging right ear. Farmer Caudill lifted the ear up and found Lazar.

All of Apple Valley was in tears. The bully had them all scared. The onslaught was chasing the deer from the woods. The trout were choking on the acid and dirt sliding down from the ridge into the streams. Farmer Caudill's farm was in danger of being covered by a mud slide—A giant black cloud was moving over Apple Valley and Buttermilk Creek.

Farmer Caudill's neighbors stole away that night, leaving what remained to strip mining bully and his explosive friends.

Poor Farmer Caudill, poor Boone, and poor Lazar. What were they to do? Lazar had his dictionary. His only possession. Maybe that would help him. He always counted on it. Boone and Farmer Caudill could not read. So whatever Lazar read they had to believe him.

After flipping through all the dictionary's pages, Lazar yelled out "Ole!"— A good three-letter word. He had found the answer.

"What? What?", his friends asked.

"Two words I found will do the job," tiny Lazar said in a booming voice. The words are:

"Rip . . . . off."

"Rip . . . . off," Boone and Farmer Caudle thought. Of course, "Rip off."

So quickly they hiked up the mountain to save their valley and creek and all the living things that remained or were able to return.

Lazar was the quarterback or field general of the night-time operation. He rode between Boone's ears as usual and Farmer Caudill rode on Boone's back.

Right on the mountain top the strip mining bully was resting. Nearby was a box marked "dynamite". A sign on the box said "B...E...W...A...R...E." The word was too big for Boone and Farmer Caudill to know. But that did not stop the little toad. He got Farmer Caudill to lift the box onto the back of Boone.

The huge box of explosives was carried to the spot where strip mine bully rested. On orders from Lazar, the toad, Farmer Caudill hauled the dynamite off Boone's back. He gently settled the dynamite onto the lap of the hulking strip mine bully, who still said nothing.

Lazar asked Farmer Caudill if he had a match. The farmer looked through his pockets but came up empty. No luck. No matches. Nothing to light the giant fire crackers with. Wait a miunte.

Farmer Caudill was chewing on a match with the phospherous tip at the dry end. So lazar snatched the match, scratched the tip against the bully's tread and lit the dynamite wicks.

"Run! Run! Run!" Lazar yelled to his friends. The farmer jumped on Boone's back and Lazar jumped into Farmer Caudill's pants cuff. Away they ran.

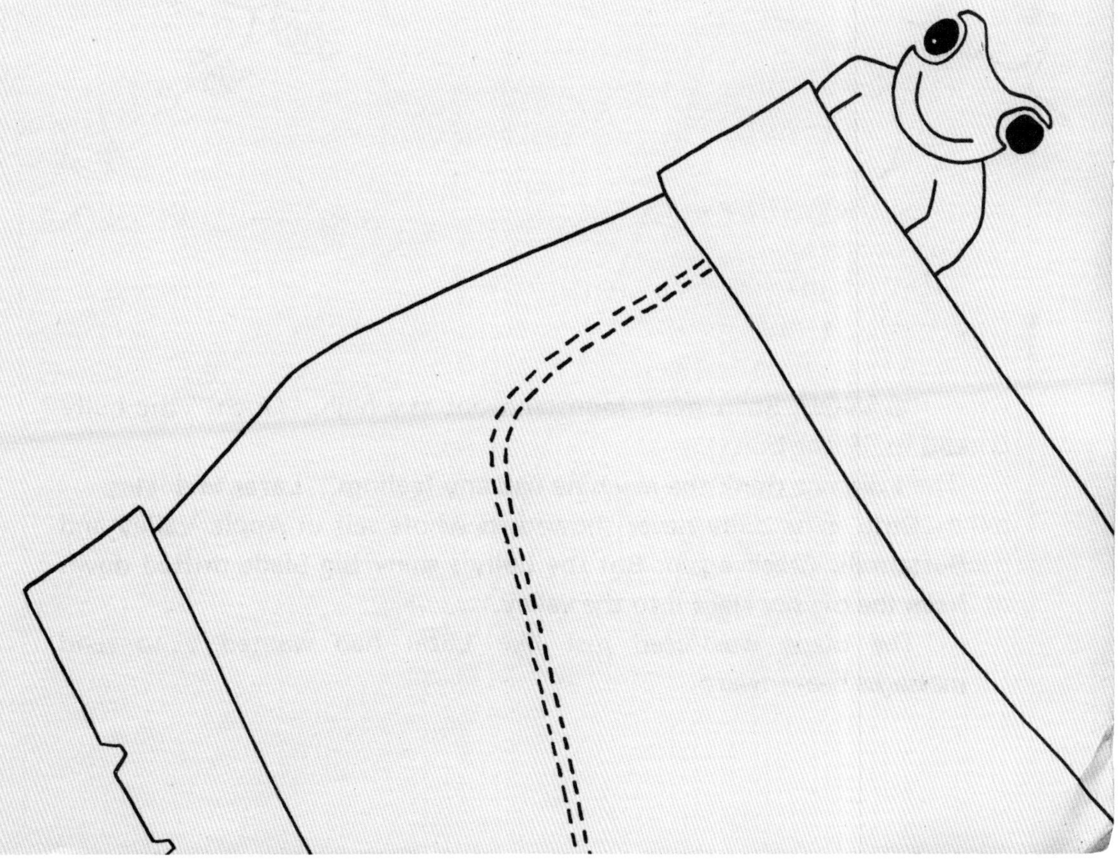

"BANG!" Strip mine monster went sky high. "Ouch!" the bully said.

"I did not think the machine had any feelings," Lazar said later.

Strip mine bully never showed its whole self in Apple Valley and Buttermilk Creek again. But the bully's shiny big blade drifted down from the big sky right into the valley.

The blade was used just like Lazar had wanted . . . to send messages heavenward.

text by Michael J. Clark
illustration and layout by Margaret Gregg
and a backword by (the other) Mike Clark

Word of the Apple Valley "rip-off" never made the evening news. Walter Cronkite didn't chuckle over it and a news reporter never came to talk to Farmer Caudill. And yet we know it happened.

The story of Apple Valley is not unique. In the high valleys and creeks and hollers of the mountain coal fields bulldozers are destroying an inheritance millions of years old. Strip mining for coal has destroyed entire mountains, killed streams, and driven people from their homes. An increasing number of mountain people have decided these practices must come to an end.

There were no "outside agitators" in Apple Valley before the dozer came—and there were none left after the "rip-off." The story of Lazar and Boone and Farmer Caudill proves, once again, that mountain people and their friends will solve their own problems if they can find the necessary tools.

So if, on some dark and moonless night you hear a loud boom echoing off a high ridge, relax; it's just General Lazar, the toad, giving orders.

— Mike Clark

Lazar and Boone Stop Strip Mining Bully Inside Back Cover

Appalachian Movement Press, Inc.
P.O. BOX 8074 • 1600 8th AVE.
HUNTINGTON, WEST VIRGINIA 25705
PHONE: (304) 523-8587

1st printing, March 1973

Surrounded on All Sides by the Slavocracy

Don West's *Freedom on the Mountains*

We'll never know all of what Don West would have covered in his book on "southern mountain history" and the abolitionist movements in the central Appalachian region, because although he had worked on it on and off since the 1940s, he never finished it. He did, however, manage to publish two distinct pieces of his manuscript with Appalachian Movement Press: the twenty-eight-page *Robert Tharin: Biography of a Mountain Abolitionist* in 1971 and, in 1973, *Freedom on the Mountains*, reproduced here for the first time.

Freedom is presented as "excerpts," which is an accurate description of this collection of talking points, anecdotes, and truncated biographies of white abolitionists. West, who taught history in various capacities throughout his life, sought to piece together a revised "people's history" of the central Appalachian region that would situate his home, rather than New England, as the birthplace of the US abolitionist movement. Locating the "Slavocracy" in the regions where plantations were concentrated, and therefore not in the mountains, West positions the Appalachian Mountains as a stronghold for Union loyalty and abolitionist sentiment (which did not necessarily correlate) and a mainline of Underground Railroad activity running along the spine of the Appalachian Mountains themselves.

More broadly, and in much of his other writings, West challenged the idea of broad Confederate support across the South during the Civil War, in particular proclaiming that support for Southern secession was rare amongst poor and working-class white people and was supported almost exclusively by the plantation-owning aristocracy. The misconception that all Southern whites supported the Confederacy, he believed, helped to continue systemic racism and class stratification in the region and fueled national stereotypes about homogenous white southerners that bore little resemblance to his modern era. Working with these ideas, West was building an antiracist praxis for liberation in the Southeast. But in some ways his attempt to promote a history that challenged myths and stereotypes also helped reinforce another myth: that of white racial innocence when it came to Appalachian settlers in the mountains.

"That [history] was important to Don. It was part of his whole mythology about how the hillbillies weren't as racist as the flatland southerners," George Brosi reflected.[14] Discussing West's methods and writing, Brosi stressed the problem of historical narratives that neglect the reality of Black self-determination at the heart of emancipation, civil rights, and liberation struggles in the US.

Appalachian Movement Press published other works that paralleled and supported West's general thesis. *Life of Reverend John Rankin, Written by Himself in His 80th Year* (1977)—a ninety-page booklet AMP contracted with the Lawrence County (Ohio) Historical Society—is a previously unpublished autobiography of an abolitionist from southeast Ohio, bordering on Huntington's Cabell County, West Virginia. Given that Rankin, who is mentioned in *Freedom*, was on West's list of influential abolitionists in the region, West likely pushed for the publishing of this book. AMP also published African American historian Carter Woodson's *Freedom and Slavery in Appalachian America* as a pamphlet in their early 1970s catalog. Woodson, who lived in Huntington and later attended Berea College in Kentucky before moving on to the University of Chicago and then Harvard, writes a romantic history of a southern West Virginia that is functionally less segregated than elsewhere in the United States. Woodson's historical lens mirrored the kind of thinking that West was following (even though desegregated communities don't necessarily mean harmonious ones).

Of his methods, West writes of visiting archives and interviewing individuals, although there's something to be said for finding what you're looking for when you're doing research on your own terms—and it's hard to imagine West doing anything on anyone else's terms, like submitting a manuscript for review by other historians. "I don't think that Don spent a lot of time seriously doing research in a comprehensive way," said Brosi. "He pulled some threads, but I think that he wasn't really a scholar. The fact that he *did* pull some of those threads is what has inspired other people." [15]

What's really at the heart of a modern critique of what Don West was up to when he was researching and writing history? Mainly that, throughout most of his writings against racism, West pulled from his personal experiences and feelings and used these to paint broad generalizations, which he then projected onto the whole of Appalachia. In doing so, he didn't challenge racism in quite the substantial way that he meant to: if this kind of creative thinking works in his poetry and editorials, it functions deceptively in his works of history.[16]

To be frank, there are compelling reasons not to republish incomplete histories like *Freedom on the Mountains*, riddled as it is with flaws in methodology and coercive framing. I include it in this book partly to honor the earnestness of West's intention to work and teach from an antiracist standpoint and partly as a key (and rare) historical document of the breadth of the Appalachian Movement Press imprint. Don West appears to have published with AMP under almost no oversight, as was his style generally, and a strident pamphlet like *Freedom* is the result.

The narratives that activists like Don West promulgated aren't rare, and they aren't isolated in past eras. These ideas come to us today in modern literature about Appalachia, some of which still relies on muddled mythologies about innocent settler history and white genetic determinism. Unfortunately, with a little sleight of hand, these ideas can easily be subverted by white supremacists and can just as well be stretched to fit the darker side of tendencies like Harry Caudill's later preoccupation with dysgenics.

If we are to move towards a liberatory, antiracist Appalachia, white Appalachians in particular must be careful not to invest in convenient narratives about regional innocence based on misleading or partial histories, nor to fall into the trap of believing in a mythical white Appalachian indigeneity.

Freedom on the Mountains was published by Appalachian Movement Press in January of 1973, and this is the first time it is being reproduced in print. *Robert Tharin: Biography of a Mountain Abolitionist* was released in 1971 as a completed chapter of West's book. That publication was transcribed and is available in *No Lonesome Road: Selected Poems and Prose*, eds. Jeff Biggers and George Brosi (Urbana: University of Illinois Press, 2004).

Freedom on the Mountains

(Excerpts from a book manuscript on Southern Mountain history.)

By Don West

35¢

Freedom on the Mountains

Front Cover

Freedom on the Mountains

Inside Front Cover

Appalachian Movement Press, Inc.

P.O. BOX 8074 • 1600 8th AVE.

HUNTINGTON, WEST VIRGINIA 25705

PHONE: (304) 523-8587

1st printing January 1973

Don West is the founder of the Appalachian South Folklife Center in Pipestem, W. Va. He has spent a lifetime in the mountains - - as a union organizer beginning in the 1930s, as a researcher of Appalachian history, as a poet, and as one concerned with education. His book of poetry, Clods of Southern Earth, sold more volumes than any book of poetry in the U. S. excepting Walt Whitman's Leaves of Grass.

THE BIRTHPLACE OF MODERN ABOLITIONISM

A memorial "To call your attention to the internal slave trade, which is carried on in the United States...Our national legislature has declared such traffic to be piracy when carried on by American citizens on the high seas; and your memorialists humbly presume that the act is no less an outrage on humanity and justice when practiced in America than in Africa, or on the ocean. We therefore petition Congress to prevent by law the extension of slavery, by a prohibition of it in any new state hereafter to be admitted into the Union...*1

THE OLD UNITED SOUTH MYTH

The Confederate school of history writers find the Appalachian South an embarrassing block to the old "united solid South" myth. Thus they may either ignore it or write it off by derogatory innuendoes. For, while the Confederacy may have done a fair job rounding up the lowland poor whites to fight its battles in the Civil War, in the mountains it can only record almost utter failure.

Such writers cannot quite overlook, try as they may however, that after all, the first conflict over slavery was not between North and South. Neither can they rightfully claim that the abolitionist movement originated in New England. That first conflict, as we have said, was within the South itself, and the abolitionist movement originated in the mountain South. This part of the South consistently opposed slavery, and it was elements in the North which eventually came to the aid of antislavery Southerners in the battle against Slavocracy.

Even Coulter, one of the more able and articulate

Freedom on the Mountains

Page 4

apologists, must admit that: "East Tennessee became the cradle of the emancipation press. In Jonesboro in 1816 the Manumission Intelligencer sprang up, soon to be followed by the Emancipator, edited by Elihu Embree..."[2]

Not only did the mountain South refuse to go with the Confederacy, and, by supporting the Union, throw the ballance in its favor, but it has been a hindrance to the propaganda battle ever since.

If, as Coulter admits, and Barton also says, "The abolitionist movement may fairly be said to have begun in in the mountains of the South,"[3] East Tennessee is the specific spot of that beginning, Coulter writes: "East Tennessee very early became the scene of vigorous attempts to organize manumission societies, and some of the earliest anti-slavery leaders who came to be best known made their start here. Samuel Doak came into the Holston River Valley before the end of the Revolution and for the next generation educated the people against slavery...in Washington Academy and Tusculum Academy which he founded. A pupil who showed the results of his teaching, fifty years later in faraway Texas, was Sam Houston."[4]

Surrounded on all sides by the Slavocracy, it was here in Greene County, Tennessee, that the Manumission Society of Tennessee was first organized at the Lost Creek Meeting House, February 15, 1815. In the leadership of this beginning were such men as Samuel Doak, John Rankin, Charles Osborn, John Canady, John Swain, Elihu Swain, John Underhill, Jesse Wills, David Maulsby, Tom Monaker, and Elihu Embree. It was here at Jonesboro that the Manumission Intelligencer was launched in 1819, followed by Embree's Emancipaior in 1820.[5]

It is interesting to note that Charles Osborn, Elihu Embree, John Rankin, and other East Tennessee mountain abolitionists were organizing anti-slavery societies and advocating unconditional and immediate emancipation when William Lloyd Garrison was only nine years old. It was this same area which later attracted Benjamin Lundy who came, after Embree's death, to use the mountain print shop to publish his Genius of Universal Emancipation.[6]

LUNDY & GARRISON INFLUENCED BY MOUNTAINEER ANTI-SLAVERY

Lundy's own decision to become an abolitionist editor is itself traceable to this East Tennessee influence. A saddle maker at Wheeling, Lundy had been outraged by seeing coffles of slaves driven by on their way South, but he had not undertaken any specific means of opposing slavery. It was not until he came in contact with the influence of Charles Osborn, who had moved from East Tennessee to Mount Pleasant, Ohio, and was publishing an anti-slavery paper there in 1817, that Lundy's real growth and development in abolitionism began. Lundy was hesitant. He did not think he could write. He mainly sent little clippings from other papers. But, he writes, "After he (Osborn) had published the Philanthropist a few months, I was surprised at receiving from him a request that I should assist in editing it. The thought that I could do such a thing had not then occurred to me. But on his repeating the request, I consented to try..."[7]

Later when Osborn sold his paper and moved on to Indiana where he became a storm center of abolitionism, Lundy was dissatisfied with the new owner's policy and decided to publish his own paper. The first issue of the Genius of Universal Emancipation was printed at Mount Pleasant, Ohio, in January 1821. In the meantime Elihu Embree of the Jonesboro, Tennessee, Emancipator had died. Lundy writes: "When the friends of the deceased Elihu Embree heard of my paper, they urged me to remove to Tennessee and use the press on which his had been printed.''''[8]

Lundy accepted the invitation and, after printing eight issues of the Genius at Mount Pleasant, moved its place of publication to Jonesboro, Tennessee.

In this way the anti-slavery sentiment and thought of the mountain South began to spread and influence wider areas, eventually reaching New England and Garrison. It came about in this way: In 1828 Lundy was on a lecture and subscription raising trip in Boston. Stopping at the same boarding house he accidentally met Garrison, who was then editing a temperance sheet. About his experience in the East, Lundy wrote: "At Boston I could hear of no abolitionist resident in the place. At the house where I stayed, I became acquainted with William Lloyd Garrison, who was also a boarder there. He had not then turned his attention to the anti-slavery question. I visited the Boston clergy, and finally got together eight of them belonging to various sects. Such an occurrence, it was said, was seldom if ever before know in that town."[9]

Garrison attended Lundy's meeting with the preachers. Later, after the influence of Lundy, John Rankin,[10] and other Southern mountaineers had converted him to a full-fledged abolitionism, Garrison wrote a sharply discouraging description of the meeting. "He (Lundy) might as well have urged the stones in the streets to cry out in behalf of the perishing captives." Garrison wrote. "O the moral cowardice, the chilling apathy, the criminal unbelief, the cruel skepticism. that were revealed on that memorable occasion! Poor Lundy! That meeting was a damper on his feelings."[11]

ELIHU EMBREE
A BRIEF BUT FLAMING ABOLITIONIST METEOR

"The abolitionists made no concessions whatever to the prevailing racial prejudice, which has served as one of the main bulwarks of the American Colonization Society."*12

Elihu Embree, Southern mountaineer, radical anti-slavery abolitionist editor, is well described in the above paragraph. Some have maintained that the mountaineer's anti-slavery thinking stemmed entirely from self-interest, that he hated slavery purely because he was unable to own slaves himself. We do not claim that this may not have had some bearing, but not with Elihu Embree. He could have owned slaves and, in fact, did at one time, by marriage. He set them free.

Neither does Embree fit Calhoun's description of the mythical South in which: 'With us the two great divisions of society are not the rich and the poor, but white and black; and all the former, the poor as well as the rich, belong to the upper classes, and are respected and treated as equals...[13]

A MOUNTAIN FOLK HERO

Elihu Embree was the kind of man who ought to be among the story book heroes for our children's reading. He was the kind we may sometimes think of maybe as representing the great hope for the American Dream. An able man, sensitive to his time, and radically outspoken, he would no doubt today be labeled "a red" or "subversive" because he was the antithesis of all that Robert E. Lee, Jackson, and Jeff Davis symbolized. He would probably be dragged before some Congressional investigating committee. If he happened to be a professor and spoke as was his want the university would doubtless see fit to release him from the faculty. That is, unless he were not sent along with men such as Dr. Willard Uphaus and others to serve time in prison.

For Embree was an editor who struck powerful blows against an existing evil. He was no pussy-footer, and his was the first outright anti-slavery paper dedicated wholly to its abolition published in the United States.

Crusaders for a just cause are never lukewarm. This is what liberals may never realize. There is no sitting on the fence or straddling the rail, or "beating the Devil around the bush" with such men. They may be jailed or executed, but with all that, the men who have meant most to man's vague gropings toward the light of the age-old dream of love and freedom have been the dedicated ones, perhaps "dedicated fools." The liberals, the fence-sitters, those who seek to pacify evil, end with Munichs.

Elihu Embree was a man on fire with an ideal--the right of all men to liberty and human dignity. He had much to do with initiating the abolitionist movement in the mountain South.

MOUNTAIN SOUTH NEVER TAP ROOT OF RACISM

Some writers, including W. J. Cash, have held that the mountain South had a particularly vicious race prejudice. This I do not agree with. Of course there was and is prejudice. But the Underground Railroad from the central South could not have run up through the mountains had there not been genuine anti-slavery sentiment and sympathy for the slave. I do not, however, maintain that this sympathy was the only reason for the mountaineer's Union loyalty. It was only part. The mountain Southerner may be said to have held the Lincoln attitude generally. To the mountain man of the 1850's whose fathers had fought the Revolution against Tory and British, the Stars and Stripes symbolized liberty and independence.

The flag must be defended, then, because of what it symbolized. The Confederacy, with all its claim to belief in individual freedom and liberty, did not convince him. Four million blacks in bondage contradicted that. Besides, the Mountaineer was also a victim of discrimination himself, virtually disfranchised by the ruling Oligarchy. All of this entered into forming his attitude.

There were some, too, who approached the problem with the crusader's zeal. Elihu Embree was one of these. Born near Jonesboro, Tennessee, on November 11, 1782, Embree was among those, many in number, who were influenced by the teachings of Dr. Samuel Doak. In the first issue of his Emancipator, he declared its purpose and reason for being was the end of slavery. Decrying the loss of many anti-slavery citizens who fled the South to go to free soil, Embree wrote in his first issue: "Thousands of first rate citizens have within twenty years past, removed from this, and other slave states, to Ohio, Indiana, and Illinois, that their eyes may be hid from seeing the cruel oppressor lacerate the backs of his slaves and that their ears may not hear the bitter cries of the oppressed. I have often regretted the loss of so much virtue from these slave states, which held too little before. Could all those who have removed from slave states on that account to even the state of Ohio, have been induced to remove and settle in Tennessee, with their high love for universal liberty and aversion of slavery, I think that Tennessee would ere this have begun to sparkle among the stars of liberty."[14]

Embree's radical impatience caused him to strike hard and sharp at times. When Savannah, Georgia, after a great fire, had refused $10,000 in relief from New York because it was stipulated to be used without regard to color, Embree who had himself sent $100 to Savannah was roused to write: "I had always thought (until those haughty slaveholders told me otherwise) that a donor has the right of directing his donation as he pleases, and I still think that where justice is not entirely turned out of doors, it continues...I pitied their circumstances when I first heard of their late calamity; I now am utterly ashamed that they are human beings, as this act of theirs disgraces human nature. But when I reflect that these monstors in human shape are citizens of America, the land of boasted LIBERTY, and that these very men have the audacity to take that sacred work in their polluted lips, I am struck with astonishment, amaze and wonder at the mercy of the Supreme Being, that instead of burning the town of Savannah, that he has not destroyed its proud inhabitants with fire unquenchable!!!"[15]

These "monsters in human shape" were the aristocratic rulers of the city of Savannah.

Some have thought Embree an impatient man, a too radical man. He published his <u>Emancipator</u>, believed in and advocated immediate emancipation ten years before Garrison's Liberator. When his critics pointed to the the practical difficulties of immediate emancipation, the difficulties of immediate emancipation, he replied: "In answer to those insurmountable difficulties, it has been observed, that as slavery is a moral evil, it ought to be removed as speedily as possible, and trust the consequence of such duty in the hands of an unerring Providence."[16]

On the problem of race mixing, so often posed as the supposedly unanswerable question, "would you want your sister to marry a Negro?" Embree had an answer. About the claim that emancipation would lead to miscegenation, he wrote; "For my part I would have less fear of mixture in consequence of their being free, than in their remaining in bondage; for I am persuaded that matters of fact will testify that mixtures are more abundant in the slave states than in the free, according to the numbers of the colored population."[17]

NOT ALL MOUNTAINEERS ACCEPTED NEGRO INFERIORITY MYTH

Nor did Embree accept the view, held by many both North and South, of the Negro's inferiority. In his paper he wrote: "With respect to the dreaded equality of the blacks with the whites...I have never been able to discover that the author of nature intended that one complexion of the human skin should stand higher in the scale of being, than another; nor do I feel any disposition to contradict the declaration of rights, established by the sages of our American Revolution; nor yet to call in question the wisdom of Deity in fixing that variety of climate, calculated to produce the diversities of light, and shade, discoverable on the surface of the human body."[18]

Embree, of course, opposed all moves to give in to Slavocracy demands, such as the Missouri Compromise. "Not another foot of slave territory," was his slogan.

Indicative of the widespread anti-slavery sentiment in the mountains is the fact that this sensitive and gentle, but radical, editor should have had such a great acceptance among the mountain people. Even the churches supported his efforts. He was deeply gratified, and before his untimely death at the age of thirty-eight, was able to write: "The Emancipator...meets the approbation of thousands...and is patronized perhaps at least equal to any other paper in the state."[19]

SAMUEL DOAK, D.D.
WHO TRAINED ANTI-SLAVERY MEN

"In East Tennessee...the stream of anti-slavery opinion was full and strong...The most prominent Presbyterian abolitionist in the region between 1800 and 1830 was the Rev. Samuel Doak, D.D." *20

Dr. Samuel Doak, leading abolitionist in East Tennessee, founder of Martin Academy, Washington College, and Tusculum Academy, which later combined to become the present Tusculum College in Tennessee, is all but lost to history. It is extremely difficult to find more than bare skeletal facts about his life. Appleton's Cyclopedia tells us he was of Scotch-Irish Presbyterian origin. He attended Lexington College in Virginia where, undoubtedly, he must have come under the influence of the West-

REV. SAMUEL DOAK, D.D.,
FOUNDER OF WASHINGTON COLLEGE, TENNESSEE.

CINCINNATI, O., FEBRUARY 12, 1896.

Freedom on the Mountains

Page 13

ern Virginia anti-slavery men such as Henry Rufner. He was graduated from Princeton and then taught two years at Hamden Sydney Institute.[21]

EDUCATED MOUNTAINEERS AGAINST SLAVERY

After moving into the Holston Settlement of East Tennessee in 1777, Doak participated in the Watauga movement and was later a member of the convention forming the State of Franklin with John Sevier. From the time he came to the Holston River Valley, and for the next generation, he "...educated the people aganist slavery.."[22]

Doak's students were noted for their anti-slavery, abolitionist thinking. Sam Houston was one of his pupils there in East Tennessee. "He inculcated upon all his students, theological and literary, the principles of immediate abolition. It is probably due to his teaching that Sam Houston gave his vote many years later against the Kansas-Nebraska Bill and vetoed the Texas ordinance of secession."[23]

John Rankin, who became a nationally known abolitionist leader and operated an Underground Railroad station at Ripley, Ohio, was another Doak pupil. Rankin studied three years -1813 to 1816- with Doak, and began his own anti-slavery activity there in the Tennessee mountains. He had helped set the Tennessee Manumission Society on its way, and his perseverance in the anti-slavery cause earned for him laurels as being one of the great inspiring forces in that movement. Even Garrison considered himself "a disciple of John Rankin," and Beecher called him "...the father of abolitionism, the Martin Luther of the Cause." Rankin always gave full credit to his old mentor, Samuel Doak.[24]

Freedom on the Mountains

Page 15

Yours Truly
John Rankin

Freedom on the Mountains

Page 16

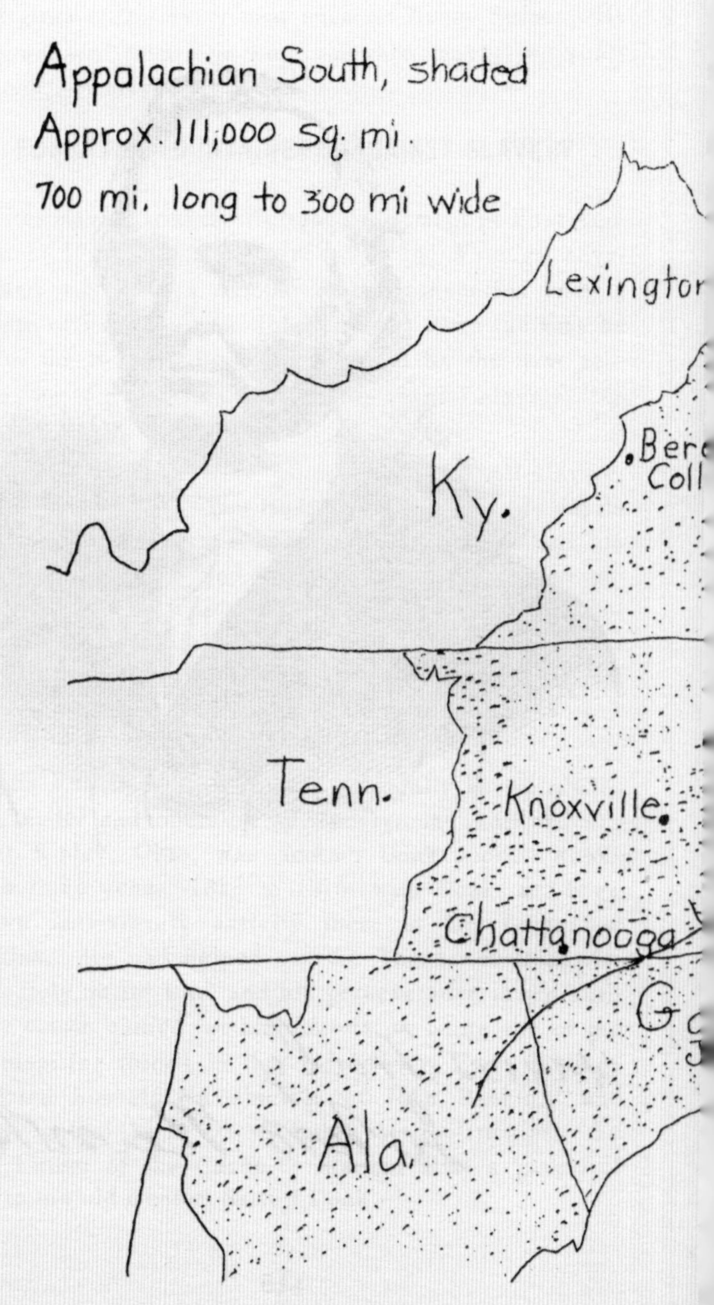

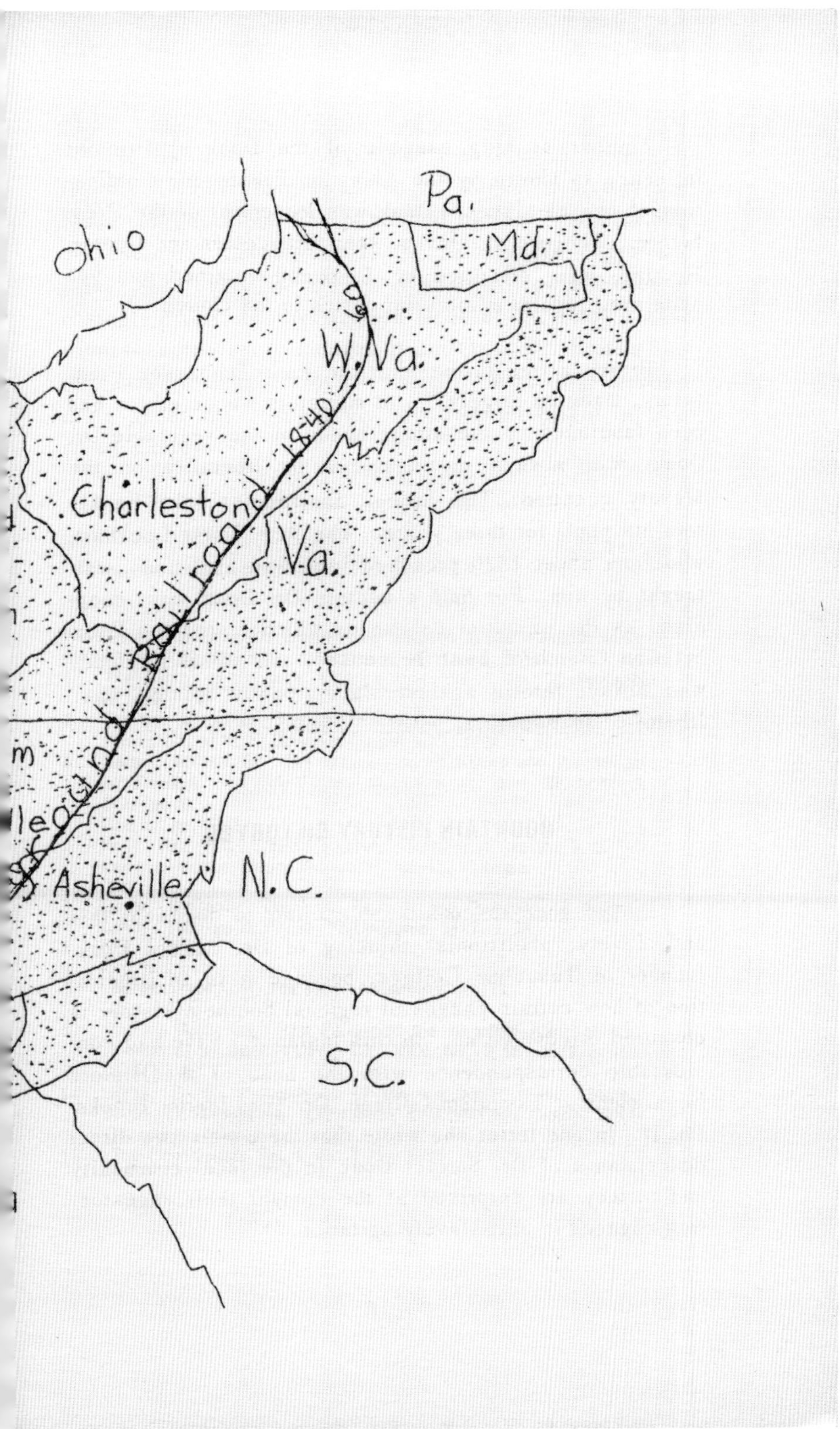

Freedom on the Mountains

Page 17

Another striking example of the Doak abolitionist influence is shown by the Abingdon Presbytery's ordination of two ex-slaves. Doak was Moderator of the Presbytery. The two ex-slaves, John Gloucester and George Erskine, were educated by Doak and ordained and set upon their regular ministerial duties in the church.[25]

Birney writes further that the East Tennessee Presbytery, made up largely "...of ministers whose ethics had been fashioned by the strong hands of the venerable Dr. Doak...was always distinguished by liberality on the slavery question...The famous abolitionist John Rankin was his pupil for three years. The Rev. Jesse Lockhart, who from about 1820 preached immediate abolition ...was taught by him...For half a century Dr. Doak was recognized as the principal column on which rested the Presbyterian Church of East Tennessee, and as his influence was always thrown against slavery-public opinion was liberal on that subject."[26]

MOUNTAIN HISTORY DISTORTED

I have gone to considerable effort to document this anti-slavery, abolitionist thinking of Dr. Samuel Doak, founder of Tusculum College, because it is an illustration of how certain phases of regional Southern history is obscured or covered up. In this instance I have had considerable correspondence with the head of the History Department at Tusculum College, Dr. Jean Ingrim Brooks Ph. D. In one letter she wrote that there were two direct descendants of Dr. Samuel Doak in the local community and"...they are surprised at the thought their ancestor was engaged in anti-slavery agitation."[27]

At Dr. Brooks' suggestion I ordered a book, The History of Tusculum, by Allen E. Ragan, a history professor at Tusculum, and published by the Tusculum Sesquicentennial Committee, 1945. It has 274 pages and I have read every one of them carefully. Nowhere, not in a single place, is any mention made of Dr. Doak's abolitionist, anti-slavery thought or activity. Dr. Brooks also informed me that the local community historian knew nothing about the anti-slavery, abolitionist origin of Tusculum College.[28]

*A memorial to Congress unanimously adopted at the eleventh annual convention of the Manumission Society of Tennessee, 1826

1 The Genius of Universal Emancipation, Vol I, No 52, September 2, 1826.

2 Coulter, E Merton, Fighting Parson of the Southern Highlands, (University of North Carolina, Chapel Hill), 1937, P. 91.

3 Barton, William E. "The Cumberland Mountains and the Struggle for Freedom" The New England Magazine, Vol. XVI, No. 1, March 1897, p. 70.

4 Coulter, pp. 90, 91.

5 Hoss, Rev. E E, "Elihu Embree, Abolitionist" in the S. C. Williams collection, Emory University, Atlanta, Georgia.

6 Ibid.

7 Lundy, Benjamin, The Life, Travels and Opinions of Benjamin Lundy, (William D. Parish, Philadelphia, 1847) p. 18.

8 Ibid. p. 20.

9 Ibid, p 25.

10 Barton, Pine Knot, The Story of Kentucky, p. 171

11 Ibid p 171

12 Dillon, Martin L, "The Failure of the American Abolitionists," Journal of Southern History, Vol XXV, No 2, May 1959, p 166

13 Ibid p 180

14 Hoss, E E, Publications of the Vanderbilt History Society, Nashivlle, Tennessee, 1897, in the S. C. Williams papers, Emory University, Atlanta.

15 The Emancipator, Vol. I, No. 2, May 1820

16. Ibid.
17. Ibid.
18 Ibid.
19 Hoss
20. Birney, William, James G. Birney and His Times, (Appleton, New York, 1890), p. 74.
21. Appleton's Cyclopedia, p. 187.
22 Coulter, pp. 90, 91.
23. Birney, p. 75
24 Hoss
25 Birney, p 76, Also Rankin, A T., The Truth Vindicated, p. 5.
26. Birney, pp. 76, 77
27 Brooks, Jean Ingram, personal letter to the writer, November 14, 1959, Greeneville, Tennessee.
28 Ibid

THE SLAVOCRACY MOVES TO SUPRESS ALL ANTI-SLAVERY THOUGHT

"In the latter part of the summer of 1835, the slave-holders generally became alarmed at the progress of the abolitionists. Meetings were held throughout the South, To excite all classes of people to the requisite degree of exasperation against them. At one of these meetings held at Clinton, Mississippi, it was resolved: "That...any individual who dares to circulate, with a view to effectuate the designs of the abolitionists, any of the incendiary tracts or newspapers..is justly worthy in the sight of God and man of immediate death!..." *1

The Southern states passed severe laws against circulating anti-slavery sentiment, pamphlets, or newspapers. Even mild-mannered Benjamin Lundy traveled under an assumed name in the South on his trip to Texas.[2] The Georgia Code of 1835 set the death punishment for circulating pamphlets calculated to incite insurrection. Prior to that, in 1831, Georgia put a price of five thousand dollars on Garrison's head.

"That the sum of five thousand dollars be, and the same is hereby appropriated, to be paid to any person or persons who shall arrest, bring to trial and prosecute to conviction under law of this State; the editor and publisher of a certain paper called the Liberator, published in the town of Boston..." *3

The Georgia attitude was typical of other Southern states. It was necessary for the Southern abolitionists to go "underground" or quit. Many turned to the underground railroad and it became more and more abolitionist in character.[4]

1. Birney, James G , The American Churches, The Bulwark of American Slavery (Charles Whipple, Newburyport, 1842), p. 8.
2. Dillon, Martin L., The Journal of Southern History, Vol. XXV. No. 2, May 1959, p. 166. Dillon quotes from the correspondence of Lundy to Elizabeth Chandler, September 6, 1832, in the Elizabeth Chandler Papers, Michigan Historical Collection, University of Michigan.
3. Acts of the General Assembly of the State of Georgia, 1831, pp. 255-256. State Archives, Atlanta.
4. Scarborough, Ruth, Opposition to Slavery in Georgia Prior to 1860, Ph. D. dissertation at George Peabody College, Nashville, 1933. P. 187.

LOYALISTS OF NORTH GEORGIA MOUNTAINS

> "In extreme North Georgia dwelt the Mountaineers...they were devoted to the Union and would have supported emancipation if it had been attempted...The mountaineers were anti-slavery in sentiment. They were an inarticulate element and their views have usually been lost..." *1

"They were inarticulate and their views" were usually lost. This is a sad truth. Therefore the total extent of anti-slavery, pro-Union thought in North Georgia is not generally known, even by the people who live there today, the direct descendants of men who volunteered for the Union Army.

An example of how a people's self image can be changed by a constant barrage of propaganda and teaching of a contrary nature was given before in the case of the two direct descendants of Dr. Samuel Doak of Tennessee who were surprised to hear that their ancestor had been an anti-slavery worker. Another is the case of Jasper, Georgia.

GEORGIA MOUNTAINEERS RAISE UNION FLAG

At Jasper, Georgia, the Union flag was raised over the courthouse every day throughout the four years of Civil War.[2] Marlin writes about these North Georgians: "...the hill people did not own slaves, were not in sympathy with those who did, and refused...to cooperate with the South. Many people of Mountain Georgia rallied to the old flag and enlisted with the forces of the union. Pick-County practically seceded from Georgia, raising the stars and stripes on the courthouse at Jasper, where they waved till after the surrender" of General Lee.[3]

A few years ago I was in Jasper, Georgia, and spoke with members of the local high school senior class. Not a single one of those pupils knew about this local flag history. In general they felt themselves to be descendants of the Slavocracy tradition. The myth of history had done an excellent job on them. They had all had regular courses in Georgia State history.

CONFEDERACY FEARED THE MOUNTAINEERS

But if the school history books fail to record the extent and seriousness of the mountaineer loyalists' threat to the Confederacy, the Confederate leaders themselves were never unaware of it. This is shown by the increasingly strong measures they sought to use in suppressing it. In early 1863 Governor Brown of Georgia had received "shocking reports" of anti-Confederacy activity in the North Georgia mountains. The report said that Confederate deserters were being sheltered by mountaineers, and that they were organizing into rebellious bands to oppose the Confederacy.

In an effort to destroy this loyalist activity, the Governor issued a proclamation in which he said it had been reported to him "that numbers of these deserters, encouraged by disloyal citizens in the mountains of Northeastern Georgia, have associated themselves together with arms in their hands and are now in rebellion against the authority of the state and the Confederate States..."[4]

The Governor's statement proceeded to order all such deserters to return to their "respective commands." He held out an olive branch of conciliation and leniency if they obeyed, but otherwise the "full penalty of the law" would be their fate. Civilians assisting them would be similarly punished.[5]

Shortly after the Georgia Governor's proclamation, the Richmond (Virginia) Enquirer editorialized that such problems were not confined to the Georgia mountains, but were general throughout the Appalachian South. "There is within the limits of the Confederacy," the Enquirer said, "certain tories and traitors...expecially in the remote mountainous regions...in which treason is not only practiced by the people but sanctioned and protected by the judges elected by these people."[6]

I have recently been to the Georgia State Archives in Atlanta. There one finds local histories of most of the mountain counties. Lloyd G. Marlin, official historian of Cherokee County, covers areas beyond his immediate county. By Marlin's account the Georgia mountaineers not only made long and dangerous journeys to join the Union Army, but those not physically fit or too old for military service often helped Sherman's foraging squads round up food and feed supplies. In reprisal the McCollum Scouts (Confederate) made vengeful raids into the mountains, laid waste the homes of loyalists, murdered and "...carried terror into the hearts of the Unionists in upper Cherokee and Pickens. One favorite way of disposing of them was to go up into upper Cherokee and Pickens and capture some, bring them down to the river near Canton and shoot them off their horses into the running stream."[7]

COURAGEOUS MOUNTAINEER DIES CURSING CONFEDERACY

Marlin gives many dramatic instances of the courageous spirit of these mountaineer loyalists on trail.

"They caught a man named Jim Pitts," he writes, "over above Salocoa, put him on a horse and swept through Beasley Gap, in Pine Log in Bartow County, where they impressed into service a methodist preacher named Fletcher Weems, and along with him a convenient rope. Stopping on the road up near Adairsville, they told Weems to do his stuff quickly, which he did. Jim Pitts preserved the indomitable courage of his race consistently cursing them all and singular, except the preacher, till they down the soul they could not conquer."[8]

Another dramatic tale is about a humble old woman whose husband was taken out and shot by the Confederates. We have it from two Sources, Marlin's history of Cherokee County, and from the local folk tradition. Both are given below, the historian's account and the folk legend taken from notes of talks with old citizens of the area.

THE HISTORIAN'S ACCOUNT

McCollum's guerillas caught an old man near Sharp Mountain Creek in Cherokee who had been with Sherman's foraging squad in Jasper the week before. "So the 'Scouts' carried him to the top of the mountain, where the Jasper road crosses it about three miles south of Jasper, hung him up, and fired two pistol balls through his heart. Next day the dead man's wife came walking across the hills from Cherokee, borrowed a little cart and yearling from a nearby farmer, and with the assistance of the farmer's son, went up to the mountain top and cut down the corpse; then she drove away alone with her dead, back to Cherokee."[9]

THE FOLK STORY

To Lucindy Larmon that day was a nightmare. It was a bundle of bad dreams all come true. Word had come that her two sons, soldiers in the Union Army, were dead in Tennessee. The messenger was hardly out of the yard when McCullum's guerillas rode up. They knew about her two sons, and they knew her man had been with Sherman's food hunting squad the week before. They had come for the settlement.

After emptying the smokehouse, they set fire to the barn and burned the dwelling house. Then they rode off, leading Lige, her man, with a rope around his neck, hands tied behind his back.

Lucindy was not a young woman, but she had grit. Like most of their neighbors, the Larmons were Union people. They had never had any sympathy for the man-hunting "paterollers" who from time to time had come into the mountains from the plantation country. Most of the able bodied men had gone off to the Union Army. The McCollum "Scouts" took advantage of their absence to wreak a merciless and sometimes ghastly vengeance.

Lucindy struck out in the direction the Confederates had gone with her man. At dawn-break she was still walking over the hills toward Pickens. At Jasper she saw old man Mance Mulkey limp out with the Union flag under his arm. He had been wounded fighting the Confederates at Knoxville, and had come back home to get well. He ran the flag up on the courthouse. Lucindy watched the wind undo its faded folds. That flag had gone up there every day since Fort Sumpter.

"Ye seed anything of them McCollum rogues, Mance?"

Freedom on the Mountains

Page 28

the old woman asked. "Hain't seed um, Cindy, but heerd devilish heap of tarnation noise and shootin' down trail yan side of town toward Sharp Top."

Lucindy wasted no time. She trudged off in the direction Mance pointed. The sun-ball rose up over Burnt Mountain like a big shiny new-ground punkin cut half in two. It lit a skyline of fiery red, but in the old woman's eyes the glow was dull.

At a spot three miles from Jasper a chestnut tree spread a huge limb out over the wagon trail. Lige Larmon, with two big bullet holes in his forehead, dangled from that limb.

The old woman staggered up under the tree. Her shoes dragged against chestnut burrs cluttered about the trail. She wiped sweat with her waist sleeve and sat down on a nearby log. For a long time she just sat there looking, with eyes that saw nothing.

Finally she stood up. The body had to be got down and buried. Lem Cantrel's widow had a bull yearlin and cart. She'd borrow them. Maybe the nine year old Cantrel boy could help a little. Lige's body was big and long and heavy.

With the yearlin yoked to the two-wheel cart, Lucindy and the boy managed to get the body down and loaded. Then with her dead, and the bull and cart, Lucindy began the trip back over the hills to Cherokee and the Graveyard.[10]

LOCAL GEORGIA MOUNTAIN HISTORIANS VERIFY ANTI-SLAVERY

Luke Tate, official historian of Pickens County, Georgia, verifies the Marlin account of the Jasper flag and other incidents. He says the last flag to fly officially below the Mason and Dixon Line after secession was there at Jasper. Governor Brown, a contradictory character and sometimes thorn in the Confederate flesh himself, refused to send troops to take the flag down at Jasper. When the planters urged him to do so, Brown said, "By no means; let it float...if the people of Pickens desire to hang it out let them do so. I will send no troops to interfere with it."[11]

Ritchie, Rabun County historian, writes: "...nearly all the delegates from the northern counties of Georgia... were against secession and in favor of staying in the Union. Practically all the citizens of Rabun County and of the entire southern mountain region were Union men."[12]

Battey, official historian of Floyd County, Georgia, lists the votes on secession as they were cast by all the counties of the old Cherokee Nation, which is mountain country. Out of a total of twenty counties only three had any votes for secession.[13]

Freedom on the Mountains

Page 30

1. Scarborough, Opposition to Slavery in Georgia, p. 226.
2. Marlin, Lloyd G, History of Cherokee County, Georgia. in State Archives, Atlanta, pp. 67, 68.
   Tate, Luke, History of Pickens County, Georgia, in State Archives, Atlanta, pp. 204, 205.
   Ward, George G., History of Gilmer County, Georgia, in manuscript, State Archives, Atlanta.
3. Marlin, p. 68.
   Tate, p. 205.
4. Kirwan, Albert D., The Confederacy (Meridian Books, New York, 1956) pp. 266, 268.
5. Ibid.
6. Ibid.
7. Marlin, p. 72.
8. Ibid. pp. 74, 75.
9. Ibid. p. 76.
10. From notes taken personally by the writer in talking to many old citizens in the Jasper area.
11. Tate, pp. 205, 206.
12. Ritchie, Andrew Jackson, Sketches of Rabun County (Georgia) History, State Archives, Atlanta, P. 267.
13. Battey, George M., Jr., A History of Rome and Floyd County, Georgia, State Archives, Atlanta, p. 134.

Freedom on the Mountains

Inside Back Cover

Freedom on the Mountains

Back Cover

Please enter my subscription to AMP!!!

NAME ______________________________

ADDRESS ______________________________

____

Enclosed is my check for $

___$7.50 for working people.

___$7.50 for students.

___$12.50 for professionals.

___$15.00 for libraries & institutions.

___$25.00 for wealthy people (income over $15,000).

___$0.00 for unemployed Appalachians.

Here's another $ ____ for ___ free subscriptions to unemployed Appalachians.

Appalachian Movement Press
P. O. Box 8074
Huntington, West Virginia 25705
(304) 523-8587

Simply Wiped Off the Map

Davitt McAteer and Thomas N. Bethell's *The Pittston Mentality: Manslaughter at Buffalo Creek*

At around eight o'clock on the grey, cold, and rainy Saturday morning of February 26, 1972, a series of coal slurry impoundment dams built entirely from "gob"—the waste mud, rock, and combustible debris from underground coal mining—collapsed above the narrow Buffalo Creek Valley in Logan County, West Virginia. The water slammed into another burning section of gob below, causing an explosion, and twenty-one million cubic feet of water, combined with one million tons of sludge, roared down and through the small community of Saunders below. The black wave coursed through the valley, utterly destroying everything in its path on a brutal eighteen-mile wash towards the town of Man at the banks of the Guyandotte River.[17] Thomas Bethell described the scale of the disaster: "Roads disappeared underneath or were torn up and flung ahead. The steel rails of the C&O Railroad were lifted and twisted like wet spaghetti, the houses were torn from their foundations and smashed against each other until there was nothing left but old lumber. Bridges were wrenched from their moorings intact and hurled hundreds of yards at a time. Pictures of Jack Kennedy and Jesus Christ rode down through the valley and disappeared under the brown sea. Along with nobody knows how many people."[18]

When the waters finally slowed, several of the sixteen mining communities along Buffalo Creek had been completely annihilated, 125 people had been killed, 7 were unaccounted for, and over 4,000 were left homeless. As Ronnie Smith was interviewed in Mimi Pickering's 1975 film on the disaster, holding a small microphone and sitting next to his young son, his stoic demeanor begins to crack as he recounts his family's last-minute evacuation in the path of the flood and the houses he saw destroyed: "This is the most tragic thing I've ever seen in my life. I'm sorry that God let me live to see it."[19]

It turned out that the Pittston Coal Company, owners and operators of the nearby mines for the past two years and the people responsible for the construction of the largest of the faulty dams that collapsed, were also entertaining thoughts about divine influence. In the immediate days after the flood, while the black water emptied into the Guyandotte River and families like Ronnie Smith's sheltered in HUD-provided trailers, Thomas Bethell recorded reporter Mary Walton's conversation with the company's New York spokesman in the pages of his activist watchdog paper, *Coal Patrol*: "An official of the Pittston Coal Company, owners of the dam, stated, 'We're investigating the damage which was caused by the flood, which we believe, of course, was an Act of God.' The dam was simply 'incapable of holding the water God poured into it.' "[20]

"The scale of it, the size of it, and the forces that were released were so beyond comprehension. We were just baffled by it," Davitt McAteer remembered about the aftermath of the dam collapse.[21]

Immediately after the monster wall of coal slurry and water crashed through the Buffalo Creek Valley, McAteer and Thomas Bethell arrived to see the horror for themselves, and they joined Beth Spence on the ground in Logan County, West Virginia. Spence, whose father ran the *Logan Banner* newspaper, took them around the valleys and hollows to see the aftermath and to speak with the residents who had survived.[22]

McAteer was intimately familiar with the explosions that occurred in underground "deep" coal mines. The young lawyer grew up in Fairmont, West Virginia, and, before he found himself slogging through the aftermath of the Pittston dam collapse, he had worked on the mine safety case study in the wake of the Farmington mine fire that killed seventy-eight miners near his hometown in 1968. That report would help lay the groundwork for the Federal Coal Mine Health and Safety Act passed by Congress in 1969. Buffalo Creek was similar in force to these underground explosions, but when released out in the open upon a populated valley, the force of destruction was "beyond the pale."[23]

McAteer remembered executives and representatives of the Pittston Coal Company arriving and surveying the area in personal helicopters, hovering safely above the destruction wrought by their faulty engineering, never engaging with the residents. "It reminded me of the Johnstown Flood, when that rich boys' resort collapsed," said McAteer.[24]

In 1881 Henry Clay Frick, Andrew Carnegie, Andrew Mellon, Robert Pitcairn, and other wealthy Pittsburgh industrialists founded, for themselves, the South Fork Fishing and Hunting Club as an escape from the smoky air of the city. Purchase of the property on which they built their exclusive resort included the South Fork Dam, an aging earthen dam with no water release control mechanism, which held the artificial Lake Conemaugh. Around this lake resort cottages were built, and within and around the water and dam, adjustments were made to improve lifestyle amenities for members only: the club could afford to stock the lake with black bass imported from Lake Erie but chose not to invest in structural repairs to the dam itself in the interests of the safety of Johnstown, Pennsylvania, situated fourteen miles downstream to the west.

On the afternoon of May 31, 1889, after days of heavy rainfall, the South Fork Dam broke. A roaring sixty-foot wall of water "swept into town with the debris of homes, wagons, dead bodies, trees, draft animals, railroad tracks and bridges, a freight car with 60 tons of pig iron, pianos and household goods, all interwoven with telephone and electric wire." Twenty-two hundred people were killed. Although a few of the industrialists who were invested members of the South Fork Club donated some money to relief efforts, and the club itself donated blankets, all later damage suits were unsuccessful: the dam failure was ruled an act of God.[25]

In the case of the 1889 Johnstown Flood, the 1972 Buffalo Creek flood, and so many other disasters like them, acts of divine intervention were, in reality, known structural-engineering problems, which had, through wanton negligence, simply been left unaddressed. "What the Hell, Our Insurance Will Cover It," read one 1972 *Coal Patrol* headline.

Thomas Bethell and Davitt McAteer make a powerful pair of investigative writers. For his part, Bethell began his career in Whitesburg, Kentucky, at the *Mountain Eagle* newspaper as a reporter (where he is still contributing editor). He carved a niche for himself twisting thorns in the sides of coal-industry executives with his hard-hitting, deeply informative independent paper, *Coal Patrol.* Six to eight pages per issue, offset printed on yellow, blue, or green paper, and bound together with one staple in the top left corner, *Coal Patrol* could be subscribed to from Bethell's office in the National Press Building in Washington, DC. Bethell wrote and distributed thirty-one issues of *Coal Patrol* between 1970 and 1973, popularizing the work of Miners for Democracy and other dissident union groups and providing reporting and commentary on "Coal-Related Developments in Labor, Industry, and Government."

"Talking about *Coal Patrol* is talking about Thomas Bethell," says a review in a 1973 issue of *Antipode: A Radical Journal of Geography.*

"Few of us know or care about the rottenness of the coal industry, but Bethell has taken away the excuse of ignorance. He writes well."[26]

Davitt McAteer's background in mining technology and engineering kept his focus on the structural issues in the Buffalo Creek situation: what went wrong with the design, "or absence of design," of the dams that failed. "It's not as though this wasn't foretold."[27] In the pages of *Coal Patrol* that April, Bethell agreed. Bringing the national news media in for a flogging over their lack of consistent attention to the wreckage in West Virginia and criticizing the "active programs designed to protect the environment" trumpeted in Pittston's full-color annual report to their stockholders the month after the flood, Bethell fumed: "In Logan County, the 'active program' until 8 a.m. February 26 involved building a dam out of slime on a foundation of dead trees, bushes, loose rocks, mine refuse, and old bits of mine machinery, and assuming that somehow it would be strong enough to hold back 150 million gallons of water. That's the Pittston way of protecting the environment."

As McAteer recalls, the pair worked quickly to write *The Pittston Mentality*. Bethell, "the better wordsmith," would "tune up" McAteer's dry, functional drafts while adding his own prose, and in that collaborative way they wrote this terrifying piece of narrative journalism.[28] *Pittston Mentality* was first published in May 1972 in the *Washington Monthly*, an upstart nonpartisan magazine out of DC, launched only a few years before and running on a shoestring budget. Appalachian Movement Press, fueled by similarly sparse resources and dedication, republished this essay on their own imprint the following month. Although the inside cover of the AMP edition claims that their printing "is unauthorized by the magazine," McAteer says that Charlie Peters, *Washington Monthly*'s founding editor in chief (and a West Virginian), was actually very much in favor of AMP's efforts. The booklet, which encapsulates so much of AMP's stance against corruption and embodies the prickly tone that they were known for, remained in print and regularly available in the AMP catalog until the printshop folded up in 1979.

The Pittston Mentality: Manslaughter at Buffalo Creek was last published in 1978 as an essay in the academic survey *Colonialism in Modern America: The Appalachian Case* by Helen Lewis, Linda Johnson, and Don Askins (Boone, NC: Appalachian Consortium Press). We republish the Appalachian Movement Press edition here.

The Pittston Mentality: Manslaughter on Buffalo Creek

by Thomas N. Bethell
and
Davitt McAteer

25¢

The Pittston Mentality

Front Cover

The Pittston Mentality

Inside Front Cover

Thomas N. Bethell is the editor of Coal Patrol, a monthly newsletter on the coal industry which is extremely informative. He is also a contributing editor for the Washington Monthly.

Davitt McAteer is a lawyer with Ralph Nader's Center for the Study of Responsive Law.

SUBSCRIBE TO COAL PATROL!!!

rates: $7.50 for individuals
$15.00 for organizations

10-15 issues per year stocked full with some very useful and important information.

write: Appalachia Information
737 National Press Building
Washington, D.C. 20004

This article was first published in the Washington Monthly of May, 1972. We publish it with the permission of Tom Bethell. It is unauthorized by the magazine.

published by:

Appalachian Movement Press, Inc.
P.O. Box 8074
Huntington, West Virginia 25705

June 1972

Buffalo Creek, in Logan County, is reasonably typical for the southern part of West Virginia—a long, winding hollow, snaking between steep ridges on both sides for more than 20 miles from the town of Saunders, at its headwaters, to the town of Man, where the creek empties into the Guyandotte River, which flows north to join the Ohio River at Huntington. The narrow valley is just wide enough for the creek, the railroad, and an almost unending line of company-built houses stretching along both sides of the tracks. There are occasional wide places in the valley where tributaries flow into Buffalo Creek, and in the wide places there used to be towns—small towns that nobody ever heard of, places like Kistler, Crown, Accoville, Braeholm, Fanco, Becco, Amherstdale, Robinette, Latrobe, Crites, Stowe, Lundale, Craneco, Lorado, and Pardee. Some of the names come from coal companies that no longer exist. As coal towns go, these were old, most of them built before World War I. They were in varying stages of decline. Some of them were not much more than post-office addresses. The old frame two-family houses were settling unevenly. Some had collapsed altogether. Others, considering their age and the haste with which they had been built, were in surprisingly good shape. As a general rule, if a house was freshly painted you could assume that a working miner lived there.

The Pittston Mentality

Page 2

The population of Buffalo Creek has fluctuated with the times, declining when the industry declined, recovering when the industry recovered. In 1970, coal had its best year since 1947, and a rosy glow of optimism suffused National Coal Association predictions for the future. Big companies opened new mines along Buffalo Creek and stepped up production in their old ones.

When coal comes up out of the ground, the impurities that come with it are separated out in preparation plants—tipples, as they are more commonly called. The coal rolls away in long, black trains; the impurities stay behind, and something has to be done with them. They have a way of accumulating with staggering speed: a ton of raw coal generally contains up to 25 per cent of extraneous material, and a good-sized tipple, handling the production of several mines at once, will separate out thousands of tons of waste every day. Miners have different names for it—"gob" or "slag" or "culm"—but whatever you call it, it still has to be piled somewhere. In the crowded hollows of West Virginia, finding places to pile slag is a problem of major proportions. As a general rule, no engineer is ever called in to consult on the best and safest locations. Instead, the company superintendent simply hunts around for some vacant space convenient to his tipple, and the slag is dumped there, either by trucks climbing up a mountainside and dumping down the slope, or by an aerial tramway strung between peaks and dumping in the middle. Whatever system is used, the slag is piled up until it is higher than the dumping spot, and then a new pile is started.

Facing the Gob

Since 1946 a tipple has been in operation at the head of Buffalo Creek. The plant was built by the Lorado Coal Mining Company, a mostly local outfit that sold out to the Buffalo Mining Company in 1964. Buffalo Mining, in turn, sold out in 1970 to the Pittston Company, which is headquartered in New York and is the largest independent producer of coal in the United States. All this time the tipple continued in operation. And all this time it grew. Originally designed to process coal from a single mine, it was expanded periodically as new mines were opened nearby. By 1972 Pittston was operating a total of eight mines in the Buffalo Creek vicinity—five of them underground, three of them stripping jobs. The coal from all eight was processed in the single tipple. On average, the tipple operated six days a week, two shifts a day, handling about 5,200 tons of raw coal daily, shipping out about 4,200 tons of cleaned coal on the long Chesapeake and Ohio trains. That meant that every day a thousand tons of gob, more or less, had to be dumped.

Three tributaries run into Buffalo Creek near the Pittston tipple. From 1947 until about 1955, the refuse was dumped along the hillside a few hundred yards upstream from the tipple, but by 1955 the available space was mostly exhausted and the tipple began dumping a little farther away, across the mouth of a small hollow where the Middle Fork tributary met the creek. At first the gob pile grew slowly—it had to, because most of the hollow behind it was occupied by miners living in company houses. But when production at the tipple increased, the growing gob pile began to menace the houses, and the miners were forced out. The houses were abandoned—some of them were knocked down for the lumber—and the gob was dumped where they had stood. The families moved away, some of them out of West Virginia entirely, some of them only a few hundred yards, settling in vacant houses in the small community of Saunders, which stood facing the gob pile at the intersection of Middle Fork and Buffalo Creek.

Saunders Was Gone

The gob pile grew, and grew, and grew more swiftly as the tipple kept expanding production. At first this grotesque black mountain was only an eyesore. Later it became a source of air pollution and a fire hazard. Gob piles may be nothing but waste, but much of that waste is flammable, and a combination of compaction and oxidation can result in spontaneous combustion. Once a fire gets going deep within a gob pile, extinguishing it is nearly impossible. The fire smoulders, sometimes bursts into open flame, fouls the sky with acrid smoke, and occasionally produces an explosion. The federal Bureau of Mines has spent millions of dollars in research on the problem, but the end result is that hundreds of gob piles are smouldering in the Appalachian coalfields right now, and nothing is being done about them. The gob pile at Middle Fork began burning years ago and kept on smouldering.

As the dumping continued, another problem arose. Tipples require vast quantities of water in the cleaning-separating process, but water can be a scarce commodity at times in West Virginia. Partly to provide itself with a reliable year-round supply of water, partly to comply with new state regulations governing stream pollution, Buffalo Mining began to build a series of settling ponds in 1964 (previously the contaminated wash water had simply been sluiced directly into Buffalo Creek, despite the objections of people who liked to fish there). The ponds were created by building retaining dams in the most immediately convenient location—on top of the huge Middle Fork gob pile. By that time the pile had reached stupefying proportions: as high as a

10-story office building, 600 feet across, stretching back into the hollow more than a quarter of a mile. Seeping down through the pile and wandering across the top, the waters of Middle Fork ran sluggishly to join the main stream of Buffalo Creek. Damming the water was a relatively easy task, using the material closest at hand: mine waste. No civil engineer in his right mind would permit the construction of a dam from such materials—as many a civil engineer would later confirm—but no engineer, it now appears, was consulted.

In operation, the settling ponds not only contained runoff water from the hills, but refuse-filled water piped from the tipple. The solid refuse would settle out and clear water could be piped back to the tipple. The first of the ponds impounded a relatively small volume of water, however, and it silted up within a couple of years. A second dam was built in 1967, slightly farther upstream. When the tipple was operating full blast, it required 500,000 gallons of water a day, pumping back between 400 and 500 gallons of waste-filled water every minute. Some of the water would seep out through the porous dam, but the waste settling to the bottom—500 tons every day—rapidly filled the pond, and a third dam was built in 1970. Again, no engineering was involved—just truckloads of mine waste, a bulldozer to push them around, and *presto!* a dam grew across the hollow, built of nothing but junk, standing on a foundation of slime and silt and dead trees. The trees were there because nobody had bothered to cut them down. It was simpler and faster just to dump on top of them.

In West Virginia, February means snow and rain. February meant it this year, as always. In Logan County, there were heavy snows and flash floods—but they were, as the state meteorologist would later point out, "nothing uncommon." At the head of Buffalo Creek, the waters rose behind Pittston's makeshift dam. Early on the morning of February 26, Pittston's local mine boss, Steve Dasovich, sent a bulldozer operator up the access road to the dam with instructions to cut a drainage ditch to relieve the pressure from the swollen lake. The access road winds around a mountainside, with the dam out of sight much of the way. When the bulldozer operator finally came around the last bend and looked through the rain at the dam, he saw with a sudden, terrible shock that it wasn't there.

The dam was gone, and 21 million cubic feet of water and an immeasurable mass of mud and rock and coal wastes were charging through the narrow valley of Buffalo Creek. From where he sat on his suddenly useless machine, the bulldozer operator could look down toward the little town of Saunders—a town consisting of nothing more than a church and some two dozen houses. Now it consisted of nothing at all. Saunders was gone, eradicated completely. Beyond Saunders, the valley curved away out of sight, but the air was filled with the terrifying sound of the flood bearing down on the 15 communities in its path.

Father of Strip-Mining

There are no slag heaps on Park Avenue and no floods will ever wash through the offices of Joseph P. Routh unless the island of Manhattan sinks into the sea. Thirty-five floors up in the Pan American building, the chairman of the Pittston Company has a commanding view. When he looks down to the street below, he can see Brinks armored trucks moving the wealth of America from place to place. The trucks belong to Joe Routh. A good deal of the money does, too.

Routh is 79 now, and he has been making money longer than most men have been alive. He was already a power to be reckoned with when the Pittston Company, which then operated a dozen anthracite mines in Pennsylvania, stumbled into bankruptcy during the Depression. A friend at Manufacturers Trust suggested to Routh that he take over the company and lead it out of the wilderness. The bank sweetened the offer with a $10-million loan—essentially unsecured, since there would be no way to recoup the loss if Pittston went under—and Routh moved in.

Anthracite, he concluded, was a dying industry. The future lay in the vast bituminous fields of Virginia and West Virginia. He unloaded most of Pittston's properties in Pennsylvania and began buying up tracts of coal in central Appalachia.

At a time when coal prices fluctuated wildly, he had discovered that the best way to tear loose a chunk of coal in time to take advantage of favorable trends was to strip it from the mountainsides, rather than go through the difficult, two-year-or-more process of engineering and constructing a deep mine. By 1950, when strip-mining was still an infant industry in Appalachia and conservationists hadn't the foggiest notion of the plague to come, one of Routh's companies, Compass Coal, was profitably tearing the hills of Harrison County, West Virginia, to shreds. Since there were no state or federal reclamation requirements, no money had to be spent on binding up the wounds. It must have been the best of all possible worlds, unless you lived near one of Routh's mines. He, of course, didn't.

Routh kept himself busy with other conquests, picking up coal companies in Kentucky, West Virginia, and Virginia, buying up trucking companies and warehouses in New York, enlarging his oil-distributing operations, hatching long-range plans for a giant refinery on the Maine coast. Money flowed from Routh's various holdings into his Manhattan office in a never-ending stream, and Routh bought Brinks, Inc., to carry the cash in his own armored cars.

An Act of God

Despite abundant evidence that he was in no danger of going soft, Routh decided in 1969 to bring in a new president. He looked around for a man to match his own toughness and found one—a 53-year-old native of West Virginia named Nicholas T. Camicia who had already made a mark in the industry as a notable scrambler. "The coal industry is run by men who got where they are by not being nice," says one former federal official in a position to know, "and when Camicia smiles, you can hear his jaws making a special effort." Routh liked him fine.

But Camicia already had a good job when Routh approached him about taking over Pittston. Routh reportedly told him to write his own ticket, possibly remembering his own reluctance to sign on until Manufacturers Trust gave him the $10 million to play with. Camicia did, in fact, write his own ticket, putting his signature to a contract that has never been publicized, but makes fascinating reading in the archives of the Securities and Exchange Commission. The contract runs until 1976 and guarantees Camicia not only a minimun salary of $100,000 (increased now to $134,000), but stipulates that a deferred salary of $25,000 will be set aside each year, compounded, and paid out to him in 120 monthly installments whenever he quits or gets fired; if he reaches retirement age before that happens, he also qualifies for a hefty pension. The contract also appears to have included some highly attractive stock options; SEC records show, for example, that Camicia picked up 7,200 shares, worth approximately $270,000, for a price of $78,000–less than a third of their market value. That wasn't all. Camicia was living comfortably in an exclusive Chicago suburb when Routh signed him up; in return for agreeing to move to New York, Camicia got Pittston to buy his house for $90,000 and furnish him, cost-free, an equivalent home within commuting distance of Manhattan. He went to work for Joe Routh, reportedly satisfied with the terms of his employment.

If ever there was any doubt that Routh and Camicia were a pair of industry touchdown-twins, it was dispelled early in 1970, when Pittston signed a contract with the Japanese steel industry. The Japanese wanted a long-term contract and were willing to make concessions to get a reliable supply of American coking coal. By 1970 Pittston had gained control of a third of all the available commercial metallurgical coal in the U. S., and no one could offer more reliability than Routh and Camicia. They would not offer it without certain stipulations, however. The contract they signed

The Pittston Mentality

Page 12

with the Japanese calls for Pittston to deliver 140 million tons of coal over the next 10 years at a reported average of $15 per ton, which is about twice the going rate elsewhere.

Pittston's directors were so happy last year that they boosted dividends twice and voted themselves a three-for-one stock split to boot. The company now has more than 50 mines working, with nine more under development, and there is no end to the good times in sight.

Is everybody happy? No. Federal mine inspectors in Appalachia are not pleased with Pittston's safety record; they never have been particularly pleased with it, but the past couple of years have been especially bad. Nine miners lost their lives in 1971 in Pittston mines (two of them in the newly acquired Buffalo Mining division), another 743 were seriously hurt, and the company's accident frequency rate was one of the highest in the coal industry. The record in 1970 was even worse: 18 dead. Investigators found that in a solid majority of the fatal accidents bad management practices (rather than personal carelessness) were to blame. "The company appears to be sincere in its desire for health and safety throughout its mines," one inspector wrote. "This desire," he added drily, "is not always fulfilled." Not always. All told, some 98 men have been killed in Pittston's mines in the past decade, and a 1963 explosion in which 22 men died still ranks as one of the worst of recent disasters. Three or four thousand men have been seriously injured or maimed in the company's mines since 1962, and the U. S. Public Health Service estimates that as many as 5,000 Pittston miners may have developed pneumoconiosis during that time. The profit margin of the new Japanese contract is a reported 24 per cent, almost three times the normal profit margin in the coal industry; you can't help marveling at how much of that money will be going back to the disabled derelicts living out their lives in Appalachia after destroying themselves to help make Joe Routh a millionaire for the third or fourth time.

Pittston's stockholders don't have to concern themselves with such things, because they don't hear about them. The company's handsome four-color annual reports talk about money, not about people. There are pictures of freshly painted oil storage tanks, spotless armored trucks, gleaming computer banks—and aerial pictures of the long, black coal trains winding their way through seemingly virgin Appalachian valleys. The pictures are taken with care: on the inside back cover of the 1971 report there is a color shot of lovely hills and hollows with a sturdy complex of mine buildings prominent in the foreground. "Aerial view of the Lorado Mine of newly acquired Buffalo Mining Company," the caption reads.

The Pittston Mentality

Page 14

Beyond the mine, railroad tracks stretch away, disappearing behind a hill. If you could see beyond that hill, you would see the massive, smouldering gob pile that stood at the head of Buffalo Creek, and on top of it the jerry-built dams that Pittston used with its preparation plant. But those things are not part of the picture, not part of the annual report. As far as Pittston's stockholders were concerned, they never existed–not until the morning of February 26, when suddenly the dams collapsed and the burning gob pile erupted and all hell broke loose.

Helicopters were still thrashing back and forth between Buffalo Creek and the nearest hospitals when reporters began calling Pittston's New York headquarters to find out what the company had been doing to cause such a monstrous disaster. Camicia and Routh weren't available, wouldn't answer the telephones, wouldn't return calls. Finally, Mary Walton of the Charleston *Gazette* flushed out a Pittston lawyer who insisted on remaining anonymous, but was willing to give the company's point of view. "It was an act of God," he said.

Dasovich's Yardstick

" 'Act of God' is a legal term," Robert Weedfall remarked when he heard about Pittston's explanation of the flood. "There are other legal terms–terms like 'involuntary manslaughter because of stupidity' and 'criminal negligence.' " Weedfall is the West Virginia state climatologist, the man who keeps track of basic acts of God such as rain and snow. He was in a better position than anyone else to know whether there could be any possibility that Pittston's dam had collapsed from natural causes, and he was convinced that it had not—could not have—not by any stretch of the imagination. There had been heavy rainfall in Logan County during the week of February 26, and considerable flooding. But it was nothing uncommon for February, Weedfall said, and he had the statistics to prove it. When reporters called him they were impressed with his conviction. Pittston officials had called, too, looking for ways to document their private theory of divine intervention. Weedfall wasn't much help.

Nor were the technical specialists of the Department of the Interior who arrived from Washington and, in the aftermath of the disaster, poked and probed among the ruins in search of clues. The U. S. Geological Survey sent a crew, as did the Bureau of Mines; the Bureau of Reclamation summoned a former chief of its Earth Dams Section from retirement. The investigators examined the remains of the dam in microscopic detail, interviewed Pittston workers and company officials (who would not talk to reporters), and pieced together a convincing account of what had happened and why. None of the investigators showed any doubt that the dams had been badly engineered. Fred Walker, the retired Bureau of Reclamation expert, went further, refusing to use the word "dam" to describe the structures. "Locally these barriers are called dams, but to me this is unacceptable nomenclature," he wrote. "These structures were created by persons completely unfamiliar with dam design, construction, and materials, and by construction methods that are completely unacceptable to engineers specializing in dam design."

West Virginia law, Walker noted, "requires permits, approval of plans, and inspection during construction for impoundments more than 10 feet deep. I was unable to find that such requirements had ever been complied with." Suggesting that similar potentially disastrous situations could be found elsewhere in the coalfields, Walker commented scathingly that "fortunately most of these barriers are built in valleys that have small watersheds above them, as apparently little if any consideration is given to the flood hazard involved."

Pittston's consideration of the flood hazard at Buffalo Creek seems to have begun at 4 p.m. on February 24—exactly 40 hours before the so-called dam collapsed—when Jack Kent and Steve Dasovich drove up to survey the situation. Kent was superintendent of Pittston's stripping operations in its Buffalo Mining division; Dasovich was superintendent of the tipple. The water was rising behind the newest of the three dams. A federal mine inspector had driven past on the previous day and recalled later that the water seemed to be about 15 feet below the top; now it was within five or six feet. According to the Bureau of Mines report, Kent and Dasovich "agreed that neither the dam nor the rising water presented danger of collapse or flooding at that time." The report makes clear that they were concerned only with the possibility of water overflowing the dam; they seem to have been untroubled by the possibility that the dam might simply give way, even though it was settling visibly in places—and even though part of it had given way almost exactly a year earlier during the rains of February, 1971. (It had been under construction then, with not much water backed up behind it, and there was little damage.) Kent stuck a measuring stick into the sludgy surface of the dam, with the top of the stick about a foot below the top of the dam. It was raining; Dasovich and Kent decided to keep an eye on things.

Kent was back at the dam 24 hours later to check his measuring stick. The water was up about a foot and a half. Rain was still falling. Kent, who lives in an imposing home a few miles below the dam, decided to start checking the water level every two hours. He found that it was rising about an inch an hour. At 3:30 a.m.

on February 26, peering at the stick with the aid of a flashlight, Kent saw to his alarm that the water was rising faster—two inches an hour, maybe more. An hour later the level was up three inches more and the measuring stick was almost covered. Kent telephoned Dasovich and asked him to come take a look. By the time Dasovich arrived the stick had disappeared entirely and the water was only about a foot below the top of the dam.

According to the Bureau of Mines investigators, Dasovich decided to cut a ditch across the dam; he had some drainage pipe on hand and intended to use it to relieve the pressure. He called some of Jack Kent's strip-mine bulldozer operators at home and told them to go to the stripping operation—some three or four miles away—and bring their machines to the dam. Kent, meanwhile, made some calls, too; "he telephoned several families in the Lorado and Saunders area after his 4:30 a.m. examination," Bureau investigators reported, "and advised them of the rising water and the possibility of the dam overflowing." Three hours before the dam broke, in other words, the disaster had been foreseen by someone in a position to do something about it. A telephone call to the state police—who could have traveled the entire length of Buffalo Creek by 7 a.m., ordering a general evacuation—might have saved more than a hundred lives. But the call was never made. And the drainage ditch was never dug, because the dam had given way before the bulldozers arrived.

Walking in Soup

You can find Jack Kent at home—his house is on high ground and survived the flood untouched—but he doesn't like to talk to reporters. His eyes tell everything; there is no need for words. Dasovich seems to have disappeared entirely—he was in a nearby hospital after the flood, being treated for shock, and nurses said later that he was hysterical, blaming himself for the tragedy. Still later he was reported to have been admitted to a private psychiatric clinic—still later, released. The federal investigators have not yet talked to him and some of them, knowing now what they do about the dam, see no need. "He knows what was up there," one of them said. "He'll *always* know what was up there."

Other men knew, too. In the community of Saunders there was general concern about the safety of the dam, and on the night of February 25, most of the families who lived nearby decided, on their own, to take refuge in a schoolhouse five miles down the creek at Lorado. The decision saved their lives; the schoolhouse survived the flood, but when the families returned to Saunders to look for their homes, there was nothing to be found. No homes, not even the foundations;

everything was gone, everything except an appalling sea of slowly settling, black, foul-smelling sludge.

Off and on during the night, in the last few hours before the dam broke, miners went up to have a look at it—there were rumors spreading that it was going to go, but no one really seemed to know. Dasovich reportedly was telling people that things were under control. About 6:30 a.m., according to the federal reports, a miner saw ominous signs of what was coming. "The dam was moving like a bridge moves under heavy traffic," he remembered later. "Water was coming through the dam. . . not much, but it was causing the lower lake to fill up fast." By 7:30, according to another eyewitness account, "the top of the dam was moving back and forth. . . the dam was settling down and shoving forward." Trying to walk anywhere in the vicinity of the dam was "like walking in soup—it had gotten real, real juicy, buddy, all the way down. I got in the car and got the hell out of there."

The top of the dam was lower on one side than on the other, apparently from foundation settling, and now the top was slumping still further, with a momentum that could not have been stopped by an army of bulldozers. One of the several federal reports theorizes that the water level rose quickly during the night, not just because rain was falling, but because the dam had been collapsing slowly into the lake for several hours. But even while the rain continued, the tipple went on pumping its 500 gallons a minute into the sludgy lake behind the dam.

30-Foot Flood

Whatever happened in the night, it was morning now, and there was enough light to see what was happening. Apparently no one saw the actual moment when the dam finally gave way. It seems to have happened very fast, the dam settling until water was running across the top, the water cutting a cleft into the dam, more water hurrying through, and then complete and total collapse, and millions of gallons of water and hundreds of thousands of tons of sludge streaming across the top of the slag pile at the beginning of catastrophe.

The water cascaded into the burning section of the slag heap and erupted in a volcanic explosion. Men were coming off shift at the tipple and saw what was happening; they saw a mushroom cloud burst into the air from the explosion, saw mud and rock thrown 300 feet into the sky, saw the windshields of their pick-up trucks covered with steaming mud. They raced back up the road and tried to use the telephone at the tipple to send out a warning, but the line was already dead. The tipple was safe—it was upstream, up another fork of the creek, out of the path of the destruction—but the men were cut off from the main stream of Buffalo Creek and there was no way they could help anyone. They could only watch as the water and sludge crested over the top of the exploding gob pile and burst into the valley, "boiling up like dry flour when you pour water on it."

The flood traveled at first at a speed of at least 30 miles an hour—in a solid wall 20 or 30 feet high. People who saw it coming as they headed up the Buffalo Creek road barely had time to throw their cars into reverse, turn around wherever there was room, and head back downstream, leaning on their horns, flashing their lights, trying to warn other people who had heard the explosions but still did not know what was happening. There was very little time to do anything. It takes a few seconds to collect your wits when you see a wall of water bearing down on you, especially when you live in a valley where there are only a few exits—hollows running at right angles to the main valley. For most of the people who died, it was like being in the barrel of a gun and seeing the bullet coming. There was nowhere to go.

That so many people did escape is something of a miracle. Nearly 5,000 people lived in the path of the flood. Probably a thousand were caught up in it, battered, left shaken and sometimes badly hurt, but alive. From the wreckage of 16 communities, the bodies of 118 people have been found. There are others still missing; the final toll may be close to 150.

The Only Life They Knew

What happens after a disaster of such magnitude? There are inquiries, of course, and inquiries are under way in West Virginia. But in Appalachian affairs, the official response tends to have a common theme. After the Farmington mine disaster killed 78 miners, it was an Interior Department assistant secretary who said brightly: "We don't know why these things happen, but they do." After the 1970 mine explosion that killed 38 men in Kentucky, it was a newly installed director of the Bureau of Mines who said: "We can almost expect one of these every year." While the search for bodies was still continuing in Logan County, West Virginia's Governor Arch Moore was already defending the Pittston Company: the sludge-built dam had served a "logical and constructive" use by filtering mine wastes that would otherwise have gone unfiltered into Buffalo Creek. It didn't seem to matter much how the thing was built. The state legislature chose not to investigate, instead, leaving to the governor the selection of an official commission which would be told to report back by the end of summer. "It's easy to say that the dam shouldn't have been there," Moore said at one point. "But it had been there for 25 years." He was technically wrong, of course, but the inference seemed to be that if a hazard simply exists long enough, it has a right to be left alone. And by the same token, the Governor made it painfully clear that he would ask the same treatment for the problems of West Virginia. The real tragedy, he said, a tragedy greater even than what had befallen the people of Buffalo Creek, was the unflattering coverage of West Virginia in the national press.

In fact there had been precious little of that. The flood had been on page one for two or three days, but it was eclipsed by the President's tour through China (from Shanghai, where he learned of the flood, Nixon sent an expression of regret, concluding from a distance of many thousands of miles that it was a terrible "natural disaster" and promising speedy federal aid), and within a week it would be forgotten, dismissed as one of those things—*Time*, for example, observed that the people of Buffalo Creek would have been well-advised to live elsewhere, but that they had stayed on in the shadow of the smouldering gob pile presumably because "that was the only life they knew."

Passing the Buck to God

The Interior Department, meanwhile, explained through Assistant Secretary Hollis Dole that there was, in its opinion, no federal responsibility in the matter, despite the fact that regulations within the 1969 Federal Coal Mine Health and Safety Act specifically cover the construction and use of gob piles and retaining dams. There were no indications that the government would move to take action against Pittston, unless it was prodded by an outraged Congress; on Capitol Hill there was no outraged Congress to be found.

There would be room for doubt, in any event, about the kind of action that Interior would take even if it were forced to do something. The Department is reluctant to think of itself as a regulatory agency, or as a federal cop, and among all of the subordinate agencies within Interior, the Bureau of Mines is a standout example of one that has refused to grasp the idea of representing the public interest. The problem might not be serious if a system of countervailing power were in operation—if, for example, the people of Buffalo Creek could have counted on the United Mine Workers to represent them against the overwhelming resources and indifference of the Pittston Company. There had been scattered efforts along Buffalo Creek to protest against the slag heaps and the sludge dams—petitions had been circulated, attention had been demanded. But the effort never went anywhere, and it never went anywhere partly because no powerful organization—like the union—chose to push it. The union hasn't pushed much of anything in some time, except perhaps the fringe benefits available to its ranking officers. The result is that on one side of the equation there is a powerful industry deeply dedicated to its own interests; on the other side there is, most of the time, nothing at all. And in the middle, where there should be an even-handed government agency, there is instead the Bureau of Mines, an organization so encrusted with age and bureaucracy that it will not even support its own inspectors when they try to do their jobs.

They had, for example, been trying to do their jobs at Pittston's mines, trying to cut down the number of men killed in needless accidents. Over the past year they had slapped thousands of violation notices on the company. The idea is that the notices will cost money; get fined often enough and hard enough, the theory goes, and you will become safety-conscious in the extreme. It hasn't worked that way. Thanks to a highly complex assessment system set up in Washington by a former lobbyist who is now in charge of the Bureau's fines-collection operation, Pittston has been able to defer, seemingly indefinitely, any payment for its sins. Specifically, over the past year inspectors had fined Pittston a total of $1,303,315 for safety violations. As of April 1, the company had appealed every one of the notices it had received, and had paid a grand total of

$275 to the government.

Meanwhile, on Buffalo Creek, the investigations continue, the reports are compiled, the survivors try to plan a future; the mines, only briefly disrupted by the raging flood, are back at work, and the long trains roll. One month after the disaster, Pittston set up an office to process claims—without, however, accepting liability. The company's official view is still that God did it—and if, by any chance, God should pass the buck back down, "we believe that the investigations of the tragedy have not progressed to the point where it is possible to assess responsibility." It's possible that such a point will never be reached. Who was responsible, for example, for deciding to spend $90,000 to buy Nicholas Camicia's house, but *not* to spend the $50,000 that it might have cost—according to one of the federal reports—to build a safe dam at the head of Buffalo Creek? There are sticky questions like that rising in the aftermath of the disaster, questions that will be hard to answer. "There is never peace in West Virginia because there is never justice," said Mother Jones, the fiery hell-raiser of West Virginia's early labor wars. On Buffalo Creek these days there is a strange kind of quiet, a peacefulness of sorts, but it is not the kind that comes with justice. □

The Pittston Mentality

Page 28

OTHER PUBLICATIONS NOW AVAILABLE

oughts of Mother Jones, edited by Jim Axelrod	10¢
:king Povertys Pocket, by Barkan & Lloyd	20¢
st Virginia Wonderland, by Bill Blizzard	15¢
at's Next?, by Ernest Seeman	75¢
ıspiracy in Coal, by Tom Bethell	20¢
: Hillbillys, by Harless and Cutler	35¢
: Socialist and Labor Star, by David Corbin	$1.00
ıhilating the Hillbilly, by Jim Branscome	15¢
: West Virginia Establishment, by Rod Harless	$1.00
: Appalachian Struggle, Past & Present, 1972 Calendar	50¢
nphlets by Don West:	
nantic Appalachia,	25¢
Time For Anger, a collection of poems	25¢
ople's Cultural Heritage in Appalachia	15¢
ert Tharin, Biography of a Mountain Abolitionist	30¢
thern Mountain Folk Tradition	20¢
g pamphlets available:	
nt Creek Miner, Labor Songs From Appalachia, by Patterson	25¢
gs of Freedom, Labor Songs From Appalachia, Part II	25¢
: IWW Songbook	40¢
ent additions:	
en Southern Labor Stirs, by Tom Tippett	
Part I, Introduction	50¢
Part II, Elizabethton	25¢
Part III, Gastonia	35¢
Part IV, Marion	40¢
All 4 parts	$1.25
West Virginia Miners Union, 1931 from Labor Age	25¢
lan and Bell, Kentucky, 1931-2, the National Miners Union from Labor Defender	40¢
l Miners Struggle in Eastern Kentucky by Paul Nyden, with a comment by Rich Kirby	25¢
Pittston Mentality: Manslaughter on Buffalo Creek by Tom Bethell and Davitt McAteer	25¢
available from Charles Kerr, publishers:	
Autobiography of Mother Jones	$2.25

When ordering please include money for postage:
20% on orders less than $5.00
15% from $5-10; and 10% over $10
Bulk rates available on request.
Mail to: AMP, Box 8074, Huntington, West Virginia 25705

The Pittston Mentality

Back Cover

Epilogue

In early May 2017, after I had begun to exhaust some of my initial online research about Appalachian Movement Press, I traveled back down to the West's Appalachian South Folklife Center to poke around. At that time I had some idea about Don and Connie West, I had Tom Woodruff's and Danie Stewart's names, and I knew that the offset presses had ended up at the ASFC in 1979. I spent a few days there, exploring the grounds on my own, meeting people as they passed through, and searching for clues and rusty printing equipment.

I slept in a tent those nights, and since there was a consistent prevailing wind combing over the hills that weekend, I pitched it to the east side of the small wooden library cabin. I hoped that the structure, full of yellowing, somewhat disorganized children's books, pulp novels, books on communism and socialism, and boxes of 1970s and 1980s periodicals could do an extra duty as a windbreak.

The first night I was there, I slept restlessly, and I woke in the morning from a particularly vivid dream. In it, I was in the main cafeteria hall at ASFC in the midst of an event: the hall was crowded and lively with maybe a hundred people socializing. Don West was there—he was much older than me, very tall, wearing a large cowboy hat that seemed a bit exaggerated. Basically, he looked like almost every photo I had seen of him. I was fascinated by his presence, and I was also intimidated. Someone I was friendly with insisted on making an introduction, interrupting a small group over which West was holding court.

"Don, this is Shaun. He's from Pittsburgh. He's trying to find out more about the Appalachian Movement Press so he can write something about them." West listened patiently while I tried to explain my

Reimagined AMP logo by artist Emily Prentice, 2019.

research. But I noticed that, as he was standing, he never really fully turned to regard me. I don't recall the exact words of his response. He was polite, but he gave me to understand that he wasn't going to bother with being impressed with my intentions until, if ever, he was presented with something meaningful, something *useful*, from whatever it was that I was up to. And then he turned back to the people he had been busy captivating.

I end this book with this dream partly to give you a funny window into my own quiet anxieties about research, history-telling, and my personal place in that process. But I also believe that the scene that my subconscious crafted is more or less what would have *actually* happened if that encounter with Don West had occurred in my waking life, in that cafeteria hall that I was sleeping nearby. I didn't know it at the time, but the character of Don West that my mind had conjured might not have been too far off the mark. If nothing else, it's concurrent with what Tom Woodruff would later paraphrase as West's first dismissive response to Danie Stewart's and his pitch about the idealistic printshop they were starting: "You're probably not serious, and you'll probably do more harm than good." I never had the pleasure of meeting Don West, as he passed away in 1992, before I knew his name.

But self-effacing humor aside, I still think often about the message underneath Don West's impatience in that dream, which was something like, "Do well by the history, because most people won't." It's an abrupt directive, and it's also the earnest, humbling request that everyone working in the research and sharing of people's history should abide by. Don West was telling me to listen and to take the time. He knew that Appalachia is a region from which many, many people have taken so much and that most of them have left very little in return. With this book, then, I leave a bit more than I have perhaps taken.

Acknowledgments

My name is featured on the front of this book, and yet the creation of volumes like this one requires a lot of cooperation between people. I used to say that I was a "self-taught historian," but now I think it's much more accurate to say that I am "community taught," because there's always someone who I can turn to.

Many of the people who made AMP what it was were happy to speak and write to me about it, at least what they could remember. I've included their stories, memories, and fragments with everything else that I could glean from reading the materials I could recover from both collectors and wet basements.

I worked to blend all of the parts of this story together while being fair to the discrepancies, contradictions, and gaps that I just couldn't fill. I've been critical where I thought it due, with respect to the challenges, conditions, and context that the people at the press experienced in their time. I've let them speak with their own voices and guide my work through listening.

So, thank you to everyone that I interviewed. Each of these people were (more or less) comfortable with me contacting them out of nowhere to discuss, in great detail, the work that they'd been doing forty and fifty years ago: Thank you, Tom Woodruff, Paul Salstrom, Miriam Ralston, John Strong Clark, Michael J. Clark, Margaret Gregg, Barbara Ervin Placier, and Errol Hess. Yvonne Farley and George Brosi, while not directly involved with AMP, were deeply important in providing additional context and firsthand accounts of the movements that AMP was integral to. Greg Carannante and Michael Fanning, who created and worked on *Mountain Call*, were also gracious with their time, as were Davitt McAteer and Jim Branscome.

Special thanks are due to Jonathon Averill, Jon Hennan, Roger May, Dr. Lou Martin, and Dr. Chuck Keeney, who all provided help that was critical bringing parts of this research into focus. I am deeply grateful to my friends Josh MacPhee, Alec "Icky" Dunn, and Craig O'Hara, who believed in my sleuthing and writing capabilities and pushed me to do the original research that led to the article I wrote for *Signal: A Journal of International Political Graphics and Culture* (PM Press) in 2017, work which has since metastasized into this book through the support and guidance of Derek Krissoff at WVU Press.

Many, many thanks to my friends in the West Virginia Mine Wars Museum for bringing me earnestly into the world of Appalachian history and welcoming me as a many-hat-wearing storyteller. Barbara Ellen Smith, on our museum board, was instrumental in finding contact information for some of the people that I could not locate.

Librarians are our history keepers! I owe a lot to the help of Jessica Eichlin and Lemley Mullett at the West Virginia Regional and History Center at West Virginia University. Thanks also to Jeremy A. Smith at East Tennessee State University and to Lindsey M. Harper and Lori Thompson at Marshall University Libraries.

Lastly, I'm reserving my deepest gratitude for my partner in love and in life, Becca Susman. It takes a lot of obsessive energy to research and write about something that nobody else has ever bothered to look for, and it takes a lot of understanding and patience to live with someone who has buried themselves in that work. Thank you for walking this road by my side and for all of your advice and real encouragement, even in the times when you thought that this was some pretty boring stuff. I'll always be your biggest fan.

Perhaps because so much of their work was focused on reprinting existing works for broader distribution, Appalachian Movement Press hasn't received much, if any, attention until now. Occasionally collectors can be found selling their publications at conferences and online. The

Appalachian South Folklife Center has multitudes of AMP's work in nonarchival storage, nearly forgotten remainders from when Mountain Freedom Press ceased operations. Selections of publications are available in only a handful of university libraries, but typically they are not collected as the output of AMP itself. These collections include West Virginia University, Marshall University (WV), Appalachian State University (NC), East Tennessee State University, Radford University (VA), and Ohio University in Athens. A small collection has been donated to the Interference Archive (NY) by both myself and the Appalachian South Folklife Center through the process of my research for this book.

Appendix

An Appalachian Movement Press Bibliography

1970

Paint Creek Miner: Famous Labor Songs from Appalachia, Charles Patterson, introduction by Tom Woodruff (fourth printing September 1972, 20 pages)
Thoughts of Mother Jones: Compiled from Her Writings and Speeches, edited by Jim Axelrod, introduction by Agnew R. Thomas, conclusion by Robert Edwards (10 pages)
A Time for Anger, Don West (multiple printings, 22 pages)
West Virginia Wonderland, William C. Blizzard (second printing September 1974, 23 pages)
What's Next? Ernest Seeman (67 pages)

1971

Annihilating the Hillbilly, Jim Branscome (17 pages)
People's Cultural Heritage in Appalachia, Don West (12 pages)
Picking Poverty's Pocket, Barry Barkan and R. Baldwin Lloyd (10 pages)

Robert Tharin: Biography of a Mountain Abolitionist, Don West (28 pages)
The Socialist and Labor Star, Huntington W. Va 1912–1915, David Alan Corbin (71 pages)
West Virginia Establishment, Rod Harless (101 pages)

1972

The Coal Miner's Struggle in Eastern Kentucky, Paul Nyden and Rich Kirby (28 pages)
Harlan & Bell Kentucky, 1931–32: The National Miner's Union, various authors (30 pages)
Il Manifesto, Ludo Abicht, Ludo Abicht, translated by Errol Hess (28 pages)
The Pittston Mentality: Manslaughter on Buffalo Creek, Tom Bethell and Davitt McAteer (27 pages)
The Shame That Is Kentucky's! The Story of the Harlan Mine War, Edward J. Costello (28 pages)
War in the Coal Fields: The Northern Fields 1931, various authors (14 pages)
The West Virginia Miner's Union 1931, Tom Tippett and A. J. Muste (20 pages)
When Southern Labor Stirs, part one, Tom Tippett (reprinted in 1978, 53 pages)
When Southern Labor Stirs, part two (Strike at Elizabethtown), Tom Tippett (reprinted in 1978, 24 pages)
When Southern Labor Stirs, part three (Strike at Gastonia), Tom Tippett (reprinted in 1978, 36 pages)
When Southern Labor Stirs, part four (Strike at Marion), Tom Tippett (reprinted in 1978, 48 pages)

1973

Coal Creek Rebellion: East Tennessee Miners v. Convict Labor System, Philip Foner and Archie Green (32 pages)
Fighting for Survival: The Bootleg Coal Industry, Paul Mattick and Louis Adamic (42 pages)
Freedom on the Mountains, Don West (28 pages)
Lazar & Boone Stop Strip Mining Bully to Save Apple Valley & Buttermilk Creek, Michael J. Clark and Margaret Gregg (24 pages)
Songs for Southern Workers: 1937 Songbook of the Kentucky Workers Alliance, Don West (24 pages)

1974

Look Out—There's a Profit in Your Appendix! Mountain Messenger/no author listed (12 pages)

1979, AS MOUNTAIN FREEDOM PRESS

Gospel Millions, Jim Haught (54 pages)

UNDATED PUBLICATIONS

Conspiracy in Coal, Tom N. Bethell (36 pages)
The Federal Government in Appalachia, Jim Branscome (43 pages)
Freedom and Slavery in Appalachian America, Dr. Carter G. Woodson (20 pages)
The Hillbillys: A Book for Children, Rod Harless and Dan Cutler (38 pages)
Miseducation in Appalachia, Jim Branscome, Mike Clark, and Bob Snyder (46 pages)
Romantic Appalachia, or, Poverty Pays If You Ain't Poor, Don West (6 pages)
Songs of Freedom: Famous Labor Songs from Appalachia Part II, Edith Fowle and Joe Glazer (16 pages)
Southern Mountain Folk Traditions and the Folksong "Stars" Syndrome, Don West (20 pages)
The Threat of Western Coal, David Green (9 pages)

KNOWN PRINTING JOBS

Green Revolution, periodical, 1975–77
Life of Reverend John Rankin, Written by Himself in His 80th Year, book contract with Lawrence County (Ohio) Historical Society, 1977
MAW: Magazine of Appalachian Women, periodical, 1977–78
The Mountain Call, periodical, 1974–78
Mountain Life & Work, periodical, 1970–?
No Willows for the Zen Cowboy, Tom W. Gibbs, 1977
Soupbean: An Anthology of Contemporary Appalachian Literature, various authors, 1977
West Virginia Green Part 1, Jack Frazier as Solar Age Press, 1976 (62 pages)

SHOPPED-OUT PUBLICATIONS

O Mountaineers! Don West, 1974 (hardback and paperback, 242 pages)

Notes

INTRODUCTION. A BRIEF HISTORY OF THE MOVEMENT PRINTSHOP IN THE UNITED STATES

1. There is no official count of movement printshops, but Lincoln Cushing's inclusive count of Bay Area shops includes twenty-five printing with offset presses—and just in this small geographic area. It is most likely that closer to three hundred shops were started between 1965 and 1985, but until someone attempts to do a real accounting, "over two hundred" seems a fair number.
2. Cushing, "Red in Black and White."
3. MacPhee, "Survival by Sharing," 81.
4. Barbara Ervin Placier, interview by Shaun Slifer via telephone, January 23, 2020.
5. Cushing and Inkworks Press, eds., *Visions of Peace and Justice*, 8.
6. Aubert, *The Detroit Printing Co-op*, 15–16.
7. MacPhee, *Liberation Support Movement*, 5.
8. MacPhee, "Survival by Sharing," 84.
9. Lincoln Cushing, "Directory of San Francisco Bay Area Political Poster Workshops, Print Shops, and Distributors," Docs Populi, last modified January 7, 2017, http://www.docspopuli.org/articles/BayAreaRadicalShops.html.
10. Cushing, "Red in Black and White."
11. Cushing and Inkworks Press, eds., *Visions of Peace and Justice*, 9.
12. Ross Newport, email exchange with author, July 5, 2019.
13. Pat Gleason, email exchange with author, January 17, 2020.

PART I. THE PRESS

1. John Hennen, "Struggle for Recognition: The Marshall University Students for a Democratic Society and the Red Scare in Huntington, 1965–1969," *West Virginia History* 52 (1993): 127–47.
2. Errol Hess, interview by author via telephone, January 23, 2020.
3. I've only seen one issue of *Free Forum* from this time period: vol.1, no.1, March 1966, preserved at the Marshall University Libraries. Thus, it's not

clear to me what the longer arc of the publication was throughout the Huntington SDS struggle, but presumably it stood as an organ for SDS and a thorn in the side of the more conservative elements of Huntington. A single issue of the satirical *Eerf Murof!* (vol. 1, no. 1) is also archived alongside this paper, as is *Free Forum* 4, no. 1, from two decades later in September of 1987.

4. Tom Woodruff, interview by author via telephone, September 6, 2019.
5. Just as immediately, the student activists' efforts spawned at least one issue of *Eerf Murof!*, a confrontational mimeographed page-by-page satire of *Free Forum*, which was also anonymous.
6. Stanley, "Appalachian Movement Press," 30–33.
7. Appalachian Regional Commission, "The Appalachian Region."
8. Lorence, *A Hard Journey*, 200.
9. George Brosi, interview by author via telephone, February 14, 2019.
10. Tom Woodruff, interview by author via telephone, July 9, 2017.
11. James Branscome, interview by author via telephone, February 12, 2019.
12. Tom Woodruff, interview by author via telephone, September 6, 2019.
13. Stanley, "Appalachian Movement Press," 30–33.
14. Tom Woodruff, interview by author via telephone, September 6, 2019.
15. John Strong Clark, interview by author via telephone, June 2, 2017.
16. Stanley, "Appalachian Movement Press," 30–33.
17. Stanley, "Appalachian Movement Press," 30–33.
18. Barbara Ervin Placier, interview by author via telephone, January 23, 2020.
19. Stanley, "Appalachian Movement Press," 30–33; Errol Hess, interview by author via telephone, January 23, 2020.
20. Stanley, "Appalachian Movement Press."
21. Errol Hess, interview by author via telephone, January 23, 2020.
22. In doing the research for this book, my difficulty in finding women who had been involved with the printshop seemed to reflect the atmosphere of AMP generally. When some men I interviewed would recall women working there, they were often remembered as someone's girlfriend or wife: roles that attached them to a man who was remembered, rather than to a skill they contributed to the printshop. I want to be careful to draw full conclusions, because it's also true that there were men and women that I reached out to for interviews who chose not to speak with me, and perhaps their memories would have built a more thorough story. Still, my intuition is that the omission of women from memory is a mirror of their omission from critical roles in the shop for most of its existence, and the words of the few women I spoke with support that idea.
23. Barbara Ervin Placier, interview by author via telephone, January 23, 2020.
24. Stanley, "Appalachian Movement Press," 30–33.
25. Tom Woodruff, interview by author via telephone, July 9, 2017.
26. Stanley, "Appalachian Movement Press," 30–33.

27. Stanley, "Appalachian Movement Press," 30–33.
28. Stanley, "Appalachian Movement Press," 30–33.
29. Tom Woodruff, interview by author via telephone, July 9, 2017.
30. Stanley, "Appalachian Movement Press," 30–33; Paul Salstrom, interview by author via telephone, September 3, 2017.
31. Critical to the internal colony idea is not only the outside industrial forces of resource extraction but the collusion of wealthy regional elites with those extractive forces. This kind of cooperation is fundamental to any colonial project, and many AMP readers would have been familiar with local and regional corruption that could have mirrored it. In "The Case for Appalachian Studies" (1974), for example, Jim Branscome details the decades of corruption in the Turner family's nepotistic hold upon the politics of Breathitt County, Kentucky. As he explains, the Turners' power had much to do with their ability to access and divert federal education funding streams into their own projects and pockets instead of to the schools in their community, to the generational detriment of the local population. With the county school district as the largest employer, and kinship and loyal voting records key to employment eligibility, residents became stuck in a cycle with no clear path out. "As always, justice is elusive," Branscome writes. "Appalachians still have no voice in the affairs of their region."
32. Walls, "Internal Colony or Internal Periphery?" 351–64.
33. Walls, "Internal Colony or Internal Periphery?" 351–64.
34. Walls, "Internal Colony or Internal Periphery?" 351–64.
35. Stanley, "Appalachian Movement Press," 30–33.
36. Penland, "The Invisible Populous of Appalachia."
37. Knollinger, "Wild, Wondering West Virginia"; Penland, "The Invisible Populous of Appalachia."
38. It was Allen Batteau who coined the term "Holy Appalachia" to describe this mythology of an untouched population of white settlers in Appalachia, which he extended to include the abolitionist history of the region and the persistent idea that the mountains were always a bastion of antiracist culture. The term "Idyllic Holler" is my own, a specific locale within Holy Appalachia that is replicated indefinitely through story.
39. Knollinger, "Wild, Wondering West Virginia."
40. Yvonne Farley, interview by author via telephone, March 25, 2019.
41. Catte, *What You Are Getting Wrong about Appalachia*, 11.
42. If place is a significant element of identity, then migration from that place can sometimes help intensify the relationship to it. A particularly legible, historical example of Appalachian identity for a reader positioned outside the region might be the activists of the Young Patriots Organization (YPO), active from the late 1960s through 1972. The YPO was comprised of working-class white Appalachians living in diaspora in Chicago, surviving in urban poverty with dwindling resources in the Uptown area of Daley's Windy City. They were what some might call

migrants and what Branscome would correct to "economic refugees." The Patriots organized from a combination of the mutual aid networks of Uptown street gangs and local SDS affiliates into a radical politicized organization. Although they experienced their oppression as Appalachian whites in an urban environment, they began working alongside the Young Lords, the Black Panthers, and Rising Up Angry as part of Chicago's original Rainbow Coalition. The Patriots took seriously the Panthers' call to "organize your own," and they organized other white Appalachians to participate in building a movement across the racial lines that otherwise typically divided working-class people.

For a short time, the Young Patriots were distinctive for having chosen Confederate flags as an early emblem of unity, in a punk spirit of transgressive costuming, which was largely meant to horrify middle-class Chicagoans. "We Are All Slaves in the Eyes of the Man," one broadsheet reads, under a drawing of the flag. Use of the symbol was eventually abandoned when it turned out to also horrify a lot of other radicals, particularly those who were not white, but some seemingly incongruent photos remain. For a history of the YPO, see Amy Sonnie and James Tracy, *Hillbilly Nationalists, Urban Race Rebels, and Black Power* (Brooklyn, NY: Melville House, 2011).

43. "Affrilachian" as a term for African Americans who identify as Appalachian is attributed to the Kentucky-born African American poet and scholar Frank X. Walker.
44. Yvonne Farley, interview by author via telephone, March 25, 2019.
45. Smith, "De-Gradations of Whiteness," 38–57.
46. Walls, "Internal Colony or Internal Periphery?" 351–64.
47. Catte, *What You Are Getting Wrong about Appalachia*.
48. Tom Woodruff, interview by author via telephone, September 6, 2019.
49. John Strong Clark, interview by author via telephone, June 2, 2017.
50. Tom Woodruff, interview by author via telephone, September 6, 2019.
51. Corbin's essay "*The Socialist and Labor Star*: The Harassment of Heresy" appears in Corbin, ed., *Gun Thugs, Rednecks, and Radicals*, 217–48.
52. Howard B. Lee's *Bloodletting in Appalachia* was published in 1969 but maintains some of the level of anti-union perspective that would have been common in other published accounts up to that point. Corbin's book brought an academic approach and a fresh viewpoint that focused on working-class life and human rights in the coalfields. This was followed in 1991 by Lon Savage's *Thunder on the Mountains*, both of which began to pave the way for a broader understanding of the West Virginia Mine Wars era.
53. Tom Woodruff, interview by author via telephone, September 6, 2019.
54. John Strong Clark, interview by author via telephone, June 2, 2017.
55. Find a Grave, "Roderick Mansfield 'Rod' Harless."
56. Tom Woodruff, interview by author via telephone, July 9, 2017.
57. Lorence, *A Hard Journey*, 54.

58. Lorence, *A Hard Journey*, 198.
59. Tom Woodruff, interview by author via telephone, July 9, 2017.
60. Tom Woodruff, foreword to *A Time for Anger*, by Don West.
61. Lorence, *A Hard Journey*, 198.
62. Yvonne Farley, interview by author via telephone, March 25, 2019.
63. Lorence, *A Hard Journey*, 27–36.
64. George Brosi, interview by author via telephone, February 14, 2019.
65. Lorence, *A Hard Journey*, 27–36.
66. The Donald Lee West FBI files are available online from the Internet Archive: https://archive.org/details/foia_West_Donald_L.-Pittsburgh-3/page/n399/mode/2up.
67. Federal Bureau of Investigation, Report on Donald Lee West, 403.
68. Carannante and Fanning, "Mountaineer of the Month: Don West," 3–8.
69. Lorence, *A Hard Journey*, 19–21.
70. Lorence, *A Hard Journey*, 228.
71. Don West, "Jesus the Quiet Revolutionary," in *No Lonesome Road: Selected Poems and Prose*, eds. Jeff Biggers and George Brosi (Urbana: University of Illinois Press, 2004), 63–65.
72. Lorence, *A Hard Journey*, 206–7.
73. Jeff Biggers, introduction to *No Lonesome Road,* by Don West, xxviii (italics are my own).
74. Yvonne Farley, interview by author via telephone, March 25, 2019.
75. *Freedom on the Mountains* is reprinted in full in this book.
76. Yvonne Farley, interview by author via telephone, March 25, 2019.
77. Lorence, *A Hard Journey*.
78. Carannante and Fanning, "Mountaineer of the Month: Don West."
79. George Brosi, interview by author via telephone, February 14, 2019.
80. Tom Woodruff, interview by author via telephone, July 9, 2017.
81. Tom Woodruff, interview by author via telephone, September 6, 2019.
82. Thomas Gibbs in email to Paul Salstrom, forwarded by Salstrom to author, February 6, 2018.
83. Michael Toothman, email with author, February 8, 2020.
84. John Strong Clark, interview by author via telephone, June 2, 2017.
85. Tom Woodruff, interview by author via telephone, September 6, 2019.
86. Paul Salstrom, email with author, February 23, 2019.
87. Since 1863, the state motto of West Virginia has been "*Montani Semper Liberi*," popularly translated from the Latin as "Mountaineers are always free." The editors of the *Mountain Call* were thus proclaiming that "Mountaineers are always well read."
88. Moize, "Turnaround Time in West Virginia," 774.
89. Greg Carannante, interview by author via telephone, August 13, 2019; Michael Fanning, interview by author via telephone, August 22, 2019; Michael Fanning, "John A. Sheppard Memorial Ecological Reservation (JASMER): Its Mission and Purpose," Big Laurel Learning Center, accessed 2017, https://www.biglaurel.org/jasmer.

90. Greg Carannante, interview by author via telephone, August 13, 2019.
91. Greg Carannante, interview by author via telephone, August 13, 2019.
92. Greg Carannante, interview by author via telephone, August 13, 2019; Michael Fanning, interview by author via telephone, August 22, 2019.
93. Greg Carannante, interview by author via telephone, August 13, 2019.
94. Greg Carannante, interview by author via telephone, August 13, 2019.
95. Greg Carannante, interview by author via telephone, August 13, 2019; a June 1976 *National Geographic* feature on West Virginia (vol. 149, no. 6, p. 774) highlights a visit to Marrowbone Ridge and the *Mountain Call* but primarily addresses the author's fascination with their difficulty in driving to the Knob.
96. Franklin, "An Oasis in Appalachia."
97. Goebel, "Jim Webb."
98. "Little Old Lady Is Tougher than Strip Miners," *Hutchinson News*, 23.
99. Paul Salstrom, interview by author via telephone, September 3, 2017.
100. Paul Salstrom, email with author, January 10, 2020.
101. Yvonne Farley, interview by author via telephone, March 25, 2019.
102. Paul Salstrom, email with author, August 2, 2019.
103. Salstrom, "The Neonatives."
104. Paul Salstrom, email with author, February 23, 2019; Douthat, "Magazine Reflects Strength of Women."
105. Paul Salstrom, email with author, February 23, 2019; Thomas Gibbs, email exchange with Paul Salstrom at unknown date 2018–19, forwarded to author August 16, 2019.
106. In many cases names could not be remembered by my interviewees, or the memories of people, events, or timing shifted in a less-than-reliable way. I've done my best to keep the threads consistent and, to the best of my understanding, true. Charlie Berry and Barbara Frazier proved elusive during the time I was writing this book.
107. Miriam Ralston, interview by author via telephone, March 14, 2019.
108. Yvonne Farley, interview by author via telephone, March 25, 2019.
109. Tom Woodruff, interview by author via telephone, September 6, 2019.
110. Yvonne Farley, interview by author via telephone, March 25, 2019.
111. Yvonne Farley, interview by author via telephone, March 25, 2019.
112. West Virginia International Women's Year Conference, Huntington, WV, June 22–23, 1977; Miriam Ralston, interview by author via telephone, March 14, 2019.
113. Montague, "A Need to Share."
114. Douthat, "Magazine Reflects Strength of Women."
115. Montague, "A Need to Share."
116. Miriam Ralston, email with author, February 20, 2019.
117. Paul Salstrom, email with author, February 23, 2019.
118. *MAW: Magazine of Appalachian Women*, no. 1 (Sept.–Oct. 1977): 3.
119. *MAW: Magazine of Appalachian Women*, no. 1 (Sept.–Oct. 1977): 3.
120. *MAW: Magazine of Appalachian Women*, no. 1 (Sept.–Oct. 1977): 1.

121. Miriam Ralston, email with author, February 20, 2019.
122. Miriam Ralston, interview by author via telephone, March 14, 2019.
123. Jack Frazier passed away in 2010 at seventy-six years old, before my research for this book began.
124. Miriam Ralston to Jeanne Hoffman, July 5, 1978, Box 25, Folder 7, General Correspondence Files, 1976–1981, Council on Appalachian Women (CAW) Records, Archives of Appalachia, East Tennessee State University, Johnson City, TN; John Strong Clark, interview by author via telephone, January 9, 2020.
125. John Strong Clark, interview by author via telephone, January 9, 2020; Paul Salstrom, email with author, February 23, 2019.
126. Miriam Ralston, interview by author via telephone, March 14, 2019.
127. Paul Salstrom, email with author, February 23, 2019.
128. Ralston, "Editorial," 4.
129. Miriam Ralston to Jeanne Hoffman, July 5, 1978, CAW Records.
130. Ralston, "Editorial," 4.
131. Miriam Ralston to Jeanne Hoffman, July 5, 1978, CAW Records.
132. Judy Gaines to Jeanne Hoffman, June 26, 1978, CAW Records.
133. Miriam Ralston to Jeanne Hoffman, July 5, 1978, CAW Records.
134. Paul Salstrom, email with author, February 23, 2019; Blevins, "The Council on Appalachian Women."
135. Yvonne Farley, email with author, August 25, 2019.
136. John Strong Clark, interview by author via telephone, January 9, 2020.
137. John Strong Clark, interview by author via telephone, June 2, 2017.
138. John Strong Clark, interview by author via telephone, June 2, 2017.
139. John Strong Clark, interview by author via telephone, January 9, 2020.
140. In my research, I was never able to ascertain whether the Alternative Energy Center had been any sort of entity beyond an address for Jack Frazier's roving residence.
141. John Strong Clark, interview by author via telephone, January 9, 2020.
142. John Strong Clark, interview by author via telephone, June 2, 2017.
143. Michael Fanning, interview by author via telephone, August 22, 2019.
144. Paul Salstrom, email with author, August 2, 2019.
145. John Strong Clark, interview by author via telephone, January 9, 2020.
146. Yvonne Farley, interview by author via telephone, March 25, 2019.
147. Change to Win, "About Us: Tom Woodruff."
148. John Strong Clark, interview by author via telephone, January 9, 2020.
149. Federal Bureau of Investigation, Report on Donald Lee West.
150. John Strong Clark, interview by author via telephone, January 9, 2020.
151. Yvonne Farley, interview by author via telephone, March 25, 2019.
152. Tom Woodruff, interview by author via telephone, July 9, 2017.

PART II. IN PRINT

1. James Branscome, interview by author via telephone, February 12, 2019.

2. James Branscome, interview by author via telephone, February 12, 2019.
3. James, "A Radical of Long Standing."
4. Lorence, *A Hard Journey: The Life of Don West*, 65–66.
5. Lorence, *A Hard Journey*.
6. Yvonne Farley, interview by author via telephone, March 25, 2019.
7. Margaret Gregg, interview by author via telephone, March 10, 2019; Michael J. Clark, interview by author via telephone, February 19, 2019.
8. Margaret Gregg, interview by author via telephone, March 10, 2019.
9. US Congress, House, Committee on Interior and Insular Affairs, Statement of Michael J. Clark, Church of the Brethren, Appalachian Caucus.
10. Montrie, *To Save the Land and People*, 156–63.
11. Farmer Caudill is named for Harry Caudill, a Kentucky lawyer and environmental activist. A decade before *Lazar & Boone* was published, Harry Caudill's public work in the 1960s was instrumental in bringing the horrors of strip mining in Appalachia to a national audience. Although Gregg and Clark would have understood Caudill in this context, by the mid-1970s, his frustration and disillusionment with the continuing poverty in Appalachia had led him to privately correspond, at least for a time, with proponents of dysgenics, which has cast a shadow over much of his later work.
12. Michael J. Clark, interview by author via telephone, February 19, 2019.
13. Michael J. Clark, interview by author via telephone, February 19, 2019.
14. George Brosi, interview by author via telephone, February 14, 2019.
15. George Brosi, interview by author via telephone, February 14, 2019.
16. For a more thorough critique of the historical deception that Appalachia was thoroughly abolitionist, see *Appalachia in the Making: The Mountain South in the Nineteenth Century*, edited by Mary Beth Pudup, Dwight B. Billings, and Altina L. Waller (Chapel Hill: University of North Carolina Press, 2000).
17. Citizens' Commission to Investigate the Buffalo Creek Disaster, *Disaster on Buffalo Creek*.
18. Thomas Bethell, "The Death of Buffalo Creek."
19. Pickering, dir., *The Buffalo Creek Flood*.
20. Bethell, "The Death of Buffalo Creek."
21. Davitt McAteer, interview by author via telephone, December 14, 2019.
22. Davitt McAteer, interview by author via telephone, December 14, 2019.
23. Davitt McAteer, interview by author via telephone, December 14, 2019.
24. Davitt McAteer, interview by author via telephone, December 14, 2019.
25. McCollester, *The Point of Pittsburgh*.
26. Hankins, "Alternative Appalachian Periodicals."
27. Davitt McAteer, interview by author via telephone, December 14, 2019.
28. Davitt McAteer, interview by author via telephone, December 14, 2019.

Bibliography

Appalachian Regional Commission. "The Appalachian Region." Accessed August 31, 2017. https://www.arc.gov/appalachian_region/TheAppalachianRegion.asp.

Aubert, Danielle. *The Detroit Printing Co-op: The Politics of the Joy of Printing*. Los Angeles: Inventory Press, 2019.

Bethell, Thomas. "The Death of Buffalo Creek." *Coal Patrol*, no. 21 (March 1, 1972).

Bethell, Thomas. "Pittston: The Arrogance of Power." *Coal Patrol*, no. 22 (April 24, 1972).

Blevins, Julie Marie. "The Council on Appalachian Women: Short Lived but Long Lasting." Master's thesis, East Tennessee State University, 2012. https://dc.etsu.edu/etd/1493/.

Carannante, Greg, and Michael Fanning. "Mountaineer of the Month: Don West—Voice of Appalachia, Man of Dignity." *Mountain Call*, no. 7 (June 1974): 3–8.

Catte, Elizabeth. *What You Are Getting Wrong about Appalachia*. Cleveland, OH: Belt Publishing, 2017.

Change to Win. "About Us: Tom Woodruff." Accessed February 17, 2020. http://www.changetowin.org/archive/content/tom-woodruff.

Citizens' Commission to Investigate the Buffalo Creek Disaster. *Disaster on Buffalo Creek: A Citizens' Report on Criminal Negligence in a West Virginia Mining Community*. Charleston, WV: 1972. http://genealogy.park.lib.wv.us/wp-content/uploads/2018/01/Disaster-on-Buffalo-Creek.pdf.

Corbin, David Alan, ed. *Gun Thugs, Rednecks, and Radicals: A Documentary History of the West Virginia Mine Wars*. Oakland, CA: PM Press, 2011.

Council on Appalachian Women Records. General Correspondence Files, 1976–1981. Archives of Appalachia. East Tennessee State University, Johnson City, Tennessee. https://archives.etsu.edu/repositories/2/resources/430.

Cushing, Lincoln. "Red in Black and White: The New Left Printing Renaissance of the 1960s and Beyond." In *Peace Press Graphics 1867–1987: Art in the Pursuit of Social Change*. Los Angeles: California State University–Long Beach Art Museum/Center for the Study of Political Graphics, 2011. http://www.docspopuli.org/articles/New_Left_Printing.html.

Cushing, Lincoln, and Inkworks Press, eds. *Visions of Peace and Justice: San Francisco Bay Area: 1974–2007*. Emeryville, CA: Inkworks Press, 2007.

Douthat, Strat. "Magazine Reflects Strength of Women." Associated Press syndicated, 1977.

Federal Bureau of Investigation. Report on Donald Lee West, compiled by Charles Paul Rose. File 100-20396. https://archive.org/details/foia_West_Donald_L.-Pittsburgh-3/page/n399/mode/2up.

Find a Grave. "Roderick Mansfield 'Rod' Harless." Created February 15, 2016. https://www.findagrave.com/memorial/158201120/roderick-mansfield-harless.

Franklin, Ben A. "An Oasis in Appalachia." *New York Times,* March 14, 1982.

Goebel, Scott. "Jim Webb: A Poet's Path of Resistance, or The Bigger the Windmill, the Better." *Journal of Kentucky Studies* 31 (June 2016): 108–21.

Hankins, Tom. "Alternative Appalachian Periodicals." *Antipode: A Radical Journal of Geography* 5, no. 1 (March 1973): 45–48. https://doi.org/10.1111/j.1467-8330.1973.tb00727.x.

Hennen, John. "Struggle for Recognition: The Marshall University Students for a Democratic Society and the Red Scare in Huntington, 1965–1969." *West Virginia History* 52 (1993): 127–47.

James, Sheryl. "A Radical of Long Standing." *St. Petersburg Times*, March 22, 1989.

Knollinger, Corey. "Wild, Wondering West Virginia: Exploring West Virginia's Native American History." West Virginia Public Broadcasting. Last Modified February 7, 2019. https://www.wvpublic.org/post/wild-wondering-west-virginia-exploring-west-virginias-native-american-history#stream/0.

"Little Old Lady Is Tougher than Strip Miners." *Hutchinson News*, September 21, 1977.

Lorence, James J. *A Hard Journey: The Life of Don West*. Urbana: University of Illinois Press, 2007.

MacPhee, Josh. *Liberation Support Movement: Building Solidarity with the African Liberation Struggle*. Brooklyn, NY: Interference Archive, 2016.

MacPhee, Josh. "Survival by Sharing—Printing over Profit." In *Signal: 05: A Journal of International Political Graphics and Culture*, edited by Alec Dunn and Josh MacPhee, 74–97. Oakland, CA: PM Press, 2016.

McAteer, J. Davitt, Katie Beall, James A. Beck Jr., Patrick C. McGinley, Celeste Monforton, Deborah C. Roberts, Beth Spence, and Suzanne Weise. *Upper Big Branch: The April 5, 2010, Explosion: A Failure of Basic Coal Mine Safety Practices: Report to the Governor of West Virginia*. Charleston, WV: Diane, 2011.

McCollester, Charlie. *The Point of Pittsburgh*. Pittsburgh: Battle of Homestead Foundation, 2008.

Moize, Elizabeth A. "Turnaround Time in West Virginia." *National Geographic*, June 1976.

Montague, Valerie. "A Need to Share, Magazine Founder Hopes Efforts Achieve Appeal." *Huntington Advertiser*, October 13, 1977.

Montrie, Chad. *To Save the Land and People*. Chapel Hill: University of North Carolina Press, 2003.

Penland, Jenny. "The Invisible Populous of Appalachia: Seeking Statutory Recognition." *Intercontinental Cry*, February 4, 2014. https://intercontinentalcry.org/invisible-populous-appalachia-seeking-statutory-recognition.

Pickering, Mimi, dir. *The Buffalo Creek Flood: An Act of Man*. Whitesburg KY: Appalshop, 1975.

Pudup, Mary Beth, Dwight B. Billings, and Altina L. Waller, eds. *Appalachia in the Making: The Mountain South in the Nineteenth Century*. Chapel Hill: University of North Carolina Press, 2000.

Ralston, Miriam. "Editorial." *MAW: Magazine of Appalachian Women*, no. 5 (July–August 1978): 4.

Salstrom, Paul. "The Neonatives: Back-to-the-Land in Appalachia's 1970s." *Appalachian Journal* 30, no. 4 (2003): 368–87.

Smith, Barbara Ellen. "De-Gradations of Whiteness: Appalachia and the Complexities of Race." *Journal of Appalachian Studies* 10, no. 1/2 (2004): 38–57.

Sonnie, Amy, James Tracy, and Roxanne Dunbar-Ortiz. *Hillbilly Nationalists, Urban Race Rebels, and Black Power: Community Organizing in Radical Times*. Brooklyn, NY: Melville House, 2011.

Stanley, Richard M. "Appalachian Movement Press." *West Virginia Illustrated*, July–August 1972.

US Congress. House. Committee on Interior and Insular Affairs. Statement of Michael J. Clark, Church of the Brethren, Appalachian Caucus. In *Regulation of Surface Mining: Hearings before the Subcommittee on the Environment and Subcommittee on Mines and Mining of the Committee on Interior and Insular Affairs*, Part 2. 93rd Cong., 1st sess., April 9, 10, 16, and 17, 1973, and May 14 and 15, 1973. Washington, DC: US Government Printing Office, 1973. https://play.google.com/books/reader?id=tep86e9LlIC&printsec=frontcover&pg=GBS.PA1119.

Walls, David. "Internal Colony or Internal Periphery?" In *Colonialism in Modern America: The Appalachian Case*, edited by Helen Matthews Lewis, Linda Johnson, and Donald Askins, 351–64. Boone, NC: Appalachian Consortium Press, 1978.

West, Don. *No Lonesome Road: Selected Poems and Prose*. Edited by Jeff Biggers and George Brosi. Urbana: University of Illinois Press, 2004.

Illustration Credits

ix Appalachian Movement Press. Used by permission.

2 West Virginia and Regional History Center, West Virginia University Libraries.

5 Marshall University Archives, Special Collections, Student Publications, Accession No. 20170302, 1966–1987.

6 *West Virginia Illustrated*, July–August 1972.

7 *Chief Justice*, Marshall University yearbook, 1965.

10 Council of the Southern Mountains.

11 *West Virginia Illustrated*, July–August 1972.

14 *West Virginia Illustrated*, July–August 1972.

15 Photograph by Amos Perrine. Used by permission.

16 Photograph by Amos Perrine. Used by permission.

18 Appalachian Movement Press. Used by permission.

21 Appalachian Movement Press. Used by permission.

22 Beehive Design Collective. Used by permission.

23 Beehive Design Collective. Used by permission.

28 Appalachian Movement Press. Used by permission.

31 Southern Appalachian Circuit of Antioch College in Beckley, WV.

41 Appalachian Movement Press. Used by permission.

49 Photography by Michael Fanning in the *Mountain Call*, no. 7 (June 1974). Used by permission.

56 West Virginia and Regional History Center, West Virginia University Libraries.

59 Photography by Michael Fanning in the *Mountain Call* 2, no. 2 (1975). Used by permission.

62 Photograph by Roger May, 2020. Used by permission.
66 Photograph of Paul Salstrom by Lois Salstrom. Used by permission.
66 Photograph by of Miriam Ralston by JB. AP Photo.
76 Photograph by Jonathon Averill. Used by permission.
77 Historic Images, Inc.
79 Appalachian Movement Press. Used by permission.
80 Appalachian Movement Press. Used by permission.
83 Mountain Freedom Press. Used by permission.
248 Logo by artist Emily Prentice, 2019.

Index

Page numbers in italics refer to figures and facsimiles.